PRISON TERMS
Representing Confinement during and after Italian Fascism

Prison Terms

Representing Confinement during and after Italian Fascism

ELLEN V. NERENBERG

UNIVERSITY OF TORONTO PRESS
Toronto Buffalo London

© University of Toronto Press 2001
Toronto Buffalo London
Printed in Canada

ISBN 0-8020-3508-6

Printed on acid-free paper

Toronto Italian Studies

National Library of Canada Cataloguing in Publication Data

Nerenberg, Ellen Victoria, 1962–
  Prison terms : representing confinement during and after Italian fascism

  (Toronto Italian studies)
  Includes bibliographical references and index.
  ISBN 0-8020-3508-6

  1. Italian literature – 20th century – History and criticism.   2. Imprisonment
in literature.   I. Title.   II. Series.

  PQ4053.P76N47 2001   850.9′355   C2001-930028-X

The frontispiece, Piranesi's *Carceri*, is reprinted courtesy of Giraudon/Art Resource,
New York. The illustration of Giuseppe Terragni's Casa del Fascio is reprinted courtesy
of Pollak/Art Resource, New York. The illustration of Guerrini, La Padula, and
Romano's Palace of Italian Civilization is reprinted courtesy of SEF/Art Resource,
New York. The illustrations of Mario Ridolfi's works are reprinted by kind permission
of Fondo Ridolfi-Frankl-Malagria, Accademia Nazionale di San Luca, Rome. All other
illustrations are reprinted by kind permission of the Ufficio Studi, Departimento
dell'Amministrazione Penitenziara.

This volume was published with financial assistance from Wesleyan University.

University of Toronto Press acknowledges the financial assistance to its publishing program of the Canada Council for the Arts and the Ontario Arts Council.

University of Toronto Press acknowledges the financial support for its publishing activities of the Government of Canada through the Book Publishing Industry Development
Program (BPIDP).

For my family

Taking possession of space is the first gesture of living things.

– Le Corbusier,
'L'espace indicible'

Everywhere you shut me in. Always you assign a place to me. Even outside the frame I form with you ... You set limits even to events that could happen with others ... You mark out boundaries, draw lines, surround, enclose. Excising, cutting out. What is your fear? That you will lose your property. What remains is an empty frame. You cling to it, dead.

– Luce Irigaray,
Elemental Passions

Contents

Acknowledgments

No book is written in complete isolation, and this one owes numerous debts to various individuals and institutions, colleagues and friends.

At University of Toronto Press, I wish to thank Ron Schoeffel, editor extraordinaire, and the two anonymous readers of my manuscript: their comments made revisions simpler and more interesting.

I am thankful to Wesleyan University for supporting portions of my research in the form of two grants. In particular, I wish to acknowledge the support of Wesleyan's Catherine and Thomas McMahon Fund. I am grateful to my colleagues in the Department of Romance Languages for the constructive criticism and support they have offered me. For their patience and excellent offices, I wish to thank Wesleyan's inter-library loan staff, without whose assistance I would not have been able to complete my research. Wesleyan colleagues deserving of special thanks include: Christina Crosby, Andrew Curran, B. Antonio Gonzàlez, Noah Isenberg, Natasha Korda, Sean McCann, Diana Sorensen, David Weisberg, and Gareth Williams. For his counsel on matters of architectural history, theory, and urban planning, and for his great acumen, I warmly thank Joseph Siry.

I owe similar debts to colleagues at my former academic home, the University of Chicago, where this project first came to life. For their intellectual rigour and encouragement, I thank Paolo Cherchi, Françoise Meltzer, and Elissa Weaver. I owe a special debt to

Rebecca West for her consistent support and sound critique. Other colleagues from Chicago – now teaching and studying elsewhere – who deserve my thanks include Nancy Henry, Jessica Burstein, Jessica Berman, Rebecca Messbarger, and Anna Maria Torriglia. Finally, I am appreciative of James Chandler's intellectual generosity even after I had left the university.

Italianists from various institutions provided support and rigorous interrogation throughout the gestation of this project. Among these I wish to thank Beverly Allen, Zygmunt Barański, Philip Cannistraro, Daniela Curti, Ruth Ben-Ghiat, Robert Dombroski, Carole Gallucci, Piero Garofalo, Nancy Harrowitz, Keala Jewell, Giancarlo Lombardi, James Miller, Robin Pickering-Iazzi, Jacqueline Reich, and Marguerite Waller.

For its gracious sponsorship during my sabbatical year, I thank the Department of Italian at New York University, particularly Stefano Albertini, Nancy Eder, and Francesco Erspamer. Without the institutional affiliation that the Casa Italiana Zerilli-Marimò afforded me, it is doubtful I would have been able to conduct extended portions of this research.

I have many debts I must acknowledge in Italy. Foremost, I thank Daniela Masci, in the office of the United States Information Services in Rome, whose ability to cleave through red tape cannot be over-praised. I recognize here my numerous debts to the Ministero di Grazia e Giustizia, without whose help I might never have seen the inside of an Italian prison (happily, as a visitor only). I am, in particular, grateful for the permission to reproduce the photographs of Italian prisons from the Fascist era that are included herein. I thank Dr Giovanni Veschi, Provveditore di Lazio, and his colleagues Dr Anacleto Benedetti, Director of Regina Coeli Prison, and Drs Paola Montesanti and Alessandra Beccaro, Vice Directors of Regina Coeli Prison. Special thanks to Dr Giorgio Linguaglossa, Dipartimento dell'Amministrazione Penitenziaria, and to Maria Ponce de Léon, who provided an initial contact. My thanks to Drs Criscuollo and Grazioso of Sollicciano Prison in the Provveditoriato di Toscana, to Dr Caterina Ciampoli, Vice Director of Opera Prison in the Provveditoriato di Lombardia, and to Dr Luigi Pagano, Director, and Dr Armanda

Rossi, Vice Director, of San Vittore Prison, Provveditoriato di Lombardia. Still at San Vittore, I give special thanks to Commander Moscariello of the Polizia Penitenziaria.

Prisons were not the only institution in Italy to give me assistance and support for this project. I therefore thank the research staff at the Archivio Nazionale Centrale in Rome and several specific staff members at the Biblioteca Nazionale Centrale in Florence who provided help at key junctures during the development of this project: Domenica Landolfi, A. Chiesalotti, and the inimitable Fabrizio Ricci. I thank as well Corrado Marcetti, director of the Fondazione Michelucci, for his assistance. Finally, I would like to thank the staff, in particular Dr Cipriani, at the Fondo Ridolfi-Frankl-Malagria, Accademia di San Luca, in Rome for their kind permission to reprint photographs from their archives.

For their remarkable generosity over time, I owe material thanks to the Annunziato family in Rome, to Carolyn Demcy in Florence, and to members of the Calvi family in Milan, Bergamo, and beyond.

Some of the material published here appeared elsewhere in more abbreviated form. I thank *Italica*, in which portions of chapter 2 first appeared as 'Tartar Control: Masculinity and the Military in Dino Buzzati's *Il deserto dei Tartari*' (74:2 [1997]). As well, I wish to thank *Annali d'Italianistica*, where portions of chapter 4 first appeared as 'Love for Sale, or, That's *Amore*: Representing Prostitution during and after Fascism' (16 [1998]). I gratefully acknowledge Bompiani, Garzanti, and Mondadori publishers for their kind permission to use material from the following works: Guido Piovène, *Lettere di una novizia* (Milan: Bompiani, 1941); Carlo Emilio Gadda, *Quer pasticciaccio brutto de via Merulana* (Milan: Garzanti, 1983); Dino Buzzati, *Il deserto dei Tartari* (Milan: Mondadori, 1979); Alba de Céspedes, *Nessuno torna indietro* (Milan: Mondadori, 1938); and Vasco Pratolini, *Cronache di poveri amanti* (Milan: Mondadori, 1993).

Finally and more than anyone, I thank Anthony Valerio. His patience, colossal editorial acuity, and unwavering support constitute a unique debt that I am uncertain I shall ever be able to repay. My recognition of that debt here is only a beginning.

PRISON TERMS

Chapter One

Introduction: Prisons and Their Analogues

Mussolini is the builder, the Fascist Regime is the construction yard, and this is the era of Italian reconstruction. The Duce's mind does not halt at intermediate phases; it goes immediately to the constructive solution. He is the architect.

Paolo Orano, quoted in Diane Ghirardo, Building New Communities, p. 24

A whole history remains to be written of spaces – which would be at the same time the history of powers (both these terms in the plural) – from the great strategies of geo-politics to the little tactics of the habitat, institutional architecture from the classroom to the design of hospitals, passing via economic and political installations ... Anchorage in space is an economico-political form which needs to be studied.

Michel Foucault, 'The Eye of Power,' p. 149

Percevoir chaque être humain comme une prison où habite un prisonnier avec tout l'univers.
[To understand each human being as though s/he were a prison, where lived a prisoner with the entire universe.]

Simone Weil, Cahiers I, p. 53

These epigraphs present the pole stars for this study, which takes as its subject the multiform representation of prison in Italy between the years 1930 and 1960. Discretely, each statement supplies a partial and perspectival frame for the material I consider here. Paolo Orano's pro-Mussolini declaration offers a local perspective saturated by Fascist rhetorical strategies of the consolidated Regime.[1] Orano presents a demiurgic Duce, who had enjoyed – by the time Orano issued this statement in 1937 – more than a decade of unopposed rule. Orano's analogy of the construction yard is noteworthy for the way it suggests a masculinist and pre-modern environment, which might at first seem at odds with its modernist dictum but actually signals its paradoxical character.[2] The Regime set about to reclaim the glory that was Imperial Rome (its 'reconstruction'), foster a particularly Italian modernist aesthetic, and, from the two, synthesize a hybrid that has come to characterize Italian art and architecture during the *ventennio*, as the Regime's two-decade tenure is known. If this seems like a tall order of business, not to mention a contradictory one, then we might remember the articulation of fascist ideology, which works, Barbara Spackman reminds us, by sundering logical associations and joining 'seemingly incompatible elements and polarities: [Fascism's] ideological specificity therefore lies not in the elements it gathers together but in the binding mechanism itself.'[3] From Orano's local and historically attentive example, we move to Michel Foucault, who, nearly forty years later, considers architectural space in a sweeping gesture that is at once locally embedded and suprahistorical, and that comprises both 'great strategies' and 'little tactics.' In the third example, Simone Weil transports us both backward and forward, back to review a locale only superficially similar to Orano's, ahead to recognize its radical subjectivity. The prison experience, she maintains, is not an extraordinary phenomenon; rather, it is constitutive.

I would not want these statements to be read as only discrete instances, an evaluation that would lack the additional significance generated by their assembly. Orano's post-Ethiopia praise paints, very nearly, a 'brave new world' that Fascism and Mussolini can construct. Orano's urban planning, if I can call it that, summons up Fascism in its autarkic phase.[4] In the early years, Fascism won mass appeal by allying social utopianism with the sense of dynamic change under the charismatic leadership of Mussolini and promised a radical reorganization of Italian politics, social institutions, and culture.[5] What the history of Fascism reveals, of course, is how easily utopianism morphs into its dystopic twin: the State's steady curtailment of civil liberties leads to corporativism, to conformity and sham consent, to economic and cultural autarky, to heightened nationalism, to the need for demographic expansion and the consequent ossification of gender roles, and so forth. The transition from Orano through Foucault to Weil similarly suggests the blurring of utopic desire and dystopic fantasy; the subject of my study, and its scope, lies in each and all of the epigraphs: during Mussolini and following his tenure, in the transition from one manifestation of power and ideology to the next, and finally in Weil's stoic belief that there is no escaping certain carceral aspects of the self.

Material and Discursive Formations: Methodological Considerations

This book is about spaces and, in particular, enclosed spaces that hold the body in check and control it. It is a study, moreover, of precise social spaces within a particular historical and cultural context, about which I will say more presently. Concerning space more generally, I follow Michel de Certeau and Elizabeth Grosz, and distinguish between 'place' and 'space.' A 'place' for de Certeau 'is the order (of whatever kind) in accord with which the elements are distributed in relationships of coexistence ... It implies an indication of stability.' A 'space,' on the other hand, is more dynamically conceived, and 'exists when one takes into consideration vectors of direction, velocities, and time variables ... In short, *space is practiced place.*'[6] Grosz makes a similar distinction, describing 'place' as a location characterized by its 'occupation, dwelling, [or] being lived in' and 'space' as 'territory which is mappable.'[7]

Discursive and material incarcerations function as a trope of continuity, linking strictures of Fascism to the postwar era of reconstruction, and the negotiation between juridical and social incarcerations centres *Prison Terms*. As the place of detainment for the juridically miscreant, prisons allow an examination of legally ratified state authority and perceived transgression of that authority. However, as social and architectural theory have helped illustrate, the State does not limit its exercise of power to the juridical arena; therefore, *Prison Terms* explores carceral sites outside the juridical domain. Of the numerous sites that offer themselves as prison analogues, in these pages I will probe four – namely, the barracks, the convent, the brothel, and the home. To be sure, these four spaces, rich in history as both built and social environments, signify in early modern social and historical contexts as well. What makes these spaces important to a discussion of literature and culture in Italy in the middle decades of the twentieth century is something we shall uncover as we go.

Some twenty years ago, Henri Lefebvre wrote that '[s]pace is permeated with social relations; it is not only supported by social relations but it is also producing and produced by social relations.'[8] Although one could profitably mine other fields with a similar purpose, I look for clues about space in the discursive and plastic arts. More specifically, I examine literary, legal, and church documents, as well as architectural theory, design, and urban planning. Aiming for a thicker description of the phenomenology of prisons, I draw into proximity the critical discourses concerning material and discursive formations. The ways in which specific spaces correspond and run counter to their received spatial practice is one of this study's underlying precepts. Blending these discourses may be seen as unequivocally beneficial to the discursive field: texts, it is generally held, always benefit from greater (historical, political, cultural, socio-economic, etc.) contextualization. Yet, architecture's study of 'actual' buildings stands to improve its critical purchase from exposure to discursive concerns. For example, the more 'interstitial' social spaces become, the more they are denoted by spatial practice rather than architectural typology. Urban geography and *habitus* valuably inform architecture, but, in some cases, architectural form yields little if no information about social spaces. The architectural mutability of the brothel, as we shall see, offers a case in point. We must attend to the discursive construction of brothels in Italy because they are not architecturally denoted: it is the practice of prostitution that creates the space of the brothel and not architecture per se. In other words, since no architectural typology for 'brothel' applies, we must turn to discursive representations in order to reconstruct it.

The notion of *habitus* furnishes a useful point of encounter between the customarily discrete zones of discursive and material production. In Pierre Bourdieu's conception, *habitus* works by drawing from a set of 'dispositions' that concern the social regulation of the body and of social comportment: it provides the social subject with a 'practical sense' ('le sens pratique') of the possible negotiations of quotidian living. Bourdieu writes that *habitus* is the 'strategy generating principle enabling agents to cope with unforseen and ever-changing situations'; moreover, it is a 'system of lasting and transposable dispositions which, integrating past experiences, functions at every moment as a matrix of perception, appreciations and actions.'[9] Although Bourdieu does not discuss gender as an explicit disposition, this oversight does not prevent Roberta Gilchrist from making use of *habitus* in her excellent *Gender and Material Culture*, refashioning Bourdieu's gender-neutral concept as the 'unconscious practical logic of gender ordered materially through architecture and space,' a successful adaptation that provides a better understanding of gender and material space.[10]

Prison Terms studies the representation of prisons and its relation to the articulation of gender during and after Fascism. Recent criticism, and literary criticism focusing on texts authored by women during the Regime in particular, has revealed undercurrents of resistance to and transgression of Fascist ideological formations of the social subject. Focusing on the Italian and German cases, feminist scholarship of the last fifteen years has examined Fascism's instrumentalization of gender. Attentive studies hailing from a variety of scholarly disciplines have illustrated the specific ways that state policies intersected with the practice of everyday life of women in these two fascist countries.[11] Although one may query, as Mabel Berezin does, the degree to which states, 'even reputedly totalitarian states, can impose meaning or identities on their citizens,' scholarship of this type exposed the imbricated registers, ranging from the juridical to the spectacular, which Fascism employed in pursuit of its collective state.[12]

This extremely useful work has had salutary effects. First, regarding women's involvement in and with the Regime, recent scholarship has served as a corrective to Marie Antonietta Macciocchi's formulation of Fascism's 'seduction' of the Italian female polity.[13] In her troublesome (to some, galling) 1976 study, Macciocchi attributes Italian women's 'seduction' by Mussolini to their intrinsic masochism. Fascist constructions of female identity were founded, she claims, on the bedrock of female masochism, which induced women to agree to (and thereby promote) reified gender roles and norms. By inculpating women for not only the rise of Fascism but its root as well, Macciocchi, as Spackman observes, 'replays and reinforces the gender politics of the scenario she criticizes [and] tropes a standard feature of the rape scenario by blaming the victim.'[14] The inquiry into the practices of 'resistant' women and cultural practitioners during the *ventennio* has refashioned the debates on fascism and culture, and provided a way out of the closed circuit of coercion and consent.

Study of the imbrications of representation and ideology has also expanded the understanding of the Fascist operation of ideology, troubling the conceptual divide between Fascism and its postwar Republican correction. To be sure, as concerns the relation between ideology and cultural production, the divide between the *ventennio* and the Republic is anything but neat. Scholarly understanding of ideology has focused on its nature and conception: either ideology is rationally conceived and deliberately executed, as Sternhell, for example, believes, or ideology is more psychosocial in formation and performance. Critics with more Marxist leanings have occupied the latter position, which, I believe, has more fully reckoned with the polysemy of dominance, hegemony, and ideological operation.[15]

Representation holds similarly important consequences for the role that gender plays in the analysis of space. My interest lies more in the representation of gender than in the study of the way women differently (and transgressively) represent women or femininity. This is largely a matter of focus, the significance of which

Rosi Braidotti underscores when she writes, "'I, woman," am affected directly and in my everyday life by what has been made of the subject of woman; I have paid in my very body for all the metaphors and images that our culture has deemed fit to produce of woman.'[16] Representation and discursive formation, the 'metaphors and images' Braidotti refers to, visit the body in a material way. Resistance to such representation takes place on a daily basis and is continually evolving and adapting; it may be expressed, for example, immediately in response to oppression, or response may come after the fact, mediated by history. This sort of diachronic operation, mediating between a contemporary and historic affront, finds literary expression in a work like Anna Banti's *Artemisia*. In her 1947 novel, the author interpolates the disorientation she felt (as a writer, woman, and Italian) following the Allied bombing of Florence during the Second World War with the disorientation she imagines Artemisia Gentileschi to have felt (as a painter and a woman) following the trial for her rape in seventeenth-century Rome.

The scholarly examination of prison literature, like the problem of the representation of issues of gender, is also marked by a divide. In the main, this criticism splits into two methodological approaches: an interest in veritable prison accounts and an interest in the metaphoric significance of confinement. For the first (materialist) tack, prison is seen as a locus of intellectual and political activity – especially for prisoners of conscience – and imprisonment is thought of as a conditioning factor in the production of writing.[17] This critical assay customarily takes up memoirs, autobiographies, and epistolary correspondence of prisoners, though this is hardly an exclusive focus. The literature of confinement, on the other hand, features 'subcategories [of] captivity of any sort and the particular experience of imprisonment.'[18] Imprisonment and prisons are more phenomenological in nature, and noncarceral space is no guarantee that freedom of body and mind will not be abridged in ways consonant with prison.

Between these two very different approaches and their distinct aims, methodologies, and assumptions, we can locate a third position, one in which a materialist discourse merges with its representational counterpart. This is John Bender's position in his investigation of the coeval rise of the novel and the penal system in England in the eighteenth century, *Imagining the Penitentiary: Fiction and the Architecture of the Mind in Eighteenth-Century England*.[19] Bender believes that the architectural design and construction of the 'new' prisons in England during the 1700s and the rise and development of the novel as literary form precisely and significantly coincide. The novel and the sense of narrative time unfolding within and from it, Bender asserts, guaranteed a space in the social imaginary for the acceptance and comprehension of the newly reformed prisons. In Italy during the corresponding period, however, the architecture of prisons no more resembles the evolving prison reform movement, spearheaded by Cesare Beccaria (whose *Dei delitti e delle pene* proved influential throughout Europe), than the development of the novel in Italy resembles that which was taking place in other European literatures. In fact, there exists an historical and architectural interval that makes the Italian case quite distinct from its English counterpart. Following unification (1870), ecclesiastical lands were deeded over to the newly formed Italian state. As a consequence, properties formerly belonging to the church were transformed into, among other things, prisons. This metamorphosis of spatial use provides for the prison palimpsest (once a monastery, now a reform school, once a convent, now a penitentiary) a phenomenon that finds a correspondingly rich expression in Italian prose literature of the period.[20] Italy's specific historical and architectural circumstances suggest a layering that hints at the ways prisons camouflage themselves. Like the third critical approach I described, in which the historical concrete is merged with the representational, *Prison Terms* seeks to make this subterfuge visible by bringing the aims of the study of confinement together with the cultural specificity of the materialist approach. Focusing on a period that reaches from deep within the consolidated Regime to fifteen years in light of the Fascist experience, this study also seeks to contribute to the understanding of Italy at mid-century, a period significant for the way it cleaved to and away from Fascism.

Prison exudes power, and my interest in it during this particular period is, I hope, plain. Power is an appropriate focus for this period in Italy, which divides between the last years of the Regime and the first of the Republic. Fascism operates, some will say, by way of an abuse of power and by steadily curtailing access to social reproduction by limiting access to space. The creation of the twelve New Towns of the Agro Pontine, their architectural and urban design, and their role in internal immigration during the *ventennio* lends support to this claim. The creation of specifically Fascist space was also the aim of such enterprises as the 1932 Mostra della Rivoluzione Fascista in Rome's Palazzo delle Esposizioni.[21] The Fascist State promoted a set of exclusionary tactics concerning social space; in order to secure and preserve the homogeneity of citizens, the State eradicated heterodox elements by removing them from view. Let these stark examples illustrate my point. Giacomo Matteotti could not intervene in Parliamentary debate from his grave (where he was dispatched by zealous *squadristi* – young Fascist militiamen – following an impassioned indictment of Mussolini on the floor of Parliament in June 1924) any more than Antonio Gramsci could from the various prison cells he called home between 1926 and 1934. Internal exile removed *sovversivi* (subversives) like Leone Ginzburg and Carlo Levi from their place of origin and stripped from them the familiar clandestine networks that made possible their active resistance to the Regime.[22]

Access to social space under Fascism exacted conformity relative to race and sexuality, a conformity achieved through exile, deportation, incarceration, or, as the 'final solution' to the dilemma of subjecthood, by extermination.[23] After an initial period of inconsistency, Italian Fascist racial policy grew to resemble that of German National Socialism, to which it was allied after 1938: Jews and Gypsies were detained or deported, and interracial commingling in the North African territories was quelled.[24] Race, however, was not the only criterion for access to social space under Fascism. Like Jewishness, homosexuality and non-normative femininity similarly imperilled the Fascist myth of heterosexuality, the family, and, consequently, the State; as with the case of Italian Jewry, the state incarcerated homosexuals and non-normative women, though not always in actual prisons. *Prison Terms* seeks to shed light on the embedded constricture that these analogical prisons epitomize. Incarceration under Fascism, I argue, can be read as an exaggeration of the conceptual incarcerations of transgressive subjects during Fascism and after. Further, the exaggerated and specific ways in which the types of incarceration under Fascism were determined by gender illuminate the way subjects are gendered within the dominant discourse of a patriarchal society like Italy at mid-century, whether under Fascist rule or not.

Prose literature of this period, the primary focus in these pages, unpacks the various analogues of containment, laying them out in explicit and suggestive episodes. The spaces I designate form a homology of prisons because they monitor, coerce, and limit the subject who must live within their walls. These are not the *bona fide* prisons of Fascism, like Primo Levi's Auschwitz or Gramsci's itinerary of Italian prisons; rather, they are those spaces refigured as prisons. For this reason, the actual prison and concentration camp – as *representatives* and not *representations* of prison – are a point of departure and not of analysis for this inquiry. The carceral homologues herein are in a state of becoming prisons for their occupants. Of the many potential carceral spaces one could profitably explore, I limit myself here to four specific instances. The barracks, the convent, the brothel, and the home take on carceral attributes which manifest on very nearly every page of the texts I consider. In some cases, the lexicon of the carceral could not be more naked: it takes little, for example, to transform the barracks in Dino Buzzati's *Il deserto dei Tartari*, of primary focus in chapter 2, into a prison; the convent in Guido Piovène's *Lettere di una novizia* or Alba de Céspedes's *Nessuno torna indietro* (considered in chapter 3) undergoes a similar facile transformation; as does the space of the brothel in chapter 4 and the domestic confines of the home in the last chapter.[25]

Imprisonment: Space, Power, and Gender

If Western experience is conceived as having originated in a sense of confinement, the theme of imprisonment may then be thought of as one metaphorical convenience among others for rendering the original feeling ... Not only are there countless texts ... but if every artistic expression exemplifies a breaking free from empirical reality, the subject also has no natural limit.[26]

Michael Keith and Steve Pile have observed in their study about the spatialization of identity that 'politics is invariably about closure; it is about the moment when boundaries become, symbolically, Berlin Walls.'[27] Politics is absent from Carnochan's description in the passage given immediately above, which, albeit useful, does not answer to the larger thematic I put forward here: namely, that systems of power have historically privileged the male social subject and, therefore, women's 'confinement' is of a quite different nature than men's. What does the sexual difference of captivity tell us? And what does it mean in this particular historical period? What does access to social space reveal about Italy's disengagement with its Fascist legacy in the postwar period? Finally, how does a study of the representation of carceral space square with the restoration of 'equality' that occupied the forefront of social and legal consideration in the newly chartered Republic?

The gendered 'constitution' of the subject begs another matter related to our interest, namely, the drafting of the Republic of Italy's constitution in 1946. The laws and rights outlined in the 1946 Constitution of the Republic of Italy were seen as inalienable and corrective of Fascism's erosion of individual liberties.[28] The Constitution in its postwar context, as do literary documents of the period, illustrates the postwar *Zeitgeist* of restoration. Concerning the approximate relation of the law and literature, Carolyn Heilbrun and Judith Resnick assert that they both 'share the activity of generating narratives that illuminate, create and reflect normative worlds, that bring experiences that might otherwise be invisible and silent into public view.'[29]

Although the Constitution was chartered, the rights that it purports were not immediately granted, a hiatus that relates more generally to the continuity into the postwar period of the centralized Italian State under Fascism. Indeed, attempts to dissolve highly centralized Italian governance did not take place until

1970, during what Claudio Pavone calls 'the constitutional thaw.'[30] We can say that jurisprudence and criminology display more continuity than discontinuity in the transition from Fascist to post-Fascist governments. As Paul Ginsborg and others have commented, defascistization of the Italian State was, in the main, a failure; as a result, traditional state structure and administration of the Italian State remained largely unaffected by the Regime's ouster. For example, 'most of the 1,879 civil servants who were dismissed (for collaborating with the government of the north) and the 671 who had been compulsorily retired were reinstated.'[31] The postwar purges of the prefecture and the judiciary were similarly ineffectual and illustrate the difficulty that Juan Linz believes to be representative of the transition from Fascism. Democracies that follow 'highly ideological and exclusionary totalitarian regimes ... face a less difficult situation than those succeeding amorphous authoritarian regimes,' which describes the Italian situation following the Regime.[32] Although Article 2 of the 27 July 1944 decree (DLL 159) stipulated the death sentence for 'members of the fascist government and fascist hierarchs guilty of having suppressed constitutional guarantees, destroyed popular liberties, created the fascist regime, compromised and betrayed the country, leading it to the present catastrophe,' no judge, as Pavone informs us, condemned a single Fascist.[33] Ironically, although clemency toward the Fascists increased, the penalization of partisans who had committed 'illegal' acts during the liberation – in some cases, for the execution of Fascists – became more stringent.[34] Ugo Betti gives voice to the fear of corruption, anticipating the taint of vestigial impropriety and the absence of reform of the judiciary, in his 1944 drama *Corruzione al palazzo della giustizia*. Consideration of the juridical character of the postwar period will lead to other related areas of the law, namely, its subversion and transgression, punishment for which returns us to the central trope of prison. As a kind of *sine qua non* of social control and engineering, prison thus becomes a powerful trope for the social control continued in Italian culture and society in the postwar period. As regards the difference gender makes in the face of the law, it is important to note that the judiciary was not only largely unchanged from the *ventennio*, it was also untouched by the presence of women, something de Céspedes elucidates in her 1948 novel *Dalla parte di lei*.[35]

The social control of women in the postwar era limns continuities between the Regime and the postwar era of reconstruction.[36] The ambivalence that is characteristic of attempts to reform the judiciary in a period of defascistization finds a correspondence in the general juridical status of women. To be sure, women made some advances (witness the general enfranchisement of 1945), but, juridically speaking, change was glacial and women were still considered and treated as subaltern subjects.[37] Although the chapters that follow will adduce literary examples of both continuity and discontinuity of fascist norms, let historical certainties serve as illustration here. As evidence of the discrepant treatment female defendants received in the penal system, we might consider the 1961 sentence of a woman accused of adultery. The Constitutional Court – which, although chartered a decade earlier, did not function until 1956 – 'upheld Article 559 of the penal code [the Rocco Code], which punished a wife's adultery more severely than that of a husband, with up to a year's imprisonment.'[38] Further, the criteria for the incarceration of unruly subjects do not alter radically from those crafted during the twenty-year tenure of the Regime. Portions of the Rocco Code (Italy's penal code promulgated in 1926 and, ratified in 1929, axiomatic to the Regime's consolidation of power) remained in effect until the 1970s. Similarly, criminology, retarded by Fascism, still employed Cesare Lombroso's (1835–1909) formulations of 'delinquency,' particularly notorious for its insistence on the predictability of female dangerousness.[39]

A momentary return to our epigraphs is required. Issues of space and power follow the category of architecture so closely that the interval between them is at times barely discernible. Foucault's theorizations of space bridge the gap between Orano and Weil, enabling me to move from one to the other. Mussolini is the builder because he has the power to build; Weil's subject, on the other hand, is a prisoner because she does not. Although Weil herself would diminish the importance that gender played as a critical category in her work, in this trio and this study it is no accident that the existential prison is given voice by a woman.

Prison Terms predicates on the concepts of space and power two interrelated ideas discussed by, among others, Foucault. The limitations of Foucault's system of the carceral and of power establish the trajectory of this study. In *Discipline and Punish*, Foucault catalogues institutions of control in the 'disciplinary society': prisons, hospitals, cloisters, schools, factories, and other places of organized activity in industrialized Europe and North America compose a carceral landscape. Lefebvre believed that Foucault was really 'more concerned with a metaphorical notion of space – "mental space" – than with lived space, "the space of people who deal with material things."'[40] However, what the Foucauldian model does not consider, neither materially nor metaphorically, is what might constitute the differences of a gendered experience of prison. Women's prisons may be a logical extension of Foucault's scheme of the carceral, but he does not explicitly discuss women as prisoners nor does he treat as 'carceral' their domains. Not that this oversight is limited to women. Foucault's 'others' include the elderly, children, and the ill, all of whom, Mary McLeod reminds us, are in the thrall of institutional power signalled by architecture and who would, she believes, disagree with Foucault that architecture, as such, exerts no power over their (daily) lives.[41] In *Prison Terms*, I show how the effect of power entreats female subjects differently than their male counterparts. Significantly, the majority of studies on detained writers reproduces Foucault's oversight. My examination of carceral analogues, on the other hand, constructs a perch that permits a full exploration of the ways in which gender differently shapes, empowers, and (dis)enfranchises.[42]

The claim that Foucault does not offer a theory of power for women is one of the more hotly contested aspects of the post-structuralist debate within feminist studies.[43] When considering women's prisons or other 'heterotopes' thought to reveal alternative social ordering, such a claim is reasonable to make.[44] Foucault's theory of power does not account for the already existing system of entitlement that accompanies gendered identity. Domination over women is strangely absent from the already existing forms of discipline that gave birth to the prison. As evidence of this, we may consider the following passage:

> The prison form antedates its systematic use in the penal system. It had already been constituted outside the legal apparatus when, throughout the social body, procedures were being elaborated for distributing individuals, fixing them in space, classifying them, extracting from them the maximum in time and forces, training their bodies, forming around them an apparatus of observation, registration and recording, constituting on them a body of knowledge that is accumulated and centralized.[45]

Who, historically, furnished bodies more perfectible for discipline and docility than women? Overlooking the fact that domination over women operated always, already in a fluid, implicit, and interstitial network, Foucault manoeuvres a change in the representation of power that starts sometime in the eighteenth century. The point is not that Foucault's thoughts could be modified to accommodate women, but, rather, that women are not explicitly considered, which undermines a theory of power as such. For Foucault, power marshals its more or less constant public force in the name of sovereignty and then, insidiously, disappears. The power of prison, as Jeremy Bentham's panopticon demonstrates, is actually its ability to threaten and to coerce conformity. The architecture of the panopticon ensures that prisoners are not certain when or whether the warden is present; thus they adhere to the rule of the prison and present a model for social control. The internalization of measures of social control is indeed useful for an understanding of women's domination, but the notion of the disappearance of punishment is not.

Prison, for Foucault, promises that punishment once publicly celebrated will be meted out in confinement. This does not really contribute much to an understanding of how power works or has worked historically for women, although removal from the visible does anticipate the deferral of residential space from the city centre to the periphery that I discuss in chapter 5. That Foucault

locates concealed power in the interstices or, as he says, in 'capil-
lary' form, is so general as to be of no use. This kind of ambiguity
led Nancy Hartsock to warn that 'power is everywhere, and so
ultimately nowhere.'[46] Foucault's revelation of concealed power
has already taken place in gendered domination and has already
experienced architectural encoding.[47] 'In the deployment of
sexuality,' Frances Bartkowski observes, 'the space of power is
extremely privatized, even closeted. Both sex and sexuality are
codified behind closed doors.'[48] While Simone de Beauvoir's clar-
ion call in *The Second Sex* – that one 'is not born, but rather
becomes a woman' – is certainly true in a developmental sense, it
is equally true that one is born into a body whose movement
through social space will be conditioned by the facticity (skin
colour, gender, etc.) of that body. 'That one is not born, but
rather becomes, a woman,' Judith Butler asserts, 'does not imply
that this "becoming" traverses a path from disembodied freedom
to cultural embodiment. Indeed, one is one's body from the start,
and only thereafter becomes one's gender.'[49]

Architecture, spatial organization, and literary representation
work together to produce cultural spaces of incarceration. The
prison articulated by way of discursive formations conceals
repression. Prisons that are culturally constructed take an otherwise explicit example of the power of the state to control its citizens by imprisonment and obscure the repressive mechanism. My
inquiry explores perhaps the most infelicitous and hostile of all
social spaces: the carceral place pretending to be something
other than it is, the prison in masquerade.[50] The peril of the concealed prison lies in its duplicitousness: in the prison *qua* prison,
the prisoner knows s/he is incarcerated, but the reasons for incarceration are not always disclosed. Giambattista Piranesi's (1720–
78) remarkable series of engravings entitled *Carceri* (Prisons)
offers a case in point. Piranesi's title is suggestive, for the engravings do not explicitly portray prisons; instead, their fragments
uncover a series of imprisonments in which escape is as tantalizing as it is impossible. Visible exits that reveal only more imprisoning walls, staircases that lead nowhere, inaccessible galleries,
and vertical openings overhead only underscore the 'trick' of

detention that Weil already suspected, namely, that we are all detained but not all of us know it. Those immured in camouflaged prisons, culturally constructed, are prisoners unknown even to themselves.

The prisoner of the carceral analogue experiences incarceration but cannot verify it. This lack of recognition renders impossible or moot the contemplation of why or how one is confined. Gramsci, for one, knew precisely why he was imprisoned, and that knowledge (attended by his unshakeable belief that it was for fighting the good fight) lightened the considerable burden of his imprisonment. The prisoner in the analogical prison experiences incarceration but is denied the verification of that experience. This is not to claim that one is better off in a juridical prison than in its cultural analogue, something that would disavow the irrefutable materiality of the experiences of Gramsci, Levi, Cesira Fiori, Camilla Ravera, and the thousands of others less well known to the Fascist State.[51] As the mass of political detainees can, and do, attest, prison in Fascist Italy was no mere metaphor.[52]

History: Fascism during and after the *Ventennio*

As its historical parameters unravel at both ends, the understanding of Italian Fascism has seen considerable revision.[53] Recent critical studies of the relation between Italian Fascism and culture illustrate the improbability that Fascist cultural practice emerges *ex novo* at the beginning of the Regime (1922).[54] Much of the recent scholarship on Italian Futurism, for instance, examines it as a kind of organic precursor to the ideological rhetoric of the Regime.[55] Indeed, fascism's characteristic 'palingenetic ultra-nationalism,' as Griffin observes, vexes notions of history and progress.[56] At its root, fascism pushes forward to a new world order that is, nevertheless, determined by a mythopoetic past. This dual motion, as I show, is not characteristic of the Regime alone, but describes the ambivalence characteristic of the postwar era, as well. Epistemological bases for fascism antedate its taking political shape in Italy, and these bases endure after the ouster of Mussolini and the fall of the Regime.

As an analysis based on narratives produced both during and after the Regime, *Prison Terms* illuminates the relationship of literary representation to ideology during the fraught middle decades of the century when questions concerning ideologies to the right and left of the political spectrum appeared at the vanguard of social concerns and cultural practices. Documentary style of the neorealist tendency was considered a kind of antidote to the censorship which resulted in, among other things, the actual incarceration of many vocally opposed to the Regime. The 'explosion of orality,' received as characteristic of literature in the immediate postwar period, belies the existence of Fascist-era strictures not thoroughly extirpated following the fall of the Regime.[57]

I have stated that prose literature gave expression to Fascism's containment of the subject, but that is not its only function: the prisoner's choice of narrative introduces a topic central to this study, that is, how the realist aesthetic characteristic of the postwar literary enterprise in Italy paved the way for fundamental revisionism that typifies the interplay of aesthetics and ideology in the postwar period and has, thus, taught us how to learn about Fascism. In the heyday of liberation and the drafting of a new constitution, everyone may have had a story to tell, but not everyone got to tell it. As Mark Mazower comments,

> Italian Jews not only found their specific experiences granted a far more peripheral position in the memory of the war than would now be the case, but in a host of practical matters concerning the restitution of their property and, in some cases, the recovery of prewar posts and jobs, they found themselves discouraged from too forceful a presentation of their grievances.[58]

The publication history of Primo Levi's *Se questo è un uomo* (Survival in Auschwitz) offers similar testimony. Rejected by all the major publishing houses upon its completion in 1948, possibly because of the saturation of the market by prisoner-of-war memoirs, Levi published a limited edition of *Se questo è un uomo* with a small Florentine publisher. It was not until 1958, and the success of such books as French writer André Schwartz-Bart's *The Last of*

the Just and other survivors' stories in the European market of letters, that Einaudi consented to publish Levi's text.[59] Further, the
publishing culture – despite the end of Regime censorship – may
not have changed so much from the years of the *ventennio*. As
Luperini observed,

> The years 1926 to 1956 seem to be divided in half by the war and by
> the apparently neat passage from Hermeticism to Neorealism. In
> reality, there was no true rupture: one moves from an ideology of
> literature to a literature of ideology and rather than a solution of
> continuity there is an inversion of the same thematic.[60]

The Italian literary enterprise of mid-century is suffused by ideology, Fascist or not, as Luperini shrewdly observes. The 'new'
realism contributed to the revision of the Fascist experience by
fabricating a greater sense of discontinuity than really existed.[61]
By fostering the exchange of the master narrative of consensus
with the master narrative of resistance (accompanied by transition from the rhetoric of Fascism to a comparable rhetoric of
Marxist-Communist neorealism), postwar aesthetics shored up
the false rupture between the Regime and the Republic.

Prose narrative is the genre of choice of Italian Fascism's
prisoners; indeed, prose (as either epistle or narrative) has ever
been the select literary form of the prisoner.[62] The 'explosion of
orality' that characterizes the immediate postwar period found a
congenial home in narrative, either prose or cinema. In a 1987
interview, Primo Levi compared his need to tell of his experience
at Auschwitz to the Ancient Mariner's similar compulsion in
Coleridge's poem of the same name:

> I really needed to tell [my story ...] I had the feeling that Catholics
> must have when they need to go to confession: it's a great relief to
> confess. Or the feeling you have if you're in therapy with a psycho-
> analyst and by telling your story, you break free of it.[63]

Unlike Gramsci, the other much-bruited prisoner of Fascism,
Levi's ability to tell his story depended on his survival. The *Lettere*

dal carcere and the *Quaderni del carcere* both testify to the fact that Gramsci, as a political prisoner, was accorded the privilege of writing, a perquisite that Levi, a Jew detained in a concentration camp, did not enjoy.[64] While in prison, writing served as Gramsci's redemption; in fact, it became one of the 'more intense moments of life,' as he wrote to his sister-in-law, Tatania.[65] Levi's deprivation (his captivity narratives, as he says above, are works of memory, of exorcism) speaks to one of the chief differences between imprisonment experienced by men and by women, a difference which is reproduced in the analogical imprisonment exemplified by the texts studied herein. The deprivation of liberty as punishment for a breach of law is contingent on a previous state of freedom that, given their condition generally and especially during Fascism, is not an appropriate assumption when evaluating women's status in prison. Again, the comparison between women and Jews seems apt: even before his deportation, Levi was not furnished with the full complement of rights and privileges extended to his Gentile compatriots, something the Racial Laws of 1938 made pellucid.[66] Women in prison, like other incarcerated heterodox subjects, are, as Elissa Gelfand and others have noted, 'twice imprisoned.'[67]

The Plan of the Current Work

The disposition of material in *Prison Terms* signifies a critical practice: I move from exploring sites for the incarceration of men to an exploration of women's carceral spaces. The negotiation between juridical and social examples of such spaces helps me to raise questions of concern to feminist inquiry. The social and discursive practices of Fascism mark a zenith for dominant discourse, where patriarchy is at its most exaggerated and exposed. When Fascism is defeated, its overdetermination of gendered subjects abates but does not vanish completely. In this way, the postwar domestic imperative forms connections to the ways Fascism instrumentalized gender. Evaluating incarcerations during and after the Regime exposes the gendered mechanism by which Fascism was presumed to have been dislodged. Whereas following the Regime the male subject was free to return to the customary liberties and entitlements of civic society (suspended or deprived by Fascism), the female subject was turned back to a social order that did not seek or guarantee her emancipation. Illustrating the detainment of female social subjects in the post-Fascist state contests both the 'liberation' of the newly formed Republic and the logic that insists on Fascism's disappearance following the Regime's ouster (July 1943).

Structuring my argument in this way allows a materially and historically grounded theorization of the gendered subject's social space in Italy as it straddles the years of Fascism and its aftermath. The spaces of *Prison Terms* integrate the overlapping ideological registers of the quotidian and the exceptional. What issues is a porous system, not entirely unlike Foucault's, wherein ideology is sometimes imposed from above and sometimes distinguishable in the ways state-ordained strictures are resisted during everyday practices. Thus, some spaces this study designates (e.g., the prison, the barracks, the concentration camp, and the internal exile known as *confino*) reveal patent intervention of the state. Other spaces, like the convent and the brothel, situated in the transom between public and private spheres of social activity, reveal how ideology determined from above dwindles but is still visible. Finally, in the ways that its representations do not change from the time of Regime dicta to the Republic, the home reveals the most infelicitous and hostile of all social spaces: the carceral pretending to be something other than it is, the prison in masquerade.[68] Shuttling back and forth between the end of the Regime and the aftermath illustrates how this motif of the carceral does not observe any strict historical periodization.

The first stop on the itinerary of prison analogues is the barracks. This enclosed space, the focus of chapter 2, signals a shift in two critical ways. First, by taking up literary texts, this chapter marks a change in the representation of prisons. The development from the first to the second chapter corresponds to the move from text to subtext, from juridical to cultural prison, from explicit to concealed repression. Second, this chapter inaugurates the study of the relation between containment, space, and gender. The barracks is the space in service to the state where masculinity is ideated and contained. Recent critical studies in the field have not often addressed the military; this notwithstanding, I argue that understanding the barracks as the space for the convergence of the State and masculinity provides purchase on the emerging discourse of masculinity during the Regime.[69]

Although the ways the Regime instrumentalized women and reproductivity have garnered considerable scholarly attention, the exploration of its corresponding administration of men has been slower to arrive.[70] *Prison Terms* offers a sustained analysis of masculinity and political commitment in Dino Buzzati's 1940 *Il deserto dei Tartari*. Concerning the rise and fall of a feckless officer in an unnamed, Italian-speaking army billeted at the nation's periphery, the novel illustrates Buzzati's critique of Fascism's fetishization of masculinity.

Architecture and *habitus* figure prominently in chapter 3, where I examine the social space of the convent. Architectural spaces in Italy employed to detain criminals were sometimes originally built for other purposes. Such is the case of former ecclesiastical lands which, following Unification, were deeded to the Italian State. In the case of convents, architecture, spatial organization and practice, and etymology – all conspire to produce carceral homologues. Consider, for example, the construction of buildings with cells, the monastic habit of seclusion, and the various derivations of 'poenitentia' which furnish, in English and Italian, both 'penitent' and 'penitentiary.' Indeed, monastic cloisters, from the Latin *claustrum* meaning enclosure, had a long history of this kind of association.[71] This kind of layering (or, considering conventual space, we could say 'veiling') produces the architectural palimpsesting of convents and prisons, which, in turn, suggests similarly layered gender roles in the literature of the specified period. As I show, the progression from layer to layer, from convent to prison, reveals no development; rather, for its perdurable carceral attributes, the convent exemplifies historical stasis.

The convent appears in three dominant modes: as the place where novices are trained, as a form of boarding school for girls and young women, and as an orphanage. Compelling young women to take vows, *monacazione forzata*, is a topos not limited to this period, and, after tracing its lineage, I examine instances of such coercion in Piovène's epistolary novel of 1941, *Lettere di una novizia*, de Céspedes's 1938 *Nessuno torna indietro*, and the short fiction of Banti and Morante. This enduring type of social control and incarceration of women corresponds to the social position of prostitutes, which I explore in chapter 4.

The brothel, the gender-specific space to which I turn in the subsequent chapter, patently displays carceral attributes, and the lack of historical development that the brothel reveals could not be clearer. Significantly, both the literary (1948) and cinematic versions (Carlo Lizzani, 1954) of Vasco Pratolini's *Cronache di poveri amanti* trace the history of the Merlin Law in Parliament during the decade 1948–58. One of the first bills introduced onto the floor of Parliament in 1948, the Merlin Law proposed radical changes in state and social policies concerning prostitution. When the bill was ratified in 1958, it was but a shadow of the earlier, progressive program proposed by Senator Angelina Merlin. Significantly, Vasco Pratolini's delineation of prostitution in *Cronache di poveri amanti* travels a path similar to the one charted by the Merlin Law, and the novel furnishes an exemplary analogy of the public discourse on prostitution in a decade-long historical moment. The absence of change in the public perception of prostitution and literary expression points to a corresponding absence of change in the representation of prostitution in Italy. Further, this absence of change, parallel to the enduring representation of the convent as a space for the confinement of women, points to the ambivalent movement of history that I discussed earlier: forward 'past' the Regime; backward to a time and context anterior to it.

From the liminally public spaces of the barracks, convent, and brothel, we turn, in chapter 5, to a putatively 'private' space, the home.

The last chapter examines the carceral formations of 'home' between 1930 and 1960 in discursive and architectural practices. I examine the ways legislature, public address, criminology, and literary representation work together to articulate 'home' in this period and to criminalize it. Fascist ideology's instrumentalization of sex and procreation represents patriarchal discourse in its most exaggerated mode. Reconstruction-era political discourse expresses the continuation of this ideology, albeit in a palliated mode: women were still bound by the dominant discourse of family, now theorized by the centrist Christian Democrats and the Communist Party (PCI) instead of the Regime.

The publication history of Carlo Emilio Gadda's *Quer pasticciaccio brutto de via Merulana* shares a common time frame with the ratification of the Merlin Law. Published first episodically in the journal *Letteratura* in 1947, and then in novel form and with an alternate ending in 1957, Gadda's masterwork portrays the contrary and ambivalent representation of the home in Fascist Italy: women are either contained within the family structure of the home or outside of it.

In addition to discursive examples of restrictive domestic spaces, this chapter also pursues material constructions, specifically in the form of housing projects and urban planning in Rome in the decade following the end of the Second World War. I examine regulation of the housing industry in the Fanfani Plan (1949) and the way it redeployed 'privacy' perceived as damaged by Fascist design, and all in service to Rome's Master Plan of 1931. Literary representation and ideology enjoy unique standing with regard to urban planning, particularly as it affected public housing. Indeed, city planning and architecture, some architectural historians have argued, were deeply influenced by the re-creation of the working class in neorealist literature and cinema.[72] For what they reveal about the postwar housing industry, urban planning, and residential design, I am interested in two coexistent Mario Ridolfi projects. These include a housing project in Rome, in Via Tiburtina (in the INA-Casa project area known as 'Il Tiburtino'), my primary focus in chapter 5, and the new prison in Nuoro (Sardegna). The concurrence of these structures (apartment complexes and prisons) suggests not their collapse into each other so much as the homologous relation between them. Though Ridolfi's prisons and apartment complexes bear little typological resemblance, their urbanistic location bespeaks a common confinement and isolation, elaborations on the theme of captivity they share. Straining away from utopian postwar rhetoric, Ridolfi's architectural designs reveal how narrow is the interval between prisons and houses, where women, already 'criminalized' in forensic discourse, criminally respond to their domestic captivity. Examination of the spatial tactics of design works to reveal the ways in which the home in Italy cannot quickly detach from its dystopic Fascist past.

Chapter Two

Barracks and Borders, Prisons and Masculinity

Ho fatto rimettere a Sir Samuel Hoare, in risposta alla lettera che egli mi aveva fatto portare la settimana scorsa, una lettera indirizzata al nostro ambasciatore a Londra, il tono della quale è apparso particolarmente amichevole. Questo dissidio che l'Inghilterra ha con noi non ha veramente alcun senso e un conflitto fra le due nazioni è davvero inconcepibile. Nè da vicino, nè da lontano, nè direttamente, nè indirettamente noi vogliamo nuocere ad alcun interesse brittanico. La nostra azione colonizzatrice nell'Africa non potrebbe compromettere nè la prosperità, nè le comunicazioni, nè la sicurezza di uno qualsiasi dei territori imperiali.
[In response to a letter that Sir Samuel Hoare brought to me last week, I have sent with him a response to our ambassador in London; its tone was particularly friendly. England's difference of opinion has no basis and a conflict between the two nations is truly inconceivable. Not from near or afar, neither directly nor indirectly do we wish to harm any British interest. It is not permissible that our colonial action in Africa compromise the prosperity, communication, or security of any imperial interest.]

Benito Mussolini, 3 October 1935, in *Opera omnia*, 27: 160

... siccome gli eserciti, i cannoni rigati, i monitors fioriscono più che mai, è bene che la nuova generazione si imprima profondamente nell'anima il rispetto, il culto, l'idolatria e, se si vuole, la superstizione della propria bandiera ... Sia opera di tutti, giovani e vecchi, grandi e piccoli, di spargerne, di fondarne il culto. Sia sentimento di tutti che la bandiera rappresenta l'Italia, la Patria, la libertà, l'indipendenza, la giustizia, la dignità, l'onore, che per questo la bandiera non si abbassa, non si macchia, non si abbandona mai, e che piuttosto si muore.

[... since armies, cannons in lines, monitors flourish more than ever, the new generation should impress profoundly upon its soul the respect, the cult, the idolatry, and, if preferred, the superstition of its own flag ... It should be everyone's task, young and old, large and small, to found and spread the cult of it [i.e., the flag]. It should be everyone's will that the flag represent Italy, the Patria, liberty, independence, justice, dignity, honour, that for this the flag should not be lowered, nor stained, and that one would rather die than abandon it.]

Massimo D'Azeglio, *I miei ricordi*, 2: 284–5

Storeys/Stories

Although his sole physical complaint is a low-grade fever, Giovanni Corte in Dino Buzzati's 1937 short story 'I sette piani' (Seven Storeys) is advised to seek medical attention in a renowned sanatorium 'in cui non si curava che quell'unica malattia' [where they treated only patients suffering from that particular illness].[1] The hospital's seven storeys represent the illness's varying degrees of gravity: the least infirm patients quarter on the seventh floor, the next healthiest on the sixth, and so on until the rooms of the truly moribund are reached at ground level. Anticipating Foucault's consideration in *Discipline and Punish*, Corte approves of this segregation from the safety of his comfortable, seventh-storey room. He observes that 'questo singolare sistema ... impediva che un malato leggero potesse venire turbato dalla vicinanza di un collega in agonia, e garantiva in ogni piano un'atmosfera omogenea' [this unique system ... proscribed placing a mildly ill patient next to one in agony and guaranteed the homogeneity of each of the clinic's floors] (23).[2] After his first relocation to the sixth floor, however, Corte 'si sentiva a disagio al pensiero che tra lui e 'l mondo normale, della gente sana, già si frapponesse un ostacolo' [felt uneasy at the thought that an obstacle came between him and the normal world of the healthy] (25). The greater the number of floors traversed, the more the distance between Corte and the 'normal world' increases: the eventual transfer to the third floor deprives him of his view of the city, and the trees serve as yet another barrier to the outside world ('solo dal terzo piano in giù la visuale era tolta dagli alberi della cinta' [the view was obscured from the third floor down by the surrounding trees]). Upon arrival, Corte had noticed that the hospital offered its own system of surveillance to the patients and saw that 'le finestre del primo piano ... sembravano lontanissime e che si scorgevano solo di sbieco. Ma non potè vedere nulla di interessante. Nella maggioranza erano *ermeticamente* sprangate dalle grigie persiane scorrevoli' [the windows of the first floor ... seemed far away and were seen only obliquely. But he couldn't see anything interesting. They were for the most part *hermetically shuttered* by the gray blinds] (22, emphasis addded).[3]

As culmination to the fantastic concatenation of bureaucratic events in this hospital administrated by the brilliant and absent 'Dottor Dati' (Doctor Data; power is everywhere, or, as Hartsock says in her critique of Foucault, 'power is everywhere and therefore nowhere'),[4] Corte is transferred to the first floor. He thinks helplessly of the six floors that 'hovered over him with their implacable weight' and wonders to himself 'in quanti anni – sì, bisognava pensare proprio ad anni – in quanti anni egli sarebbe riuscito a risalire fino all'orlo di quel precipizio?' [how many years – yes, years – would it take for him to climb back up to the edge of the precipice?] (33). At 3:30 that afternoon, his room is inexplicably plunged into darkness. Corte 'voltò il capo ... e vide che le persiane scorrevoli, obbedienti a un misterioso commando, scendevano lentamente, chiudendo il passo alla luce' [turned his head and saw the Persian blinds, as if by some mysterious order, slowly lower, plunging the room in darkness] (33).[5]

'I sette piani' reveals Buzzati's interest in the way spatial organization subtends social and power relations. Buzzati trains his focus on an architect in his 1961 novel *Un amore*. The name of this shaper of space, Dorigo, is so sharply reminiscent of Drogo, the protagonist of Buzzati's 1940 novel *Il deserto dei Tartari* and our prime interest in these pages, that it has led critics to make connections between the two works of fiction.[6] 'I sette piani' shares this interest in spatial organization and draws attention to the intersection of penal, juridical, and medical systems. In its portrayal of the protagonist's ever-diminishing autonomy, this short story yields a version in miniature of *Il deserto dei Tartari*. Could Giovanni *Corte* be a 'shorter' ('corto' from the Italian meaning 'short') or abbreviated version of Giovanni Drogo? Both Drogo and Corte acquiesce to the omnipotence of institutions (medicine and the military) and to the *habitus*, or practice, of the architectural spaces of these institutions (the hospital and the barracks). These power constructs victimize both principals: Corte bows to the superior knowledge of Doctor Data and accepts his transfer and ultimate death, and Drogo accepts the expert medical knowledge of the portentous Dottor Rovina (Doctor Ruin), who recommends his removal from the fort, a move which ultimately results in his death.[7] Moreover, both narratives share a common historical frame. Composed in the late 1930s, Drogo's and Corte's acquiescence (and the ensuing disasters) resembles the 'consensus' of the Italian polity that Renzo De Felice theorized as a prime contributing factor to Italian Fascism's robustness throughout its second decade.[8] Like Corte in the sanatorium, the longer Drogo remains at the fort, the greater the distance that yawns between him and the 'normal' world of friends, family, and lovers.[9] Both characters' spatial itineraries share a common topography: they rise to a crest (the seventh floor of the hospital; Fort Bastiani, the mountain aerie), and descend symbolically and materially. As Corte reluctantly descends the hospital's seven storeys, so Drogo hesitantly leaves the mountaintop fort for the town below at the novel's close. For both, the descent presages certain death.

'Confino/Confine' (Confinement/Confines)

Dino Buzzati was on his way to Addis Ababa in 1939 when he gave the manuscript of his just completed novel to Leo Longanesi. Buzzati had been assigned as correspondent to the Ethiopian capital's bureau of the *Corriere della sera*, in whose Milan office he had worked for the six previous years as an editor. That job had been so dull, he told Alberico Sala in a later interview, that it served as the anti-inspiration for his novel about the evanescence of time in a barracks perched at a kingdom's edge. After Buzzati's death, Indro Montanelli added that the novelist had utilized more than the job's monotony of labour: he had also based his characters on his journalist colleagues. As Montanelli observed, 'the story of men inside a phantasmatic fortress who had grown old in their futile expectation of glorious events was nothing else than the editorial board meetings in the newsroom at the *Corriere della Sera*.'[10]

Longanesi thought the novel was fine but that its title needed revision: *La fortezza* (The Fortress) smacked too much of the military, it would not market well, it would mislead the reader, it would disappoint. With the outbreak of the Second World War barely months away, Longanesi's advice seemed prescient. But perhaps the editor hesitated to remind the author of the obvious allusion to *The Castle*, since so many critics had found his work to be derivative of Kafka's, a comparison Buzzati resisted and, evidently, resented.[11] Thus, upon his editor's recommendation and perhaps in response to his experience of Africa, Buzzati rechristened the novel *Il deserto dei Tartari*.[12] Acknowledging the importance of Africa in his novelistic landscape, Buzzati himself would say, after the novel's publication in 1940, that 'L'Abissinia, allora, era come un *western* favoloso ... L'Africa, soprattutto l'Africa dei deserti, mi ha fatto un'immensa impressione' [Abyssinia was like some fantastic *western* ... Africa and above all its deserts impressed me enormously].[13] For Buzzati, Abyssinia becomes the colonial frontier, the stage upon which Italy could play out its national fantasies and pretensions of greater presence in the geopolitical theatre.[14] Buzzati offers this Abyssinia as the corollary to the American frontier, the location of the 'western' and the 'New Frontier' where, as Andrew Ross has observed, 'an ideal masculine way of life [is ...] shown to be threatened with extinction.'[15] *Il deserto*, as I argue, displays a similar preoccupation with masculinity menaced from across a frontier. Indeed, this novel about the rise and fall of a hapless officer in an unidentified yet Italian-speaking army posted at the edge of the nation illustrates Buzzati's critique of Fascism's fetishization of masculinity.

As 'I sette piani' demonstrates, Buzzati's depiction of existential imprisonment is not limited to *Il deserto*. By the same token, a fixation on borders is not unique to the novel either, for Buzzati's *oeuvre* is shot through with it. Panafieu maintains that the frontier and border emblematize the psychological struggle against bureaucracy and modernist fragmentation so characteristic of the author's fiction.

Although in some instances the border's removal from the centre is thought to provide safe harbour, this is not at all the case for Buzzati and may not be the case even in a general sense. Far from offering some kind of marginal position from which one could theorize new and resistant political strategies, the border reifies the binary of centric and ex-centric. This is the precise opposite of what Bhabha describes when he writes that 'it is from the affective experience of social marginality that we must conceive a political strategy of empowerment and articulation.'[16] Borders, as Primo Levi warned in his 1978 *La chiave a stella* (The Monkey's Wrench), 'are where wars start.'[17] Thus, the border's geographic removal does not ensure less scrutiny or social control than might occur at the centre, presumably a more perilous place for its proximity to organs of government vested with authority over the execution of social control (e.g., police forces, secret police, etc.). R. Shields, for example, asserts that margins must exist in relation to centres: margins are either that which is excluded from the centre or the the location of everything that stands in opposition to the centre.[18] Edgar Morin emphasized the fluidity he sees as characteristic of the frontier, a place marked by its potential for transformation. He writes: 'All frontiers, including the membrane of living beings, *including the frontier of nations*, are at the same time as they are barriers, places of communication and exchange. They are the places of dissociation and association, of separation and articulation' (emphasis added).[19]

The prison imagery used to characterize Fort Bastiani implicates the flow of power in the nation, whose outer reaches the garrison ostensibly protects and defends. With the fort's soldiers, Buzzati represents the instability of *amor patriae*, national character, and masculinity under Fascism. These are the issues – enacted in a barracks that stands in the porous zone of the nation's flickering borders – that are constituted and dissolved, knit together and unravelled.

Like the topos of prison and border, Buzzati had used a military setting previously in his fiction. The military is found in the form of the forest rangers in *Bàrnabo delle montagne* (1933), and in *Il segreto del Bosco Vecchio* (1935) in Colonel Procolo, who 'tiene una autoritarietà e gerarchizzante maniera' [displays the authoritarianism and hierarchical manner] so exemplary of the career military man.[20] The military life was, Buzzati felt, of paramount importance to the setting of *Il deserto*, as well. As he told Sala, he chose the barracks because 'la vita militare corrispondeva alla mia natura' [the military corresponds to my nature] and because 'l'ambiente militare, specificamente quello di una fortezza al confine esemplifica il tema della speranza e della vita, che passa inutilmente' [the military atmosphere, specifically that of a fortress on a border, exemplifies the theme of hope and of a life that passes by uselessly].[21] Above all, in a military setting, Buzzati's story would carry the weight of an 'allegoria riguardante tutti gli uomini' [allegory for mankind]. By 'uomini,' Buzzati means here 'mankind,' but his barracks and Drogo's failure are also an allegory for Italian 'men' labouring under the Fascist articulation of masculinity.

Fort Bastiani, as the soldiers' barracks, is a likely place to look for a portrayal of the cult of manliness so central to the Fascist execution of power. The repeated imagery of flaccidity that is used to portray this privileged space relates to a double sense of anxiety over masculinity and national boundary. By way of this motif of flaccidity, Drogo's ineptitude, and the Stato Maggiore's strategic blunders, *Il deserto*, composed in 1939 and published the next year, challenges the conventional depiction of masculinity during the *ventennio*, widely characterized as consistently 'active' and 'virile,' to which the parading of Mussolini's image through various media attests, a topic I return to below. Moreover, this flaccidity impugns Fort Bastiani's principal function, which is to preserve and maintain the nation's boundaries.

The spatial and phenomenological relation between the barracks and the prison signals two critical shifts. First, concentrating primarily – though not exclusively – on literary texts heralds a change in the representation of prisons. The move from the preceding chapter to the current one corresponds to the transition from text to subtext, from juridical to cultural prison, from explicit to concealed repression. Second, this focus inaugurates my study of the relation between containment, space, and gender. In subsequent chapters, I examine spaces designated for the confinement of women, spaces wherein women are confined and where 'femininity' – produced through a variety of cultural practices – is encoded and enforced. Here I investigate the barracks, a site that traditionally isolates men, so that we may study masculinity and its cultural production in Italy at mid-century. Space as a critical category leads to a consideration of *habitus*, which I discussed in the preceding chapter, and to a consideration of geography, the charting of space. Indeed, one of the central episodes in the novel concerns a surveying expedition. The concern for the way the body negotiates the architectural space of the barracks leads me to consider the discursive apparatus of military fashion for what it discloses about the male body and masculinity within the military.[22]

The imprisoning barracks of *Il deserto dei Tartari* perch at the nation's very edge; what does the conjunction of borders and barracks disclose? The military, as Klaus Theweleit established in *Male Fantasies*, his study of the Freikorpsmen in Germany during the interwar years, constructs the barracks as a privileged space; the barracks house those who serve the state and is a place where masculinity is articulated, ideated, and contained. Although recent critical studies of Italian Fascism have not often addressed the military, I argue that an understanding of the barracks gives one purchase on the emerging discourse concerning masculinity during the Regime.[23] I maintain that the absence of theorizing regarding the role of masculinity in the military proper derives from the notion that it was already the obvious repository for the kind of monolithic masculinity Fascism sought to promote.

Marginal Masculinity

*Un posto di confine è sempre un posto di confine, effettivamente ... Una volta
la Fortezza Bastiani era un grande onore. Adesso dicono che è una frontiera
morta, non pensano che la frontiera è sempre frontiera ...*
[A border posting is nevertheless always located at a border ... Being posted
to Fort Bastiani was once a great honour. Now they say it's a dead frontier;
they don't believe that the border is always the border.]

Il deserto dei Tartari, p. 20

For its predication on borders and its protagonist's inability to
negotiate boundaries successfully and to consummate his soldierly duties, *Il deserto dei Tartari* is more than a portrait of existential torment or a modernist reflection on the passage of time.[24]
Critics' resistance to reading *Il deserto* as political allegory voids it
of its historical and cultural context.[25] For Buzzati's novel, as I will
show, is an allegory of anxiety enacted on parallel planes. *Il deserto*
illustrates both existential angst and the Empire's apprehensions
over defining and defending its borders. We should not confuse
this permeability often present in the borderlands with some of
the more sanguine theoretical observations concerning borders'
freedom of movement, polyphony, and equal exchange in the
studies of, for example, Morin and Bhabha.[26] Perhaps in a time of
diminished nationalistic ferment the border's penetrability could
be seen through more optimistic eyes. In the present reading,
the border hypostatizes the nation in its bellicose, aggrandizing
mode: advance, conquer, advance again to stabilize the most
recent line of demarcation. Drogo's failure to recognize this
mode is his downfall and the locus of Buzzati's distinction. The
representations of impotence, flaccidity, and castration make up
the calculus of subject positions with regard to masculinity; in
order to demonstrate how they work to engender anxiety, several
framing comments regarding the mutually entailing roles of the
military and virility are required.

While Fascism's essentialization of women has been widely
analysed, investigations of its corresponding treatment of men

have been slower to appear.[27] As concerns the damage that the discourse of virility inflicts on female subjectivity, it is true that 'the humanist discourse of *virtù*, the genealogical precedent to the rhetoric of virility, may work at times in an emancipatory fashion ... [and] may also ... "castrate women."'[28] Equally true is the assertion that masculinity holds castrating potential for men, which is at once the same and different from its castration of women in any sense, whether specifically Freudian, generally psychoanalytic, or socio-political. The same may be said of the act of castration itself, which deprives the victim-subject of force or potency (*vis*), and achieves different results when redeployed under a system of sexual difference. The Fascist cult of virility paints the backdrop against which we watch Drogo the *inetto* (the inept anti-hero) struggle and fail. As for most barracks, the absence of women is one of Fort Bastiani's virilizing factors. The fort, the province of soldiers, is paired with the effete, civilized (indeed, feminized) town life. Cosmopolitanism and all it offers contradicts Fascism's doctrinaire 'virile' activities. The rhetoric of virility Spackman identifies implicates women during the Regime but does not affect them alone. Virility was codified and normalized by Fascism, and its principal emblem was progeny: manhood meant children.[29] Needless to say, there could have been no prolific mothers without some prolific dissemination.

Mussolini's demographic design, unveiled in the 1927 'Discorso dell'Ascensione,' makes up part of the new imperative of reproductivity. The exhortation from the Duce (himself a good family man) to copulate and propagate was even legalized through a series of tax incentives stipulated by the law of 19 December 1926. The first article established that come January of the new year,

> è istituita ... una imposta personale progressiva sui celibi dai 25 a 65 anni compiuti ... sarà dovuta dai celibi pel solo fatto del loro stato e verrà integrata con altra contribuzione a base progressiva in ragione del reddito complessivo di ciascuno di essi.[30]

[there will be the levying of a progressive personal tax against

unmarried men between 25 and 65 years of age ... it will be owed to
the sole fact of their marital status and will be imposed with other
contributions on a progressive base and owed to the complete tax
of each.]

Using the same logic, men with large families were given tax
breaks.[31]

Vigorous mythologizing, legally supported and ratified, helped
create monolithic masculinity. The youthful Fascist who 'displayed raw energy in dare-devil sports, including the conquest of
the female animal' and later 'in maturity ... begat quantities of
children and boasted of his near insatiable sexual desire'[32] must
have seen the direct connection between sexual performance
and Party adherence. A full range of reactions to the perception
of this connection are imaginable, from acceptance to rejection,
from approval to anxiety. As Carlo Scorza declared, 'We must
make the bachelors and those who desert the nuptial bed
ashamed of their potential power to have children. It is necessary
to make them bow their foreheads in the dust.'[33] Passerini tells of
Turin's Luigi Vercellotti, who had failed in his bid for PNF
(National Fascist Party) membership because he refused to
'andare a casa e saltare adosso alla moglie' [go home and mount
his wife] at the Party's command.[34] In the mid-1930s, Giorgio Gattei, Bologna's mayor – with no irony – exhorted his constituents
to 'chiavate e lasciatelo dentro!' [screw and leave it in!], adding
that it was by 'ordine del partito' [order of the Party].[35] Although
the system of taxation established the Party's (and consequently
the State's) juridical right to require numerous births, it was also
thought that the Party, as the moral guardian of the Italian public, had the responsibility to encourage prolific procreation.

Propaganda served to disseminate the cult of virility, a goal it
achieved partially through the repeated presentation of the
Duce's image in a variety of media. In instructions to the press
corps governing reproduction of his image, it was decreed that
Mussolini not be 'shown participating in "non virile" activities ...
like dancing, but instead [be] shown participating in vigorous
sports such as riding, flying, motorcycling, etc.'[36] In fact, Musso-

lini's putative manliness was paraded so often before the eyes of the Italian polity that the repeated images of his body became part of and helped reproduce what Karen Pinkus describes as 'a universal language [wherein] ... the body itself enacts a performative utterance.'[37] Spackman concurs, adding that 'during the 1930s, the Duce's body ... became the single most compelling binding mechanism of the fascist regime.'[38]

Italy required a strong hand and discipline, and the military became the ideal locale for the display of discipline. Manly Mussolini, it seemed, had no peers in Italy's military. Despite the fact that Italy lagged woefully far behind other European powers in terms of military technological advancement, the Italian populace need not have feared: with Mussolini at the helm, there existed no perceived threat of Italy's exclusion from important technological discovery or military engagement. The Italian Fascist war machine was not adequately mechanized and the philosophy of arming the troops (the focus on the 'uomo-fante,' or infantry) turned out to be antiquated androcentrism.[39] Indeed, a resistance to technological change may have contributed to the way in which the military – particularly in the form of the air corps – was appropriated as a topos by the *romanzo rosa* (the romance novel), the literary genre of choice of a mass female reading public.[40] A proponent of the Fascist military declared that 'chi confondeva il "silenzio" con "l'inazione" dimenticava che la presenza di Mussolini e Vallero alla testa dell'esercito impediva qualsiasi staticità' [whoever confused 'silence' with 'inaction' forgot that the presence of Mussolini and Vallero at the head of the Army prevented any stasis].[41] Nothing could have been further from the truth.

Mussolini's 'genius' lay not in tactics or strategy (or, we note, in military experience). His call to arms displays characteristic (which is to say, abstract) rhetorical feints. As he freely admitted early in his political career,

> Noi non c'intendiamo affatto di strategia, nè di tattica militare, ma conosciamo molto bene il meccanismo interiore dell'anima popolare, perchè le stesse folle che portano oggi le stellette noi

le abbiamo avute nel pugno, in tempi non troppo lontani, e sappiamo le parole che bisogna dire e quelle che non si devono dire,
sappiamo quali molle devono essere toccate, perchè questi uomini
'scattino' nell'azione.[42]

[We do not understand strategy at all, nor military tactics; however,
we know very well the interior mechanism of the popular spirit, for
the same crowds that today wear the pins, we held those very pins
in our fists, not so long ago, and we know the words that need to be
said and those that should not be said, we know which buttons to
push so that these men will 'explode' into action.]

Like a good Futurist, Mussolini mechanized his troops, not their
arms. Soldiers and, above all, their officers became a kind of gre-
nade, and Mussolini readied the pin for removal and activation
('scattare'). At a time when most nations strove for an increase in
mechanized arms and greater firepower, the Italian Army instead
continued to privilege military intelligence and strategy, thereby
increasing the need for good soldiers and better officers who
would model the desired military attributes to their troops.

The figure of the 'uomo-fante,' mechanized along the lines of
Futurist fantasy, has not been adequately plumbed for its cultural
significance in this period. The training of good Fascists began
not in the barracks but in grammar school. By the time Buzzati
wrote *Il deserto*, an entire generation of Italian boys had grown
and developed under Fascist doctrine. In fact, historian Bruno
Wanrooij has convincingly demonstrated the primacy of the
youth factor in the consolidation of Fascist power in the '20s,
which sought to offer Giolitti's beleaguered Italy youthful, exu-
berant political reform.[43] The young soldiers at Fort Bastiani
might very well be the same generation historians have described
participating in the various Fascist youth organizations (e.g., Gioventù italiana del Littorio [GIL], Opera nazionale Ballila [ONB],
Fasci giovanili di combattimento, etc.) instituted in the '20s and
early '30s.[44] Young men carried the Fascist notion of masculinity
with them to the barracks, where their life was given in service to
the nation, bolstering credence in the old Fascist saw 'Tutto nello

Stato, niente al di fuori dello Stato, nulla contra lo Stato' [Every-thing within the State, nothing outside of the State, nothing against the State]. Thus, the barracks offers a simulacrum of male life during Fascism. This simulacrum – a reproduction with no reproductivity – relies entirely on the kind of spectral masculinity congenial to the concerns of Fascism's discursive and icono-graphic practices but strips away the all-important manifestation of that masculinity, namely, issue.

Theweleit demonstrates just how powerful the barracks were for the lessons of power, sexuality, and nationalism learned there. *Male Fantasies* analyses the elite German Freikorps's conceptions of women portrayed in their diaries and memoirs following the Great War. Although Theweleit's subject is Germany during the 1920s, his analysis sheds light on the instructive character of the barracks. The repeated use of flaccidity to portray this privileged space indicates the doubled sense of anxiety over masculinity and national boundaries.[45]

Army of the Flaccid Flag

The flag is by far the most significant symbol for flaccidity in Buz-zati's novel. The image of the flag in *Il deserto* relates to three cate-gories of symbols: the flag in its broadest social sense as a 'vehicle for conveying attitudes toward a social unit of which one is a member';[46] the flag as a sign whose power of communication depends on its display; and the flag as a symbol of armed force and military identity.[47] If understood according to a psychosexual schema, then the slackened flag in this *1940* novel about the *mili-tary* sounds the counterpoint in the master symphony of Fascist virility.

The 1930s, significantly, saw a proliferation of new flags intro-duced for the armed services as a means of celebrating and legiti-mating military control. These flags differ radically from the traditional *tricolore* in colour composition, size, shape, and mate-rial. Each division of the armed forces appears to have wanted its own flag. This proliferation is illustrated by the number of laws – no less than thirteen between 1934 and 1943, a greater number than between Unification (1870) and the Great War – granting flags to the different military units and specifying their treatment and status.[48] That these newly designed flags were of some importance to the representation of state and military power is demonstrated by their swift eradication following the end of the Second World War; the *Regio decreto*, declared on 25 October 1947, recalled all of these special division flags and reinstated the *tricolore* as the official flag for all of the armed forces.[49]

The first appearance of the flaccid flag in *Il deserto* neatly coincides with Drogo's first unobstructed view of Fort Bastiani. As he rounds the bend in the road that leads to the fort on the hilltop, he sees that 'un lieve soffio di vento fece ondeggiare una bandiera sopra il forte, che prima *pendeva floscia confondendosi con l'antenna*' [a light breeze ruffled the flag above the fort that earlier *had hung limply clinging to the pole*] (emphasis added).[50] The fluttering is the hope that something will happen; it is just enough movement to believe, year after year, that something will transpire other than interminable nothingness. Drogo's anticlimactic tragedy is that nothing ever does happen to/for him at the fort. His life is a series of foregone chances and near hits; the breeze comes close enough to stir, but the flag, like Drogo, never quite extends itself. As they approach the garrison, the commanding officer tells Drogo that Fort Bastiani has fallen onto hard times: 'Una volta ... era un grande onore. Adesso dicono che è una frontiera morta' [Once ... it was a great honour. Now they say that it's a dead frontier] (20). Drogo's first approach performs a significant structural task in the novel, and the flag seen at this time has manifold meanings.[51] First, it metonymically assumes the character of the nation; though it does not fly, the flag's position above the fort announces the national affiliation of this remote territory. Second, the flag is a symbol that functions within the novel's economy, a sign that demonstrates *in nuce* Drogo's dilemma: all the energy the fort can summon to greet the novel's hero (or anti-hero) is a slight movement of the flag, a twitch.

In the novel's central episode, the limp flag returns to symbolize anticipation and frustration. In this episode, a platoon is

ordered to establish contact with the Tartar soldiers who come to
survey the area and plot anew the national boundaries. The soldiers (and Drogo with them) had hoped for battle with the unidentified black mass on the horizon inching toward the fort; the
imagined sortie would provide a much-needed *raison d'être* for
these inactive soldiers. The swell of anticipation at the thought of
actual combat stirs the flag: 'Il vento agitava la bandiera alzata sul
tetto del forte' [The wind stirred the flag above the fort] (115).
The company convened before him, Colonel Filmore waits
before issuing orders. Just as Filmore is about to utter, in nearly
Tassian cadence, 'Signori ufficiali ... ecco giunta finalmente l'ora
che aspettiamo da molti anni' [My fellow officers ... finally the
hour we have so long awaited has arrived] (121), the King's mes-
senger enters.[52] Filmore reads the letter and announces that
instead of the enemy platoon so reviled and devoutly wished for,
the soldiers from the Northern Kingdom are surveyors 'incaricati
di stabilire la linea di confine, come venne fatto da noi molti anni
addietro' [charged with establishing the border, as we ourselves
did many years ago] (123). The response is a collective frisson of
disappointment, a sort of shrivelling, withering disappointment
that produces the slackened flag, the national metonym. In
concert with the soldiers' frustration, the flag that had only a
moment earlier fluttered in the breeze falls lifeless once again: 'la
bandiera sul tetto si era afflosciata' [the flag on the rooftop had
fallen limp] (124).[53]

Two related and consonant interpretations of the once more
flaccid flag present themselves. The first localizes the event and
its symbolism: the Tartars pose no threat to the nation at this
point in time ('i loro fucili erano scarichi, le daghe senza filo'
[their rifles unloaded, their bayonets dull]), and although polic-
ing their activities is important for national intelligence, it is only
nominally a military expedition. The second, more general, reading of this scene sees this limp flag in relation to, and in concert
with, the system of impotence.

The discussion of flaccidity is perhaps best understood in the
wider political context of what Panafieu calls the 'Discorso
dell'impotenza' [the discourse of impotence]. Mussolini articu-

lated the 'strong thought' of Fascism early in the *ventennio*. In the 'Discorso a Milano Associazione Costituzionale' [Speech to Constitutional Assembly in Milan] of 4 October 1924, he declared that '... un popolo, per giungere alla potenza, ha bisogno della disciplina. La potenza è la risultante di una coordinazione di sforzi di tutti i cittadini che si sentono al loro posto' [a people, to reach their potential, must have discipline. Power is the result of the coordination of forces of all citizens who work from their respective positions.][54] Nearly a year later he clarified the concept in the 'Discorso a Vercelli' [The Speech at Vercelli], saying

> la potenza è la potenza delle anime; la potenza che è una creazione sistematica, che è una eredità del passato, ma sulla quale sarebbe da parassiti vivacchiare; la potenza che deve essere una creazione quotidiana di sforzi assidui ... E questa potenza è il risultato dello sforzo concorde di tutto il popolo.[55]

> [strength (or 'potency') is strength of character; strength is a systematic creation which is a legacy of the past, but if we were to live on that legacy alone it would be as parasites; strength which must be a daily creation of concentrated efforts ... And this strength is the result of the concerted efforts of the nation.]

Impotence, on the other hand, represents *potenza*'s inverse in the economy of political philosophy. Panafieu relates impotence to the idea of *impegno*, or civic engagement, on which literary reputation pivoted in the postwar period. Echoing Romano Luperini's description of the 'inversion' of ideology in the postwar period, marking the exchange of 'an ideology of literature to a literature of ideology,'[56] Panafieu observes that

> Buzzati resterà ... molto sintomatico dell'odierna crisi nei rapporti fra letteratura e società, fra opposte istanze che scelgono un estetizzante disimpegno sociale o invece optano per un proselitismo ideologico partigiano e finalmente oppressivo sotto una apparenza di altruismo.[57]

[Buzzati will remain ... highly symptomatic of the actual crisis of the relationship between literature and society, between opposed instances that choose an aestheticizing social lack of engagement or opt instead for an ideological and partisan proselytism, which is finally oppression in the guise of altruism.]

Expanding Panafieu's matrix of 'impotence,' or political power-lessness, I would emphasize that parabola from which his metaphor derives its force: sexual impotence. This impotence manifests itself in a sustained series of flaccid images and images of paralysed wonderment when confronted by the 'vaginal' enemy embodied in the desert.

The image of the perpetually limp flag operates in tandem with the desert, whose significance should be obvious in a novel of this name: the desert is that space which belongs to the enemy Other; it is unknown, the inscrutable territory that must either be crossed or defended against. In an interview with Panafieu, Buzzati speaks of the desert as a soporific, describing it 'come la droga' [like a drug]. In fact, perhaps we ought to call Drogo motionless before the desert, *drogato* – drugged – instead. Drogo is fascinated by the desert and asks special permission to access the fort's lookout so that he may see beyond the walls. Soldiers have claimed, Morel tells him, that despite the habitual fogs they have seen fantastic visions, that even Major Ortiz has seen a 'lunga macchia nera' [long black stain]. Drogo is mesmerized by the 'other world' that he sees across the expanse of the desert:

Dove mai Drogo aveva già visto quel mondo? C'era forse vissuto in sogno o l'aveva costruito leggendo qualche antica fiaba? Gli pareva di riconoscerle, le basse rupi in rovina, la valle tortuosa senza piante nè verde, quei precipizi a sghembo e infine *quel triangolo di desolata pianura* che le rocce davanti non riuscivano a nascondere. Echi profondissimi dell'animo suo si erano ridestati e lui non li sapeva capire. (33, emphasis added)

[Where had Drogo seen this world before? Had he been there in his dreams or had the idea for it come by reading some fairy tale of old? He seemed to be able to discern things – the crumbling rocks, the winding valley where neither trees nor vegetation grew, the sheer slopes and finally that *triangle of desolate plain* that the rocks could not conceal. The scene profoundly affected him in a way he couldn't understand.]

The Tartar's 'triangle' surfaces yet again, tantalizing Drogo with its exotic difference. It is a memory of something already – we might say, following Freud – 'uncannily' experienced, a place visited in a dream or through the structured fantasy of literature. Significantly, out of this 'lunga macchia nera' emerges the enemy.

What is the dark triangle save a vaginal icon, and a powerful one at that? According to Freud,

> It often happens that neurotic men declare they feel there is something uncanny about the female genital organs. This unheimlich place, however, is the entrance to the former Heim [home] of all human beings, to the place where each of us lived once upon a time and in the beginning. There is a joke saying that 'Love is home-sickness'; and whenever a man dreams of a place or a country and says to himself, while he is dreaming: 'this place is familiar to me, I've been here before,' we may interpret the place as being his mother's genitals or her body ... the prefix 'un' is the token of repression.[58]

The fear of vaginal potency may be related to the fiction of the *vagina dentata*, but surely the fact that the dark triangle produces – indeed, gives birth to – the enemy is the more palpable danger.[59] Gillian Rose has pointed out that the geographical category of landscape, which Drogo's desert exemplifies, has a long history of association with the 'feminine.' The pleasure of looking at landscapes is very much, according to Rose, about a male (and typically heterosexual male) gaze.[60] That Buzzati attributes tropes to the stereotypical castrating potential of the vaginal desert will win him no points in feminist annals, but nor should it endanger the way *Il deserto* systematically subverts images of masculinity. A fructive union of the 'vaginalized' desert and the army of the flaccid flag requires penetrating the boundary, and this the Stato Maggiore categorically proscribes. Significantly, geography and military texts of the '20s and '30s shore up such literary expression of a 'vaginalized' frontier. Periodicals such as *Stato maggiore, Esercito e nazione*, and *Nazione militare* appearing between 1932 and 1938 define the borderlands to the north of Friuli, since d'Annunizio's 1919 occupation of Fiume, a district long coveted by irredentists – the very zone that offers itself so readily as the border Fort Bastiani so imperfectly maintains – as 'il bacino di Iugoslavia' [the pelvic basin of Yugoslavia].[61] This conflation of military and gynecological/obstetrical language articulates the corresponding sexual anxiety writ large on the body of the nation.[62] Strict maintenance of the national boundary, the fort's mission, forbids unauthorized ventures into the desert. The debacle of Drogo's watch and the surveying expedition are two important episodes for a reading of the relationship of boundary, masculinity, and Drogo's ineptitude. Both scenes convey his impaired sense of military protocol and reveal that transgressing boundaries results in death. Both episodes, moreover, show the peril and hostility of the border, the kind of danger one would expect to be displayed in a 1940 novel.

Drogo's watch at the New Redoubt demonstrates the impaired military judgment that will cost him any career advancement whatsoever; additionally, this episode helps establish Buzzati's opposition of soldier/non-soldier that he refines in the later episode devoted to the surveying expedition. Drogo is initially excited by the prospect of sole command of the watch at the New Redoubt, where he, for twenty-four hours, is more important than the king. The movement Drogo detects across the plane of the demilitarized zone shocks him and is as thrilling as the thought of engagement had been for the entire garrison before the identity of the Tartar surveying expedition had been discovered. The small black speck that Drogo views through his glass is finally discernible: a riderless, presumably harmless, horse. The horse shocks Drogo, for it '*spezzava la regola*, riportava le antiche leggende del nord ... *riempiva della sua illogica presenza l'intero deserto*' [*broke the rule*, it brought back ancient legends of the

North ... *it filled the entire desert with its irrational presence*] (95, emphasis added). Drogo adopts a 'wait and see' attitude; he conforms to the 'più minute formalità del servizio di guardia' [most minute formalities of the guard] to show Tronk and the others that 'il cavallo ... non lo aveva turbato; *e trovava questo molto militare*' [the horse ... did not disturb him; and *he found this to be a very military attitude*] (97, emphasis added). His by-the-book refusal to venture outside of the Redoubt's perimeters and collect the horse forces Private Lazzari to break rank on the return march. Apparently, the horse – Fiocco – is his. The changing of the guard is a Byzantine affair at Bastiani, requiring three passwords deployed at precise moments. Stranded outside the fort's walls without the new password, Lazzari 'si ricordò in un lampo le duri leggi della Fortezza, si sentì perduto' [remembered in a flash the hard and fast rules of the Fortress, he knew he was lost] (102). He calls out to the soldier on duty, even using his nickname, and identifies himself. The soldier does not respond to such intimacy, however, for the individual, Lazzari's nicknamed comrade-in-arms, has been replaced by an anonymous Every Soldier:

> ... la sentinella non era più 'Moretto,' era semplicemente un soldato con la faccia dura che adesso alzava lentamente il fucile ... la sentinella non era più il Moretto con cui tutti i camerati scherzavano liberamente, era soltanto una sentinella della Fortezza, in uniforme di panno azzurro scuro con la bandoliera di mascarizzo, assolutamente identica a tutte le altre nella notte, una sentinella qualsiasi aveva mirato ed ora premeva il grilletto. (102)

> [... the sentinel was no longer Moretto but simply a soldier with a hardened face who now slowly raised his rifle ... the sentinel was no longer Moretto whom all the soldiers joked with, he was only a sentinel at the Fortress, in a uniform of dark blue stuff with a leather bandolier, absolutely identical to all the others in the darkness, Any Soldier who took aim and was now pulling the trigger.]

Moretto, now 'semplicemente un soldato,' 'soltanto una sentinella,' in his uniform 'assolutamente identica a tutte le altre' [simply a soldier, only a sentinel; absolutely identical to all the others] has no choice but to shoot his one-time comrade who has been foolish enough to muck around out of bounds, outside Bastiani's walls, outside established law and order, outside language. After all, Lazzari is shot for not knowing the password. Moretto has become Every Soldier; not only the 'soldier male' of criticism investigating the cultural articulations of masculinity, but the very paradigm from which this critique has wrought its symbolic significance, a *male soldier*. Moretto's 'faccia dura,' his hardened face, recalls the 'armoured' body of Theweleit's *Freikorpsmänner*, those soldiers acutely aware of the boundaries of their bodies, boundaries carved out by their military uniform, which is itself prophylaxis for the contagion of the civilian (read: hysterical and feminine) mass.[63]

Buzzati's soldiers have no friends or intimates, no identities with nicknames; they have comrades who share their duties and follow common regulations. When discipline disappears, anomie follows. Like Drogo during the time of his orientation to the fort, Lazzari reveals faulty civilians' logic. He has failed to realize that military life razes individual difference in favour of the regulation requisite to national security. Lazzari is the non-soldier; Martelli/ Moretto, the exemplary one who puts aside friendship and identity for order. That Lazzari misgauged the situation signalled his demise; that it happened under his command is Drogo's tragedy. As the Division Commandant reminds him during his furlough, Lazzari's death may have been accidental, but it happened on Drogo's watch.

The Divisive *divisa* (uniform): Military Fashion and Masculinity

Like the proliferation of flags during the '30s, the uniforms designed by divisions of Italy's armed forces signal a heightened military presence. Military fashion operates outside an intervening economic or ideological apparatus: it is unbuffered ideology.[64] While the Duce performed a strong and typical version of masculinity through a series of staged events, the Italian armed forces crafted, through military dress and spectacle, a similar projection of masculinity appropriate to received notions of the military.[65] And the welter of detail concerning the distinction between divisions staggers the imagination. Consider only the collar of the basic uniform (not field or dress uniforms, which were more complicated still): 43 separate divisions of the armed forces wore 21 different yet extremely similar collars. At times only piping of a different colour at the collar's edge distinguishes between regiments.[66] No wonder Prosdocimo, the company tailor, admonishes Drogo for commissioning a cloak with a shorter than regulation collar: 'La moda vorrà il collo basso ... ma per noi militari la moda non c'entra. La moda ha da essere il regolamento' [Fashion calls for a short collar ... but fashion doesn't matter for a soldier. Fashion is what regulation wants it to be] (56). Although Prosdocimo will not alter the collar, out of observance of military regulation, there is in his refusal the sense that Drogo should not care about his cloak, when in fact Drogo does care. Thus, an oblique representation of the 1930s European belief that fashion is a feminizing business.[67]

Uniforms play a similarly important role in the episode of the surveying expedition, in which Buzzati opposes the hulking Captain Monti and his brutish masculinity to the slimly elegant (and fey) Lieutenant Angustina. As they set out from the fort, Monti notices Angustina's shoes, unsuitable for their outing, but says nothing. 'Il capitano Monti aveva scarpe grosse con chiodi, simili ai quelli dei soldati. Soltanto Angustina portava stivali' [Captain Monti wore climbing boots equipped with cleats, like those the enlisted men wore. Only Angustina wore dress boots] (126). Monti tries repeatedly to provoke Angustina, to elicit some kind of acknowledgment of his (Angustina's) discomfort during the hike and therefore recognition of his (Monti's) superior soldierly rectitude. When this strategy fails, he forces the pace of the march until Angustina, sweating and pale, notices that the Tartars have already gained the summit of the peak that divides the two nations. Just below, Angustina acts out his farce, playing cards with death after Monti quits the game, and maintaining 'la bella figura' in the face of the enemy and of his own demise.

Shoes alone do not distinguish Angustina from the company;

clothing for Angustina, and significantly for Drogo, provides the means to a non-regulative and more individualized identity. Angustina's elegant cloak, especially as he displays it in his death tableau, is distinctive for its polysemy. A soldier's uniform ensures soldierly demeanour, discipline, behaviour; what is more, it erects a boundary between the 'armored' soldierly self and the streaming, fluid, and inchoate non-military mass. A soldier in uniform 'assolutamente identica a tutte le altre' is reliable, manageable, and predictable, as we saw in the episode of Lazzari's death. In the final tableau of the surveying expedition, the fall and folds of Angustina's singular cloak are particularly suggestive. Gilles Deleuze discusses the way that the 'fold' of fabric, like the folds in Angustina's flowing cape, operates simultaneously with the body that it covers and against it, in the sense that it covers or obscures the body beneath.[68] Angustina's cloak, however, cannot protect him from the elements.

As he sits dying, his cloak gathered around him, the lieutenant recalls 'un vecchio quadro rappresentante la fine del Principe Sebastiano' [an old portrait illustrating the death of Prince Sebastian] (141) in one of the meeting rooms at the fort. Mortally wounded, the prince appears leaning against a tree trunk, 'il mantello ricadente con armoniose pieghe; nulla c'era nella immagine della sgradevole crudeltà fisica della morte' [his cloak falling in pleasing folds around him; the image gave no idea of the cruel reality of death]. Angustina clearly recalls the early-twentieth-century figure of the dandy, a parallel nowhere clearer than in his death scene. As Richard Dellamora outlines, the figure of the dandy in English society symbolized bourgeois desire for the appearance of the aristocratic.[69] Moribund Angustina offers a picture of 'nobiltà ed estrema eleganza' [nobility and extreme elegance; emphasis added] at the moment of death, and Angustina 'oh non ch'egli ci pensasse, andava assomigliando al Principe Sebastiano ferito nel cuore' [oh, not that he was thinking about it, but Angustina resembled Prince Sebastian wounded in the heart]. The wounded 'Prince' Sebastian hints also at another wounded Sebastian, specifically, Saint Sebastian, notable for his recurrence within a homosocial iconography where his martyrdom (the piercing of the arrows) implies sexual ecstasy and, by extension, male masochism. Indeed, Angustina, whose very name would seem to derive from 'angustiare' (which Devoto and Oli define as 'procurare afflizione, addolorare intimamente, essere in pena, *tormentarsi*'; emphasis added), appears to embody male masochism.[70]

It is worth observing that Angustina's death tableau recalls not only painting, as the omniscient narrator observes, but other plastic arts as well, among them sculpture and architecture in a decorative mode. Frozen by the cold, the smile literally frozen on his lips, the lieutenant's body and countenance clearly suggest the hardened surface of statuary. Further, the pleats of his cloak, reminiscent of the 'pleasing' folds of Prince Sebastian's mantle in the painting imply architecture in a decorative mode; moreover, the pleats help explain one of the more elusive episodes of the novel. Paulette Singley and Deborah Fausch make an early-twentieth-century connection between drapery and architecture. They remind us that in the year in which he published *Vers une architecture* (1923), Le Corbusier also dedicated a series of lectures to the subject of drapery at the École des Beaux Arts.[71] Buzzati uses the fold as a narrative device, employing it to collapse time and distance in the novel. He folds back in space the mountain peak so that he may compare it to the fort across the valley and thereby draw Angustina into proximity with Drogo. Simultaneously, he weaves oneiric time (in the form of Drogo's dream) into the narrative present.

Buzzati makes use of two obvious typographical departures to draw attention to the structuring mechanism of the fold. In the first of two passages that feature these interventions, Captain Monti suggests that Angustina join him and the others in the lea of the outcropping:

'Grazie, capitano,' disse con fatica Angustina e riuscendogli troppo difficile parlare, alzò lievemente una mano, facendo un segno, come a dire che non importava, che erano tutte sciocchezze senza il minimo peso. (*Alla fine il capo degli spiriti gli rivolse un gesto imperioso e Angustina, con la sua aria annoiata, scavalcò il davanzale e si sedette graziosamente nella portantina. La fatata carrozza mosse dolcemente per partire.*) (132, emphasis in original)

['Thanks, Captain,' Angustina said with effort and, finding it too difficult to speak, lifted his hand and made a small gesture, as if to say that nothing mattered, that they were all jokes without the slightest importance. (*Finally the head spirit imperiously signalled Angustina, who, with his customary boredom, leapt over the windowsill to sit gracefully in the carriage. The fateful coach serenely began its departure.*)]

The Roman font signifies Angustina, while the italics interpolate a dream of Drogo's the reader remembers from its first recounting several chapters earlier. Not content to cordon off the two discrete spheres by typographical font alone, Buzzati also encloses Drogo's dream in parentheses.

Shortly after this, Buzzati once more uses the same conspicuous device of embedding within the same paragraph these two spheres and fonts. Closer still to death, Angustina tries to speak and

Due parole e la testa di Angustina si ripiegò in avanti abbandonata a se stessa. Una delle sue mani giacque bianca e rigida entro la piega del mantello, la bocca riuscì a chiudersi, di nuovo sulle labbra andò formandosi un sottile sorriso. (*Traendolo via la portantina, egli staccò gli sguardi dall'amico e volse il capo dinanzi, in direzione del corteo, con una specie di curiosità divertita e diffidente. Così si allontanò nella notte, con nobiltà quasi inumana. Il magico corteo andò serpeggiando lentamente nel cielo, sempre più in alto, divenne una confusa scia, poi un minimo ciuffetto di nebbia, poi nulla.*) (132–3, emphasis in original)

[Two words and Angustina's head fell forward on his chest. One of his hands lay white and rigid in a fold of his mantle, his mouth closed and, again, his lips spread in a subtle smile. (*As the carriage took him away, with a sort of diffident and amused curiosity, he turned his gaze from his friend in the direction the cortège was taking. And away he went into the night with an almost other-worldly nobility. The magical cortège twisting its way slowly through the sky, ever upward, became a hazy trail, then a small puff of fog, then nothing.*)]

The intermingling of typographical fonts, an otherwise unique occurrence in the novel, is made all the more conspicuous for its appearance twice on the same page. That this device should also appear at the structurally prominent point of closure of chapter 15, the precise midway point of the novel (which consists of thirty chapters), cannot be accidental. Flagged typographically, the fold overlaps Angustina and Buzzati side-by-side not only geographically but temporally, as well. Just prior to this typographical merge, the narrator imagines that 'perhaps' Drogo, on watch at the fort across the valley, can see the lanterns at the top of the crest. Drogo, like Angustina, had had the opportunity to make the expedition, but had demurred. When Buzzati warps Angustina and Drogo into the same fabric, he advances their union, their sartorial tastes, their mien, in opposition to Captain Monti and the other soldiers, 'pur essendo ben più vigorosi e spavaldi, il capitano, il sergente e tutti gli altri soldati sembrarono l'un l'altro *rozzi bifolchi*' [even though they were much more vigorous and brave, the Captain, the sergeant, and all the enlisted men looked like *rubes*] (131, emphasis added). That these dandified officers should both meet their end in the novel testifies to their subversive menace, as well as to the power of dominant military culture.

The 'sartorial gaze' I have been discussing could go further in establishing a connection between nation-building and actual (as in architectural) construction than might otherwise be supposed.[72] Even before the platoon's return to Fort Bastiani and the garrison learns of Angustina's hero's death 'in the line of duty,' Drogo realizes that the expedition was a missed opportunity to profile his courage and desire to serve. Looking out over the desert, he realizes that in lieu of combat, the mission could have provided him with his *raison d'être* as a career military man. Although at first it seemed pointless to him, he was sorry he had not gone along, for 'non soltanto in guerra ... si poteva trovare qualche cosa di degno' [one could accomplish something worthy not only during wartime] (141). Once again, 'troppo tardi, l'occasione gli era passata vicina e lui l'aveva lasciata andare' [too late, the opportunity had passed close by and left him behind] (141). His absence on the expedition does not go unobserved, and Angustina's hero's accolades underscore still further his missed opportunity. Had he only asked, Ortiz says to him at the funeral, he could have had the chance, like Angustina, to defend his country and to die a hero. Angustina made the most of his miserable posting and 'è morto come in battaglia ... Come se avesse preso una pallottola' [it is as if he dies in a battle ... As though he had taken a bullet]. He is, Ortiz allows, 'un eroe, c'è poco da dire ...' [a hero, there's nothing else to say] (145).

Only a misguided and befuddled sovereign or capricious state would consider Angustina a hero and create a barracks situation in which soldiers should be forced to fire on their mates to satisfy regulations. The Division Commandant does not comprehend Angustina's posthumous honours. He tells Drogo during their interview in town that 'per una stupida ostinazione compromettere la linea del confine ... Non so come abbiano ... bèh, lasciamo stare!' [to compromise the national border out of sheer stubbornness ... I don't know how it ... Oh well, better to forget about it] (168, ellipses in original). For the Commandant, the nation's boundaries must not be 'compromised' and their protection is the task of every soldier (especially those at Bastiani). A soldier (worse still, an officer) who plays cards while on reconnaissance at a mountain summit and dies of pneumonia is not the stuff of heroes and legends. Although Angustina's final action maintains 'bella figura' in the face of the enemy, it shows tragically poor military judgment. Angustina's heroic elevation is an ironic condemnation of the nation, of the military, and of Fascist soldierhood.

Military fashion garnered much attention during the *ventennio*, and particularly during the '30s, but action and discipline took precedence over 'bella figura.' Tölölyan notes that the nation cannot tolerate difference within its ranks and establishes ghettoes and promulgates exclusionary laws based on race to ensure homogeneity within its perimeters.[73] The military, and particularly one of Buzzati's chimerical stripes, wages the battle of homogeneity on both fronts, interior and exterior. The Stato Maggiore can no more countenance difference within its ranks than can the nation within its boundaries. Furthermore, this pair of episodes reveals the peril of the border, the crossing of which results in death. Drogo's indoctrination at Bastiani during his first four years includes lessons on soldierly duty, service, and heroism, the very lessons young men were learning all over Italy during the *ventennio.*

Community, *impegno*, and Critique

The recent scholarship of nationalism maintains that sexuality, especially one of a homosocial flavour, is part and parcel of the nation-state.[74] Anderson believes that the nation 'is always conceived as a deep, horizontal comradeship.'[75] As Theweleit demonstrates, a political enemy can be perceived as a sexual threat. Similarly, Neil Hertz analyses 'the way in which, in the context of the 1848 Revolution and the Commune, a political threat may be presented as a sexual threat.'[76] The Tartars present such a threat. They embody the fearful combination of both sons and lovers: born of the dark triangle of the northern forest, they are brave (and successful) soldiers whose contact with 'the dark triangle' neither undermines nor damages their virility. Unlike the minimal platoon that came to survey the boundaries so many years earlier, the Tartars come in armed, dangerous droves at the novel's end; Drogo surveys the desert and sees 'un denso brulichio di uomini e convogli che scendeva verso la Fortezza' [a dense mass of men and convoys that were making their way toward the Fortress] (223). When the image multiplies vertiginously, Drogo loses consciousness and 'svenuto, *si afflosciò* sul parapetto come un fantoccio' [having fainted, he *fell limp* on the parapet, like a puppet] (223, emphasis added). Drogo's limp and wasted body is the pure and poetic response to the invasion. For decades he lived beneath the lifeless flag of Fort Bastiani, forgetting Ortiz's maxim that 'un posto di confine è sempre un posto di confine ... la frontiera è sempre frontiera ...' [a border posting is always a border posting ... the frontier is always the frontier]. The novel's close sublates the spheres of national and masculine sex-

ual anxiety: Drogo's inanimate body dangling from its inert pup-
pet's strings (si afflosciò ... come un fantoccio) represents a sharp
antithesis to a colonially-minded, aggrandizing Italy endeavour-
ing to enlarge its territories and extend its borders.

In a novel written at the dawn of the Second World War, the
illustration of such a crisis of masculinity (and military heroism at
that) surprises. Leo Longanesi advised Buzzati to change the title
of his manuscript and, considering censorship in the Regime at
this time, he was right to do so; La fortezza was too militaristic.
Buzzati wrote boldly and critically of the military and of masculinity, fashioning a tale of failed officers and impotent armies strug-
gling to defend the nation's borders at a time when Italy was
preparing, as it were, to gird its loins for war.

Buzzati was not appreciated in postwar Italy and this is surprising, for Il deserto certainly undermines the prevailing portrayals of
manly men and competent soldiers and, thus, offers an incisive
critique of the Regime. As literary allegory, Il deserto formally
defies certain narrative conventions of chronology. As political
allegory, it issues a similar challenge. The timelessness characteristic of allegory duly creates an achronological sense of history,
which helps prepare the terrain for possible ideological continuities between Regime and Republic. Buzzati's 1940 critique of the
military should have passed muster in the postwar climate of revisionism but, significantly, did not.

The reorganization of the military in post-Fascist Italy reveals
continuities with the Regime-era practices. In the preceding
chapter, I mentioned the failure of defascistization with regard to
the judiciary, and efforts to 'purge' the military of its fascist sympathizers fared no better.[77] Ginsborg tells us that 'the democratic
and innovative spirit of the partisans did not succeed in permeat-
ing the armed forces, and no effective reform took place.'[78] As
Domenico has noted, Marshal Badoglio's postwar efforts at
reconfiguring the military were less of a dismantling than a reorganization of the existing hierarchy. This conservative impulse
should perhaps not give surprise; as Giuseppe Di Palma notes,
Badoglio had 'earned his baton and the leadership of the joint
chiefs of staff for masterminding the invasion of Ethiopia under

Mussolini.'[79] At times, Marshal Badoglio even reassigned the same personnel to the 'new' armed forces. Domenico writes that the 'Blackshirt Militia ... was simply reconstituted into the Italian army, a disastrous move since at one stroke the royalist ground forces received a strong dose of ideological authoritarianism.'[80]

Whether it meant staying in Rome and joining Badoglio, or continuing an alliance with Mussolini in Salò, the armed forces of Fascism did not disband following the events of July 1943. Although Badoglio, the first non-Fascist prime minister of the interim period, publicly dissolved the PNF, other of the Regime's appurtenances of power remained in place. Fascists, even high-ranking Party members, found places (sometimes prominent places) in Badoglio's restructured armed forces. Some of the officers Badoglio recycled included Guido Jung, Mario Roatta, Tommaso Penetta, Antonio Sorice, Renato Prunas, and Navy Admiral Raffaele De Courten.[81] Whereas attempts to re-educate enlisted men may have been more successful, the officers presented another story. The attempt at reorientation toward a non-fascist military was greeted with tremendous indifference by the officer corps; as Domenico tells us, Mussolini himself wrote to Badoglio, offering his services to the newly constituted militia.

Chapter Three

Penitents and Penitentiaries: Interstices, Resistance, Freedom

Un conseil qu'une bonne et sage superieure devrait suivre avec toutes celles pour qui leur couvent est une prison; et le couvent est une pour moi mille fois plus affreuse que celles qui renferment les malfaiteurs; il faut que j'en sorte ou que j'y perisse.
[One piece of advice that a good and wise mother superior should follow with all those for whom her convent is a prison; and it is one for me, a prison a thousand times more terrible than the one that houses criminals; I must get out of here lest I die.]

Denis Diderot, La religieuse, p. 62.

L'impossibilità di scriverti subito e di evitare a tempo qualche iniziativa catastrofica ... mi empiva di un vero furore, ti assicuro. Mi sembrava di essere doppiamente carcerato, poichè anche tu ti mettevi a non riconoscermi nessuna volontà, a ordinare la mia vita come ti saltava in testa, senza voler ascoltare il mio parere, che pure sono in carcere, so cos'è, ne ho i segni dolorosi sulla pelle.
[My inability to write immediately and warn you off of some catastrophic initiative enraged me, let me assure you. It seemed I suffered from a double imprisonment, for even you conceded me no agency, even you decided to order my life in any way that came to mind without even listening to my opinion; yet *I* am the one in jail, I know what prison is: I wear its marks on my skin.]

Antonio Gramsci, letter to his sister-in-law, 6 September 1928, in *Lettere dal carcere*, p. 227

Misprisions

Just released from the *carcere giudiziario* (trial-pending jail), Curzio Malaparte was on board a southbound train from Rome when he met a soldier of the occupying German armed forces. Someone in the crowded compartment asked the haggard-looking Malaparte whether he was returning from the front, whereupon the soldier scoffed that Italy no longer had a front, nor were cries of 'viva il Duce' heard any longer. He hadn't left the front, Malaparte explained, but, rather, Regina Coeli. 'Che cos'è Regina Coeli?' the soldier queried. 'Un convento?' [What is this Regina Coeli? A convent?].[1] Not a convent, Malaparte corrected, a prison. But the soldier disagreed: 'Ormai non c'è più prigione. Più sbirri, più carcerieri, più prigione. Più nulla ... Finita la prigione, finita l'Italia' [There is no more prison in Italy. No more police force, no more jailers, no more jails ... Prisons are finished, Italy is finished] (619). The other passengers laughed bitterly at this: 'Tutti si misero a ridere guardando il soldato ... Tutti nello scompartimento, nel corridoio, negli altri scomparti-menti, negli altri corridoi, negli altri vagoni, tutti ridevano, tutto il treno rideva, dalla testa alla coda, sussultando e torcendosi sui binari' [Everybody started to laugh ... Everyone in our compart-ment laughed, in the corridor, in the òther compartments, in the other corridors, in the other cars, everybody laughed. From engine to caboose, the train itself laughed, shimmying and twist-ing on the tracks] (619).

Malaparte's remembrance from *Kaputt*, his dark memoir of the immediate postwar, locks onto the subject of this chapter, which examines the carceral space of the convent. The soldier's mispri-sion is ironic in two, contradictory ways. First, by August 1943, one month following Mussolini's ouster and the date of the epi-sode reported in *Kaputt*, martial law of the Third Reich had dis-placed Italy's penal system. The new order of discipline and surveillance superseded the need for specific prisons like Regina Coeli. As Malaparte notices, in Italy it is always 'la prigione, ancora la prigione, sempre la prigione ... Nient'altro che pri-gione, sgherri, e uomini ammanettati, questa è l'Italia' [prison, still prison, always prison in Italy. Nothing but prison, cops, and men in shackles: that's Italy] (617). The second irony in the sol-dier's statement concerns his near accuracy; at a linguistic level, he correctly recognizes the Latin as the Pope's and not Caesar's, but that is only part of the story. Ecclesiastical history buttresses his mistake: founded in 1643 by Anna Colonna Barberini, Regina Coeli had served as the convent for the Salesian order for more than two hundred years.[2] Following Unification (1870), however, when many Church properties came under State control, the convent's role changed: since 1884 Regina Coeli had operated as Rome's largest and most centrally located jail, where those accused of crimes varying in seriousness awaited trial.[3] The architectural and cultural layering of Regina Coeli's identity, once a convent and now a prison, was so well known that it was popularized in song: 'Le Mantellate so' delle suore, ma a Roma so sortanto celle scure; 'na campana sono a tutte l'ore, ma Cristo nun ce sta drento a 'ste mura' [The Mantellate are nuns, but in Rome they are only dark cells; the bells ring at all hours, but Christ is not within the walls].[4]

The kind of cultural and material palimpsest that Regina Coeli offers is not unique. Many of Italy's jails at one point had been convents, monasteries, or other ecclesiastical buildings whose spatial organization felicitously coincided with the newly unified Italian state's need to isolate and punish unruly subjects. The practice of interning criminals in ecclesiastical properties for their incarceration and 're-education' was centuries in the making in Italy before the definitive transfer to the State following Unification of the *ius puniendi* (the right to punish).[5] Luigi Settembrini tells us in his *Lettere dall'ergastolo* that *garibaldini* (comrades of Giuseppe Garibaldi) called their colleagues imprisoned in Neapolitan prisons 'monache,' and they called the island prison of Santo Stefano 'il convento.'[6] Similarly, and more to the point in the present context, Camilla Ravera observed that she felt upon entering prison as though she 'entered a convent [and was] living among the novices.'[7] A century before Malaparte, Silvio Pellico had noticed a similar architectural conflation of prisons and convents. In Milan's Santa Margherita jail, he marvelled that

un secolo fa questo era un monastero: avrebbero mai le sante e le pentitenti vergini che lo abitavano, imaginato che le loro celle suonerebbero oggi, non più di femminei gemiti e d'inni devoti, ma di bestemmie e di canzoni invereconde, e che conterebbero uomini d'ogni fatta, e per lo più, destinati agli ergastoli o alle forche?[8]

[this was a convent a century ago: would the saintly and penitent virgins who lived here ever have imagined that their cells would ring today not with feminine laments and devout hymns but with blasphemy and bawdy songs, and that they would contain every sort of man, all of them destined, for the most part, for a life sentence or the gallows?]

Although Pellico, in this passage from *Le mie prigioni*, thinks to contrast his carceral space with its prior monastic use, he actually joins for comparison the similar spatial arrangements of convents and prisons. Small, uniform cells (each with its own window) distributed along corridors leading to common meeting areas was a spatial configuration as serviceable to a penitent as a penitentiary user. Malaparte extends Pellico's comparison, revealing how the soldier's simple misprision belies the ways that the convent and the jail, both institutions of social control, form imbrications within a penal system.

The preceding chapters traced some institutional continuities between the Fascist Regime and the new Republic and explored some of the tensions created between spatial organization and practice. Moving into the carceral space of the convent, we see a similar lack of change. The absence of the convent's architectural development corresponds to the unchanging daily life of the nuns themselves, as well as to the absence of change in women's space within society. The urban geography surrounding Regina Coeli embodies the historical diachrony I described briefly in chapter 1, there illustrated by Anna Banti's novel *Artemisia*, in which author and subject console each other across the ages. Bordered by Via della Mantellate (of the song I partially reproduce above) and Via San Francesco de Sales, the complex of Regina Coeli reaches back from the banks of the Tiber toward the base of the Gianiculum; opposite Ponte Mazzini, it is equidistant between the Vatican and the Roman Forum, between Church and State, between Rome's recent and imperial past. The temporal palimp-sest Regina Coeli produces (first a property of the Church and then of the Capital) is hardly unusual in Rome, where such frag-ments and bricolage exemplify postmodern geography.[9] The jumble of cultural and architectural uses of Regina Coeli's space troubles the notion of historical progress of women during this period, something amply shown in the literary texts I examine in this chapter. As ecclesiastical historian Giancarlo Rocca observes, convent life of the twentieth century, its 'practical aspects of daily life, from the cloister to the scrupulous adherence to the dress code, remained more or less what it had been in the Nineteenth Century.'[10] Similarly, R. Hostie observes that 'the lifestyle [of the convents] did not evolve between 1900 and 1965. Crossing the threshold of the cloister the nuns returned many times each day to a world whose style recalls that of the year 1900.'[11] We see how easily Malaparte's soldier lapses and how his mistake almost makes sense. Moreover, we see the great architectural correspon-dences between the spaces for the confinement of women and for the detention of criminals. At once linguistic, architectural, and cultural, this conflation begs the following question: was the spatial organization of the convent *always* carceral? If the answer is yes, then what does the representation of the carceral convent in the period we are considering mean?

The literary representation of convents in this period explicitly recalls the established topos of the convent as the place for the isolation and confinement of women, a phenomenon which dates from the early modern period in Europe and whose literary expressions span several national literatures. Immurement and the coercion of vows is, for example, the script for such varied texts as the seventeenth-century epistolary novel Guilleragues's *Les lettres portugaises* (Letters of a Portuguese Nun) and Diderot's *La religieuse* (The Nun) in the eighteenth century. In the nine-teenth century and in a context specific to Italy, forced vows are the germ for the acclaimed episodes of Geltrude in Manzoni's *Fermo e Lucia* (Fermo and Lucia) and Gertrude, 'La Monaca di Monza' (The Nun of Monza), in his *I promessi sposi* (The Betrothed).[12]

Gramsci's reference to his own double imprisonment, which appears as an epigraph to this chapter, underscores his feeling of helplessness and the way incarceration infantalizes him. The forced vocation of nuns and their confinement to and within convents displays a similarly multi-layered imprisonment, and yet the nuns occupy a carceral homologue only.[13] Already isolated from society, the punishment of nuns within convent walls can be seen as the double incarceration I mentioned in chapter 1. For example, the history of Suor Virginia Maria de Leyva, from whose history Manzoni, by way of Ripamonti, draws Gertrude in *I promessi sposi*, is an excellent example of such doubled incarceration of women within the convent. Marianna de Leyva (1575–1650) was forced to take vows at the convent of Santa Margherita in Monza. In the years following her vows, she began a sexual liaison with a wealthy young man from the area, Giampaolo Osio, from which relationship issued several children. The lovers were discovered and condemned in 1607. For her crimes, it was ordered that Suor Virigina Maria be

> placed in a small cell within said monastery and that she be shut up in it; that the entrance to the cell be walled up with rock or and that it be completely sealed. We order that the aforementioned Sister Virginia Maria be respectively taken and confined to this prison and that she be immured there forever, for as long as she lives, in such a way that she must remain and live there as a prisoner, serving this life sentence, night and day, both in pain and in penance for her sins ... Never, so long as she shall live may she be enabled or permitted to leave ... Let it be ordered that only a small hole in the wall of this prison be left open, through which food and other items necessary to her sustenance be passed, so that she shall not die of hunger and we further ... order that the cell be furnished with another small opening in the walls – perhaps a small window – so that she may have light and air.[14]

Conventual confinement is a prime example of the social control of women and of manifest importance to the texts I examine here. Coercion takes shape in the time-honoured tradition of the compelling of young women to take the veil, but also as the regulation of young women's desires and their access to social space and, therefore (following Lefebvre), social production as well.[15]

Hitherto, I have explored some primary considerations of prisons, imprisonment, and social control. In the preceding chapter, I focused on the development of imprisonment from prison text to subtext. Like the barracks, the convent also imparts valuable lessons concerning gendered identity.

The convent isolates women from the public sphere and, especially, public view.[16] The convent has never, however, freed women from the social ordering of gender. The walls of the cloister are integral in preserving the nuns' modesty and have been variously interpreted over time. To be sure, nuns throughout the ages have commented on their virtual imprisonment, but there are other voices among them that describe the walls as a haven and as the physical marker of a community of women. The walls as welcome barrier to the outside world find literary expression in this period in a work like Gianna Manzini's 1928 *Tempo innamorato*, where Clementina seeks refuge from her ruined marriage within the walls of a convent boarding school outside Florence. Despite her false consciousness and aphasia, the convent – in particular, the convent cell – provides Alessandra a similar refuge in de Céspedes's *Dalla parte di lei* (The Best of Husbands) of twenty years later. Walls and their apertures (e.g., windows, doorways, etc.) are important architectural features conditioning the experience of the convent. The presence of windows and doorways in these convent jails conditions *habitus*, or the unconscious practice of negotiating space, and I will explore their significance in the several texts under examination here.

Freedom of movement will figure importantly in the carceral aspects of the spaces investigated here. Movement, comportment, and spatial negotiation vary in the texts I explore in these pages. Generally, I understand inhibited movement as an indication of constraint; similarly, I take stealth movement as an indication of resistance. The representation of women's movement in these literary texts, however, will vary with access to social space.[17] Convents reveal not only restraint, which, given the rich literary history of immured nuns, is not surprising, but they reveal strategies for resisting such inhibition, as well.

With the brothel and the home, the convent produces normativity among women and gendered identity in general. Offering potential community and solidarity, the convent is a location for imagined utopia, which, like any other, always presents its constitutive opposite; as a consequence, dystopic visions of the convent appear as well.[18] Literary representations, these works included, slip between utopian and dystopian visions of women's community. This notion of community, which is founded on an approximate familial situation ('sisters' and 'mothers'), also reveals the changing attitudes of familial relationships between women, daughters and mothers, sisters, and mothers and daughters. Convents negotiate separation and union, freedom and captivity. In the pages that follow, I will trace the struggle between freedom and confinement in the convent settings of Guido Piovène's epistolary novel, *Lettere di una novizia* (1941), Alba de Céspedes's 1938 *Nessuno torna indietro*, and selected short fiction of Anna Banti and Elsa Morante.

Educating Rita: Forced Vows in Guido Piovène's
Lettere di una novizia

Un libro che venisse di fuori, un giornale, una voce alla radio erano spiragli che s'aprivano erano come il sole che filtra, il poco cielo che s'intravede dalle celle dei prigionieri.

[A book that came from the outside, a newspaper, a voice on the radio were like glimpses of the sun filtering through darkness, that small bit of sky that can be seen in prisoners' cells.]

Alba de Céspedes, 'In casa e fuori,' *Mercurio* 3: 19–20 (March–April 1946), 6

Art. 169. Le finestre della clausura devono tenere all'interno le tende, affinché non possano sguardi estranei penetrare nella casa.

[Article 169. The windows of the cloister must feature interior blinds so that one may not peer in from without.]

Constitution of the Daughters of Our Lady of the Sacred Heart, quoted in Giancarlo Rocca, *Donne religiose*, p. 263

Although a nun's vows are meant to be taken freely, and the regulations inherent to convent life something she has chosen, literature and history have revealed a different practice. Even though the practice of *monacazione forzata* (compelling a young woman to take religious vows) was a documented phenomenon from the early modern period, Guido Piovène's 1941 epistolary novel, *Lettere di una novizia*, makes ample use of the topos.[19] Like the way Corte's path in Buzzati's story approximates the sanatorium to the prison, as we saw in the preceding chapter, Rita's trajectory in *Lettere* makes convents and prisons commensurable. Piovène's conflation of convent and prison, I argue, provides a basis for the critique of church, state, and society. Disciplining Rita draws both Church and State together and bespeaks their collusion during the *ventennio*, something liberally illustrated by the Lateran Accord of 1929, which stipulated and guaranteed autonomy for both parties and ensured for Catholicism its continued role as the religion of the Italian State. Rita's confinement, in both convent and prison, stands also for the rigid hierarchy of the Fascist State and its judicial malfeasance. Piovène's revivification of the storied practice of *monacazione forzata* reads against the grain of his allegiance to the Regime: despite his good standing with the PNF (National Fascist Party), despite the fact that he worked as a journalist throughout the *ventennio*, despite his occasional involvement in the Duce's speech-writing, and that he worked as a Regime censor, *Lettere di una novizia* offers grounds for the implicit critique of Fascism.[20] Like Malaparte's soldier, Rita's odyssey shows that the convent and prison are permeable, superimposable structures.

Critics traditionally view this novel as a contest between good and evil and have seen Rita as a prevaricator destined for a fall.[21] A collection of letters sent among a small group of interlocutors, the novel narrates the story of Rita Passi's sure progress from convent to prison. The majority of the letters are authored by Rita and Don Paolo, a priest whose help she enlists to put a stop to her vow-taking. The letters follow not so much historical chronology as Rita's very fallible memory; one of Piovène's aims in fragmenting the narrative is to accentuate the difference between 'objective' truth and Rita's subjective rendering of the events. When she is ten, Rita is sent to board at the convent she had attended as a day scholar. Six years later, on school holiday, she returns home and, for the first time, she and her mother, Elisa, experience friendship and intimacy. Rita falls in love twice that summer, with her mother and with Giuliano Verdi, a young man from the neighbourhood. Excepting Elisa and a distant uncle, Rita has no living relatives, and few friends, and these two relationships are the only intimate ones she has ever enjoyed. But when Rita's camaraderie with her mother sours and Giuliano dies in a hunting accident clouded by mystery, Elisa returns her daughter to the convent. The letters that both mother and daughter send Don Paolo attest that this time Rita will never leave. With Don Paolo's help, she escapes and hides for several days at the house of a widow nearby. When both her mothers (Elisa and the Mother Superior, Giulietta Noventa) discover her whereabouts, they send Elisa's gardener to find Rita and return her to the convent. Rita kills Giacomo the gardener, apparently in self-defence, is arrested, and tried for the murder of Giuliano Verdi. All the letters in the novel serve as state's evidence at the trial. Rita is convicted of murder and sent to prison, where she eventually dies of pneumonia.

The development of Rita's carceral itinerary is gauged in linguistic and geographical terms. As the novel unfolds, Rita's perception of her imprisoned status becomes more acute. From a novice who describes herself merely as 'non sicura della mia vocazione' [not sure of my vocation][22] at the novel's start, Rita's language crystallizes into that of prisoner. It is not long before she describes herself as 'l'accusata' [the accused] who must 'difendermi ad ogni costo' [defend myself at any cost]. As Don Paolo's suspicions of Rita's credibility mount and he decides to cut off their correspondence, Rita chastises him for judging her before the fact. 'Dunque è deciso,' she says, 'io sono condannata' [So you've decided: I'm judged guilty]. During her trial, Rita describes herself as worse than a prisoner. When asked why she had lied to Don Paolo in her letters, she asks: 'Non sarà nemmeno permesso a una bestia cacciata di cercare una strada come può per fuggire?' [Wouldn't even a trapped animal be permitted to look for a way to escape if it could?] (229).

This psychological and linguistic escalation is crafted also in spatial terms. Rita's itinerary illustrates her clear confinement within architectural structures, punctuated as it is by her inability to find any relief from confinement 'outside' of them. But this is not all: Rita's wanderings outside (e.g., the woods and landscape) not only perpetually return her to still other places of confinement, but her episodes out-of-doors seem to guarantee her further confinement.[23] Her tenure 'outside' the convent on summer holiday ends in her permanent return. As Elisa writes, the only way to save Rita from an accusation of murder is 'tenerla nel convento. Soltanto il convento può ormai separarla da un mondo in cui non può più tornare' [to keep her in the convent. By now the convent alone can separate her from a world she cannot return to] (125). During her holiday, Rita leaves the confines of her house in search of Giuliano, whose death, significantly, takes place outdoors. Her stint at the widow Zorzi's, away from the convent, yields another death (Giacomo's) that suggests Rita's still further involvement.

Rita craves the outside and Piovène closely associates her with the surrounding landscape of the Veneto region. Landscape and weather, as critics have noted, underscore Piovène's moral ambiguity.[24] The weather is described variously as hazy, shadowy (*afoso, ombroso*); the land seems to 'sollevarsi e contrarsi nella lente d'aria calda e tremolante di vapori' [rise and contract under the lens made of the heat and tremulous vapours] (26). Don Paolo writes to Rita that he finds her conscience 'foggy' ('la vostra coscienza è nebbiosa' [71]). Rita herself writes that after living with her mother, she discerned 'una nebbiolina ovattata ... mi velava la mente' [my mind was veiled as if in a milky kind of fog] (100). In the preface Piovène establishes the relationship between 'Rita personaggio – Rita paesaggio' [Rita as character – Rita as landscape]. Of the landscape surrounding his native Vicenza, Piovène wrote that 'una delle bellezze di questa terra sono certamente le nebbie di vario e incerto colore, tanto che il paesaggio non giunge a definirsi per intero, che voglia essere tutti i paesaggi nell'infinito della sua ambiguità ... Rita, la mia protagonista, vive con me come un paesaggio' [the fogs of different and uncertain colours are one of the beauties of this area; so much so that the landscape cannot really define itself entirely, it is almost as if in the infinity of ambiguity it wants to be every landscape ... Rita, my protagonist, lives with me like a fog] (8). The fog covers this novel like a veil, shrouding any truth that may exist concerning the events leading to Rita's demise.[25] The inability to see through the fog and the language of letters results in Rita's conviction, sentence, and, ultimately, her death.

The inside/outside opposition is especially pointed in Piovène's use of windows, which he invests with great function and significance in the novel's plot. *Lettere di una novizia* is organized around moments of potential liberation which are then thwarted. In captivity narratives, the window and its ability to frame the (unimprisoned) world outside has a tradition of some importance. The window scenes in Piovène recall several episodes in Pellico's prison chronicle and reinforce the very palpable undercurrent of the carceral. For Pellico, every stop on his prison itinerary features a window: the episode of the deaf-mute in Milan's Santa Margherita, the scene with the boys in the Piazza San Marco when he is detained in Venice, and the episode with Oroboni in Austria's Spielberg.

The notion of the frustrated potential of liberation may be illustrated by the motif of the window and the social and architectural function the window serves. In the text, two significant episodes involve windows.[26] The first occurs after Rita has escaped from the convent and is staying secretly with the widow Zorzi. Given her fugitive status, neither the playful tone nor the actions Rita describes in her letters are appropriate. The widow, she writes to Don Paolo, 'mi ha fatta una scena ieri perchè, dalla cucina, mi sono affacciata un istante a una finestra sulla strada' [made a stink yesterday because, for a moment in the kitchen, I looked out of the window facing the street] (193). This, it turns out, is Rita's undoing, for a woman passing the window sees and recognizes her and reports her truancy to the Mother Superior.

The second moment when windows figure prominently occurs

shortly after this. Don Paolo, sensing Rita's imminent discovery and the attendant revelation of his own complicity, advises immediate departure. Rita inexplicably hesitates and writes a desperate letter to Michele Sacco, the young man who lives in the house adjacent to Signora Zorzi's. In his letter to a friend following the trial, Michele recounts the wordless exchange he had had with Rita two days before she sends him her letter. When Michele enters the courtyard between their two houses, away from the street, he writes that

> alzando il capo scorsi il viso di una ragazza alla finestra ... Mentre guardavo, la ragazza mi scorse: io salutai, per atto di educazione; subito essa mi rispose. Il giorno dopo la vidi altre due volte, e la seconda, non rispondendo al saluto, mi fece segno di andarmene, con gesti disperati coi quali pareva accennare a un pericolo grave; vedendo che non capivo, mi fece poi altro segno, quasi per dire: aspetta, ti spiegherò. (204)

> [raising my head I noticed the face of a young woman at the window. When I looked, she noticed me; I waved, just out of courtesy; she immediately waved back. The next day I saw her twice more, and the second time, not waving back to me, she motioned for me to leave with gestures that seemed to hint at serious danger; seeing that I didn't understand, she made a sign, almost as if to say: wait, I'll explain it to you.]

In the first instance, Rita is spied at the widow's kitchen window. It is inadvert and actually triggers the series of events leading to the novel's climax. In the second, the window functions as a threshold between inside and outside, private and public. Rita's movements become more and more interiorized; she no longer has access to the street and must communicate through the courtyard window. Although she sends a letter to Michele explaining her predicament, he has already understood, through her gestures, the predicament of her circumstances.

While windows serve a clear function of plot in the novel, they are also imbued with symbolic significance and correspond to the inside/outside negotiation I described earlier. Figuratively, the window serves as conduit and indicates permeability. For Louis Marin, the window flags the eruption of the future into the present. The window 'signs an instant of pure difference; ... it is an indication of a presence traced in an event: the signal of an imminence of a fracture, an imminence which is immanence.'[27] Not only architectural apertures 'that herald transition,' as Lefebvre maintains, windows and doors in *Lettere di una novizia* also serve as framing mechanisms. As the window frames Rita's predicament, it also frames the difficult relationship with her mother. Rita is failed by her mothers in the novel: Elisa, her biological mother, and Giulietta Noventa, her Mother Superior.

In a kind of retarded symbiosis, the Passi mother and daughter shut themselves up in their home and shut out impinging external forces. They receive no guests, for example, and the single time a relative comes to visit he throws open the windows that Rita's mother 'teneva sempre semichiuse' [always kept halfway closed] and shouts, '[C]he aria chiusa! Che buio!' [How suffocating it is! How dark it is in here!] (88–9). Rita is at first delighted and gratified that her mother should treat her more as a friend than a daughter and believes that 'i miei affetti infantili non persero il loro incanto, ma da quel momento sembrarono appartenere tutti a lei' [the bloom wasn't off the rose of my childhood affections, but from that moment they seemed to belong only to her] (84). Her mother, Rita feels, abdicated the responsibility of her education, and, following the death of her grandmother, she had only the nuns as female role models. It is not surprising that such a scarce display of female comportment should cause Rita's diminshed capacity for seeing herself clearly or judging her impulses. Rita cannot, in fact, regard herself clearly: Don Giuseppe, when he visits her shortly before she is scheduled to take her vows, observes that, as a novice, she is not permitted to see her own reflection in a mirror so that she might measure how joyful she looks. The frame of the window pane and the reflective window (i.e., the mirror) coalesce in Rita's memory. Writing to Elisa from prison, Rita finally 'sees' her mother, and is able to frame their relationship with some coherence and objectivity. She remembers leaving their garden one evening and stopping outside her mother's door, which was,

> apert[a] e tu ti guardavi nello specchio, indossando un abito rosa del quale aggiustavi le pieghe e le ampie maniche simili alle ali floscie. Forse non eri contenta, perchè ti volgevi a metà, o sollevavi un braccio con l'ala pendente poi l'abbandonavi pentita e ti guardavi scoraggiata. A me il tuo parve un graziossimo ballo, sotto la luce del tuo volto gentile raccolto in quel rosa di fiore. (246)

> [open and you were looking at yourself in the mirror. You were wearing a pink dress and you played with the folds and the loose sleeves that looked like limp wings. Perhaps you weren't happy with what you saw, because you turned away from the mirror and lifted an arm with the 'wing' trailing down. Then you stopped and looked discouraged. To me it looked as though you were dancing gracefully and in that light your face had taken on the gentle glow of the dress's pink colour, like a rose.]

Elisa's trailing sleeve captures her daughter's eye and imagination and is a symbol of constraint for both women. Given Rita's struggles with taking the veil, it is not far-fetched to see this whimsical pink chiffon, so notable in feminine aspect, as a kind of displaced veil. For Elisa, it is as though her 'wings' are clipped; despite the relative social and sexual freedom accorded widows, she is unable to fly. The tendency to make this kind of displacement attaches to Rita's inability to 'see' or frame her situation correctly or, indeed, report on it truthfully.

Piovène revivifies the topos of *monacazione forzata*, even replicating characteristics acknowledged in historical documents describing it. Historical texts confirm that the convent has served as the site where a young woman's wishes collide with those of her family. The extensive bibliography detailing *monacazione forzata* demonstrates that the notion of convents as places of incarceration is not limited to the twentieth century, nor is it especially feminist in outlook.[28] Social historians who have studied the 1427 *Catasto* (tax book) and the *Monte dei doti* (dowry investments) of Florence and Florentine *libri di famiglia* (household accounts) dating from the Renaissance observe a repeated pattern; as the cost of dowries and the pressure to find a suitable husband for their daughters escalate, families will dower one daughter at the market rate and give her sister or sisters to the Church. Typically, the tithe given to the Church for the vocation of a girl in the Renaissance was about one-third the cost of a dowry.[29] Tomassino Lancillotti, a chronicle writer from Modena, observes in 1542 that

> Li cittadini per dare grande dote a una figliola cacciano le altre in le sore ... et scavezano poi el colo, et le gambe a quelle che maridano et alla sora la scavezano tutta de osse in ossa, et quando sono serate nel monestero el se crede che maledissano el di' et la hora che le ge furno cacciate dentro, et doventano arabiate quando doveriano doventare beate.[30]

> [to endow one daughter with a large dowry, the townspeople cast the others to the Sisters ... [if] they broke the neck and the legs of the ones who married, [then] they broke every bone of the Sister, and when they are locked away in the convent it is believed that they curse the day and the hour that they were thrown in there, and they become enraged at the very moment when they are to become beatified.]

Lancillotti's sixteenth-century description offers an archetype. Certainly his description of some women's fate in the mid-1500s aptly characterizes Manzoni's Gertrude. Further, Lancillotti's delineation of a woman angered in the moment of what should be her beatification sharply resembles Rita at the climax of *Lettere di una novizia*. After the gardener's death, Don Paolo's messengers try to calm the errant novice. She turns 'furente: gli occhi le si dilatarono, le traboccarono di luce; sprizzava dalla sua rabbia la vitalità di un'ossessa' [infuriated: her eyes dilated, flooded with light, she spat with rage like someone obsessed] (224).

By way of introduction into the concerns of the carceral and of gendered spaces, *Lettere di una novizia* typifies certain trends. Rita's case supports the particular socio-history of young women coerced into the convent, expressed first by Lancillotti and echoed in the eighteenth century by Diderot and in the nineteenth by Manzoni. Her transformation makes an exemplary illustration of the concomitance of convents and prisons in mid-twentieth-century Italian narrative. As Rita Passi demonstrates in *Lettere di una novizia*, it is really only 'due passi' [a hop and a skip] from convent to prison.

The Power of Sisterhood? Habitat and *habitus* in Alba de Céspedes's *Nessuno torna indietro*

Un grande romanzo ... contro gli uomini. Sostengo insomma che si può benissimo fare a meno di loro, dimostro che se li sopportiamo è soltanto per secolare tradizione di schiavitù e non per attrazione del sesso. Dico ... della istintiva ripugnanza che la donna prova per l'uomo; dell'assurdità della posizione sociale della donna nel matrimonio. Un libro rivoluzionario.

[A great novel ... against men. I maintain that we can do very well without them, I show that if we tolerate them it's only out of a centuries-old tradition of slavery, not because we are really attracted to them. I address the instinctual repugnance that a woman feels for a man, about the absurdity of women's social position in the marriage. A revolutionary book.]

Alba de Céspedes, Nessuno torna indietro, p. 181

Alba de Céspedes sets her 1938 best-selling novel *Nessuno torna indietro* in Il Grimaldi, a convent located in the fashionable residential district near Rome's Villa Borghese. In keeping with some religious orders' custom of providing hospitality to travellers and working women away from their families, de Céspedes's convent functions as a boarding house for young women enrolled at the university. Piovène develops Rita's forced vocation throughout his narrative until it culminates in the final portrait of her in a state prison, which is a nearly exact substitution for her convent immurement. In de Céspedes's novel, however, there is little doubt from the novel's beginning that Il Grimaldi is a prison, where the boarders struggle under the yoke of regulations that they, unlike the nuns they live among, did not choose to accept.

The carceral convent setting aligns de Céspedes's novel with popular cinema of the 1930s, which developed the genre of the boarding-school drama and the schoolgirl comedy.[31] The confinement *Nessuno torna indietro* delineates would have been readily identifiable to a contemporary reader even slightly familiar with this genre. In Italy such films as Goffredo Alessandrini's 1934 *Seconda B* (Tenth Grade, Class B), Vittorio De Sica's 1938 *Maddalena, Zero in condotta* (Maddalena, Zero in Conduct), and Mario Mattoli's *Ore 9, lezione di chimica* (Nine O'clock Chemistry Class) of the same year acquainted viewers with the theme of young women living away from home in environments designed to domesticate their unruly adolescent behaviours.[32] In her review for *Nuova antologia*, Maria Borgese writes that *Nessuno torna indietro* recalls two specific films in this genre, *Ragazze in uniforme (Mädchen in Uniforme)* and *Prigione senza sbarre* (Prison without Bars), which featured young women in boarding school and reform institutions.[33] De Céspedes culls more than the setting for *Il Grimaldi* from these films, and as a point of entry to an examination of *Nessuno torna indietro*, the important parallels and divergences between the novel and Leontine Sagan's 1931 *Mädchen in Uniforme* warrant inspection.

Now viewed as a classic in the early history of gay and lesbian cinema, Sagan's film tells the story of Manuela, a new student at a Potsdam boarding school. Like many of her classmates, Manuela develops a crush on her teacher, Fräulein von Bernburg. The Fräulein's firm yet compassionate manner opposes the reigning authoritarian Prussian pedagogy, embodied in the film by the headmistress and her minions. After a student performance of Schiller's *Don Carlos*, a slightly drunken Manuela publicly announces her admiration and love for von Bernburg. The headmistress responds by confining the young woman to seclusion in the infirmary. As von Bernburg confronts the principal, the alienated Manuela prepares to throw herself headlong down the central stairway. Although Sagan shot two alternative endings, only one was ever screened in Germany.[34] In this version, Manuela is saved by her companions, who rally to support her, and reunites with her beloved von Bernburg, who has herself courageously resigned from the faculty.

The conspicuous similarities between Sagan's project and de Céspedes's make the distinctions between them just as striking. Twinning the protagonists is perhaps the most evident similarity: both characters share close versions of the same name (Manuela/ Emanuela), and their respective arrivals initiate the action for both stories. Both the film and the novel share the common thematic of the experiences of young women away from home and family, and both are set in a highly structured environment. Moreover, an ideology repressive to women is central to both projects, Fascism for the novelist and, for the film-maker, Prussianism, an *ante litteram* Nazism. Although its deployment yields different results for the two narratives, a homoerotic subtext is also a common feature. The substitution of Rome for Potsdam is the most obvious difference between de Céspedes's novel and Sagan's film. Relocation to a convent setting and the outcome of the lesbian sub-theme are the two other prominent distinctions, which, in concert, work to produce very different representations of the possibility of community among women and resistance to dominant, in this case, Fascist, culture.

De Céspedes uses the patent carceral aspect of the convent to allegorize the condition of women held captive by the misogyny of a Regime that exploited reproductivity.[35] This incarceration finds abundant textual expression, which I will explore presently. Hitherto, critical readings of the novel have fruitfully teased out tactics the young boarders employ to resist the gendered conformity advocated by Regime propagandists.[36] However, while the system of surveillance limned by the author greatly affects the young boarders, they are not the only women confined within the architectural space of Il Grimaldi. De Céspedes, I suggest, balances the community of young boarders with that of the nuns in *Nessuno torna indietro* to explore the issues of liberation, resistance, and solidarity among women during Italian Fascism. The novel offers portraits of women in two different communities: young (secular) women living temporarily in a convent and the more permanent community of the nuns themselves. I will trace the relation in both groups between habitat and *habitus* to suggest that the nuns, the novel's invisible women, offer de Céspedes yet another opportunity to strategize opposition and acquiescence to the Regime.

Nessuno torna indietro traces two years (1934–6) in the lives of eight young women: Anna, Augusta, Emanuela, Milly, Silvia, Valentina, Vinca, and Xenia. Emanuela is clearly the protagonist of the group: the novel begins with her arrival at Il Grimaldi and ends with her departure.[37] Recently arrived, Emanuela is invited to join a study group of students enrolled in the faculty of literature, which includes the novel's seven other principal players. Emanuela's obvious lack of interest in her studies makes the others wonder why she has come to Rome. She puts them off with a vague story about her parents travelling to America – it would be unseemly if not unthinkable for her to live unchaperoned in her native Florence during their absence – but her real reason is Stefania, her illegitimate daughter, who lives in a boarding school herself in Monte Mario. Xenia fails her exams and, stealing a valuable ring from Emanuela, travels to Milan, where she finds work, admiration, and unforeseen affluence. Anna and Valentina return to their native Puglia for the summer, one to her parents' rich farmland, the other to experience her uncles' avarice and her mother's humiliation. Augusta, the eldest and the 'failed intellectual,' rarely leaves her room, where she scratches out 'great novels' and rails against men and matrimony. Silvia, the 'successful' intellectual, slaves for one of her professors and ultimately secures a position in a Littoria high school.[38] The elderly Mother Superior retires to the order's Mother House in Genoa, and Suor Lorenza becomes the new abbess. Milly dies and Valentina withdraws into her fantasies. Vinca, the Spanish student, falls in love with another Spaniard, worries about his involvement in the Spanish Civil War, and flouts the sisters' regulations. Emanuela becomes engaged to another student, Andrea, who rejects her when he learns that she kept the truth about Stefania from him for over a year. Both Augusta and Valentina, those remaining of the original eight, reject Emanuela at the novel's close for the same reasons. Emanuela collects her daughter, books passage, sets sail, and the novel ends.

The experience of their collective regulation unites Il Grimaldi's boarders in community. The convent has rules and privileges, lights out, and curfews like any boarding school; the characters repeatedly declare they feel 'caged,' 'imprisoned,' 'buried alive,' and so forth. The strategies de Céspedes offers for resisting these regulations are reminiscent of the ones used by inmates. Milly and Emanuela, for example, tap messages to each other on the walls separating their rooms in a re-enactment of classic prison communication.[39] Similarly, the semi-secret meetings of the young women after lights out reproduces a common practice among convicts. On her first visit to the nightly rendez-vous, Emanuela is told by the young women that she must at least pretend to study when Suor Prudenzina makes her nightly rounds. 'Fa finta di studiare,' they tell her, 'se no ti manderà in camera tua' [Pretend to study or else she'll send you back to your room].[40] Significantly, the practice of gathering together in prison so that they might educate themselves and each other was so common an occurrence that it led some incarcerated women to christen prison 'the proletarian university.' Indeed, for some women detained by the State, these meetings constituted the only post-elementary school education they received.[41] And although the reading and writing used by the boarders to engage the world outside Il Grimaldi suggests the practice of prison memoirs and coded correspondences, it is more likely that de Céspedes is portraying women's limited choice of university faculties in which they could enrol during the 1930s: literature was one of the few fields women were permitted to pursue, and, as a result, female students dominated the faculty.[42] In one of this chapter's epigraphs from Gramsci's *Lettere dal carcere* (Letters from Prison), the prisoner reminds his sister-in-law that he wears the marks of prison 'on his skin,' and we even find subtle reference to tattooing in de Céspedes's novel. Scarification and tattooing were such common practices among male inmates that it led late-nineteenth-century forensic psychiatrist Cesare Lombroso to examine the topic among female prisoners in his 1892 study *La donna delinquente* (The Female Offender).

The spatial negotiation of the convent bespeaks the boarders' confinement and their methods for resisting it. Although the young women are subject to control and surveillance within their own rooms, their nightly meeting, migratory and therefore unpredictable, indicates a fluid and effective means of combatting the convent's rigidity.[43] From their successful navigation of Il Grimaldi's regulated space, the young women distil possibilities for other oppositions to convent and convention. Emanuela, for example, after attending her gathering, gropes her way from Silvia's upper-storey room to her own on the first floor. Although terrified by the profound dark of the convent after lights out, she repeats her blind fumblings down corridors, landings, and stairwells so that she may find the company of the others. The compensation of movement for impaired vision is similarly available elsewhere in the text as a strategy for contestation. Despite the poor vision that de Céspedes emphasizes throughout the narrative, Silvia, too, in Professor Belluzzi's opinion, will 'farà strada,' that is, she will both find and make her way and be successful in so doing. Milly's correspondence with the organist offers another meditation on movement's relation to impaired vision. Though she rarely leaves her room because of her illness, Milly braves her father's censure and composes letters in Braille to her blind suitor in Milan. These letters are indeed a 'moving' experience for the bedridden woman, and reading the Braille takes on a corporality that compensates for her own immobile and infirm body. The words, she says, 'entrano nei pori, si fondano col sangue, il nostro corpo le assimila come l'aria' [enter into your pores, fuse with your blood, our bodies take them in like air] (52). In its portrayal of women's choices in the face of social strictures, *Nessuno torna indietro* is as comforting today as it must have been when it was published in 1938, deep within the consolidated Regime.[44] Although Fascism sought to curb women's life choices by exhorting them through spectacular and juridical practices to conform to the state, the future is nevertheless uncertain for the young

Piranesi, *Carceri*. Piranesi's engravings do not explicitly portray prisons; instead, their fragments uncover a series of imprisonments from which escape is as tantalizing as it is impossible. The visible exits reveal only more imprisoning walls; staircases lead nowhere; and inaccessible galleries and vertical openings overhead only underscore the 'trick' of detention, namely, that we are all detained but not all of us know it.

Prison, Genoa, Fascist period. Many of Italy's jails had previously been convents, monasteries, or other ecclesiastical buildings whose spatial organization felicitously coincided with the newly unified Italian state's need to isolate and punish unruly subjects. In some of the older prisons, including Rome's Regina Coeli as well as this prison in Genoa, Mass was celebrated at the point of conjuncture of the various wings, at the very heart of the penal institution.

Prison, Reggio Calabria, women's section, Fascist period. Domestic chores characteristic of women's work in the world outside prison walls are perpetuated in a prison setting, where female inmates did the washing, for example, for the entire prison population.

Giuseppe Terragni, Casa del Fascio, Como, 1932–6. Terragni's Casa del Fascio in Como features two conspicuous elements: its synthetic character and its transparency. Terragni's design for the Casa del Fascio creates synthesis by establishing a host of oppositions, including, for example, a traditional as opposed to a modern tectonic conception (the mural surface over against the grid frame), natural as opposed to artificial light (admitted by the open bays on the top floor), and the alternation of strip and sash windows. The configuration of the windows and natural illumination of the building yield the salient point concerning the transparency of the 'benign' Regime.

Guerrini, La Padula, and Romano, Palace of Italian Civilization, 1938–9.
The synthetic aim of this building is clear from the series of arched windows, which are clearly meant to recall the exterior of the Colosseum. The
arches were designed for the display of statues commemorating heroes
from the history of Italian civilization.

Mario Ridolfi, with Wolfgang Frankl, prison, Nuoro (Sardegna), 1953–5. The prison in Nuoro is seen as part of a barren and remote landscape.

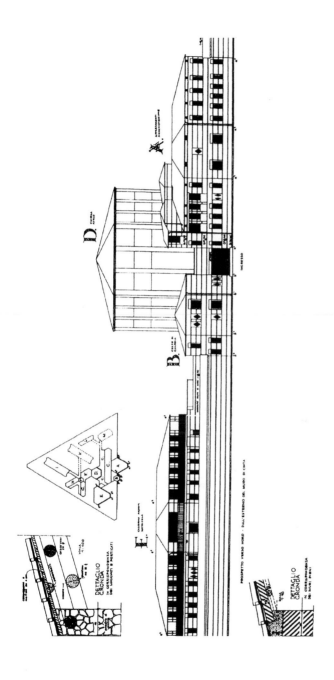

Mario Ridolfi, with Wolfgang Frankl, prison, Nuoro (Sardegna), drawing.

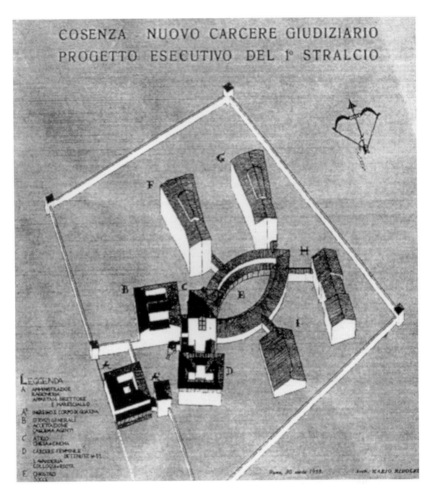

Mario Ridolfi, prison, Cosenza, drawing, 1953–5.

Mario Ridolfi, INA-Casa, lot F, Tiburtino, 1949–54. Manfredo Tafuri describes the Tiburtino complex as 'an affirmation of both rage and hope, even if the mythologies that sustained it made its rage impotent and its hope ambiguous.'

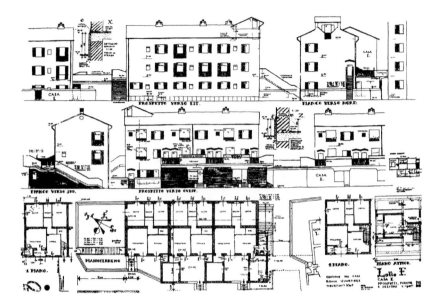

Mario Ridolfi, INA-Casa, drawings, lot F, Tiburtino, 1949–54.

Mario Ridolfi, with Wolfgang Frankl, residential tower, Viale Etiopia, 1948–54. Ridolfi's postwar designs for prisons and apartment complexes reveal common urbanistic locations and elaborate on the themes of isolation, captivity, and surveillance.

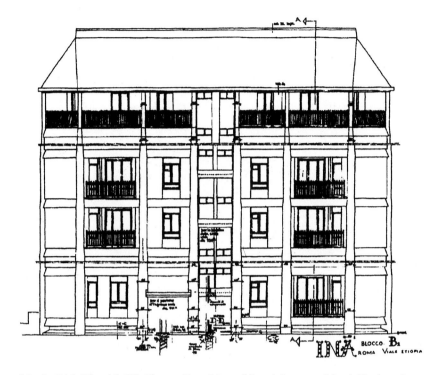

Mario Ridolfi, with Wolfgang Frankl, residential tower, block B, drawing, Viale Etiopia, 1948–54.

women of de Céspedes's novel. They must move – even fumblingly – toward their destination, however obscure it may appear. To refer to Silvia's evocative imagery from which the novel draws its title, the far side of the bridge the young women are traversing lies shrouded in fog. Though these young women do not suffer from Rita's wilful blindess, they will not all succeed in crossing the bridge: some will make it to the other side, Silvia says, and some will not, but no one turns back. These young women, Emanuela chief among them, feel their way blindly, groping for opportunities beyond those Fascism afforded women.

However robust solidarity among women in *Nessuno torna indietro* appears, it does not fall victim to the blindness it tropes; rather, de Céspedes 'sees' community among women with great acuity. Although the novel tells the story of women coming together in uncharted moments of resistance, it significantly does not lionize that resistance nor the notion of community among women. On the contrary, the novel attends to elements of potential division and discord that impugn a utopian vision of women's community in the absolute. Some divisive elements include industry, femininity, romantic and erotic love, class, matrimony, and maternity. To gain critical purchase on this matrix of issues, I will focus on the tension between production and reproduction as represented by three of the eight characters, Emanuela, Silvia, and Augusta.

Realizing that hard work can tangibly affect one's future, de Céspedes's pensioners – none more than Silvia – prize industry. Silvia is a diligent student and divides her time between preparation for the defence of her thesis and Professor Belluzzi's study, where she works as his research assistant. Pickering-Iazzi has examined Silvia's negotiation of urban geography and the ways in which de Céspedes contextualizes Silvia's state of mind in culturally urban terms. I will therefore focus on her practice of *habitus*, the way architecture – and not urban geography – materially orders gender.

In Virginia Woolf's estimation, women's autonomy was composed of equal spatial and economic parts. As she writes in her influential essay, 'a woman must have money and a room of her

own if she is to write fiction.'[45] Economics plays its role within Il
Grimaldi as well, where the socio-economic status of the boarders
is spatially rendered. For example, whereas the pensioners of
greater means lodge on the lower floors in rooms with an endless
source of electric light, their upper-storey counterparts, Silvia
among them, are left in the dark every evening.

Specific interior spaces have no particular hold over Silvia. De
Céspedes introduces the reader to this character in (for her) a
rare moment of relaxation. As she waits for the others to join her
in her room for the nightly meeting, Silvia stretches out on her
bed and appears to be resting. Though de Céspedes hereafter
concentrates on Silvia in motion (thinking, studying, working),
this interlude allows the author to survey the room. Like Silvia
herself, the room seems to be in 'mourning': like her dark
clothes, so evocative of Southern Italian women, Silvia's room is
draped in black. The corner window takes in little light during
the day and at night the room seems especially dark. Notwithstanding the funereal ambiance, Silvia is at ease there and so are
her companions, who help themselves to the figs her family sends
from Calabria. However comfortable she may find her room, Silvia nonetheless forgets it when away. Returning from summer
holiday, she says to Suor Lorenza, only recently appointed to the
position of Mother Superior, that 'durante questi mesi di vacanza,
al paese, quasi non ricordavo più com'era la mia camera, dove
stava il cassettone' [while I was home during vacation I almost
couldn't remember how my room was, where the chest stood ...]
(180).

Work dictates Silvia's choice of housing and her *habitus*.
Whether at Il Grimaldi or the Littoria boarding house, where she
later takes a room, Silvia's quarters are way stations occasioned by
and related to work. Overcome during the final preparation for
her thesis defence, she rarely leaves her room. Many Grimaldi
residents industriously study during the exam period, but Silvia's
diligence is noteworthy:

Scendeva a mangiare, risalita, talvolta senza scambiare parola.
Sotto la porta della sua camera si vedeva la luce rossa della candela

passare fino a notte inoltrata ... 'Non ce la faccio più,' la ragazza
pensava ... S'era dimagrita, l'ansia la divorava: il viso dove
s'accendevano i piccoli occhi graziosamente strabici, si mostrava
piccolo e ossuto come quello di un rosicante. (228)

[She went down to eat and came back up again to her room, sometimes without speaking a word. The candle's red glow was visible
under her door late into the night ... 'I can't take it anymore,' she
thought ... She lost weight, anxiety devoured her: her face, where
shone those two gracefully crossed eyes, was pinched and bony, like
a rodent's.]

Silvia's austerity within the setting of Il Grimaldi is reminiscent of
religious asceticism. As witnessed in the passage just above, the
discipline she uses to prepare her thesis includes taking meals in
silence and long periods of work in solitude. As well, Silvia's
weight loss is significant. Although it may premise the disappear-
ing body Pinkus locates in Italian advertising of the 1930s, Silvia's
consideration (and disavowal) of her body specifically concerns
gender; within this convent setting, she therefore evokes more
convincingly the history of the holy fasting of religious women
than of disembodied homunculi like Rayon Man.[46] This popularized version of a holy woman anticipates the explosion of interest
in such topics during the immediate postwar period, illustrated
particularly well in the Miracle of the Assumption and in the
wealth of postwar feature-length films depicting holy women,
such as, for example, Antonio Leonviola's 1943 *Rita da Cascia*,
Aurelio Battistoni's 1946 *Vita e miracoli della Beata Madre Cabrini*,
Oreste Palella's 1947 *Caterina da Siena*, Augusto Genina's 1949
Cielo sulla palude, Mario Bonnard's 1950 *Margherita da Cortona*,
Don Emilio Cordero's *Mater Dei* of the same year, Alberto Lattuada's 1952 *Anna*, Roberto Rossellini's 1954 *Giovanna d'Arco al
rogo*, Leonviola's 1956 *Il suo più grande amore*, Mario Camerini's
1956 *Suor Letizia*, Oreste Palella's 1957 *Io, Caterina*, and Lattuada's
1960 *Lettere di una novizia*, based on the Piovène novel I examined
earlier.[47] De Céspedes does not associate Silvia with the eucharis-
tic frenzy that Caroline Walker Bynum and Rudolph Bell have

examined in communities of religious women, but her weight loss suggests particularly an abnegation of the body not unlike those of religious women in earlier historical periods and especially in Italy.[48] The imprimatur of labour on Silvia's body might be another inscription of her resistance to feminine bodily tropes under Fascism.[49]

As pageants of sexual difference, spaces outside the claustral setting of Il Grimaldi force Silvia to see herself as others do: a brilliant woman, but an ugly one.[50] Outside Il Grimaldi and in the company of her companions, Silvia occasionally 'notava che gli uomini, passando, guardavano sempre Vinca o Emanuela, e si sentiva umiliata, avvilita dal suo fisico scostante' [noticed that the men who passed always looked at Vinca or Emanuela and she felt humiliated and discouraged by her unmemorable body] (65). For Silvia, the lack of male attention ratifies her sisters' declaration that she is 'un maschio anche lei' [a boy, too] (136), a tomboy in her older brother's dungarees. Silvia does not outgrow this androgyny, and Belluzzi's disregard for her womanliness is disappointing. It is precisely because of her capabilities and her familiarity with the professor's work that Silvia's presence in Belluzzi's study goes unnoticed. The professor's wife, Dora, on the other hand, even if she has no conception of the work he does, comes into his study with 'quel modo ... grazioso e disinvolto' [that graceful and nonchalant way] (115). Comparing herself to Signora Belluzzi and other women who enter rooms 'gracefully and nonchalantly,' Silvia observes that Dora 'entra come una donna mentre io sto accanto a lui come un compagno. Non si accorge neppure di non essere più solo quando entro io nello studio. Io sto di qua, dalla parte degli uomini' [comes into the room like a woman while I sit here beside him like a colleague. He's not even aware of not being alone any longer when I come into the room. Here I am, like a man in the company of men] (115).

As the Regime promised it would, labour strips away femininity, and the opposition of industry to maternity is one of the faultlines of the boarding-school community. Fascism predicated notions of femininity on reproduction, and its theoreticians extolled the virtues and attributes of 'prolific mothers.'[51] Just as Silvia's industry defies the Fascist construction of femininity, so does Emanuela's beauty and grace contravene the Fascist typology of motherhood: pregnancy and childbirth have left no visible trace on Emanuela's publicly appreciated figure. Notwithstanding their common goal – unnamed resistance to Regime strictures – these comparable efforts nevertheless oppose each other.

The discernibility of labour proves an impediment to solidarity among the young women. De Céspedes, for example, opposes Silvia to Emanuela in numerous ways and on multiple occasions. From southern Italy, Silvia is dark, her homeliness is repeatedly observed, her brilliance publicly celebrated, and her industry evident. Emanuela, on the other hand, is Florentine, beautiful, stylish, and wealthy, and her lack of study is interpreted by all as laziness. Silvia's labour is plainly visible and Emanuela's labour (e.g., following parturition, her motherhood) is not only invisible, it is concealed. When her daughter contracts scarlet fever and Emanuela spends several days at her bedside, Silvia suspects that she has simply been idling, away from the convent. Although Emanuela is wealthy and may never need to work, Silvia tries to convince her that

> non si può, nella vita, fare nulla ... tu dovresti fare qualche cosa. Già, tu non conosci la soddisfazione intima, profonda, di costruirsi giorno per giorno la strada su cui camminare, da guardare al domani come a un frutto da cogliere. Né la gioia di sentirsi stanchi la sera, stanchi di non aver vissuto un'altra giornata, ma di esserla fatta con le proprie mani, quella giornata, così come un operaio squadra la pietra. (216)

> [you can't do nothing in life ... that you should do something. Of course, you don't know the intimate and profound satisfaction of building, day after day, the road that takes you into your future, of looking at the next day as if it were a fruit you could pick. You don't know the joy of feeling tired in the evening, not tired from having lived another day but from having created it with your own hands, like a worker who splits stone.]

De Céspedes carefully points out that it is Emanuela's secrecy about Stefania and not the child herself (nor her illegitimacy) that pits the remaining boarders against her at the novel's end. Significantly, Augusta calls her a 'ladra,' a thief, linking her deceit to Xenia, who also conceals the truth from her comrades and steals a valuable ring from Emanuela at the novel's beginning. Indeed, Silvia observes, 'Forse la colpa è nostra. L'abbiamo accusata di aver agito segretamente, invece dovevamo aiutarla, offrirle tutto ciò che avevamo. Dove sarà adesso?' [Maybe it's our fault. We accused her of acting secretively, and we should have helped her instead, offering her everything we had. Where is she now?] (39).

Like secrecy, men and marriage threaten the community of boarders. Largely an optimist about supportive relationships between women, Silvia recognizes the strain that the presence of men would have on their group. 'Se ci fosse un uomo,' she says, 'non avremmo osato parlare, neppure davanti a mio padre io avrei potuto ... Noi donne siamo sincere soltanto tra donne. C'è una solidarietà singolare tra noi' [If a man had been present we wouldn't have dared to talk, even if it were my father I probably wouldn't be able to ... We women are sincere only amongst ourselves. There's a singular soldiarity among us] (86). Augusta sees marriage as a divisive element among the boarders. She remarks that 'l'anno scorso è andata via una ragazza, si è sposata. Era una di quelle che divideva ogni ora con noi: nemmeno una cartolina. Eppure aveva promesso ...' [last year a girl left to get married. She was with us all the time and hasn't even sent a postcard. And yet she promised ...] (23).

Augusta's tenure at Il Grimaldi and her thoughts concerning men, marriage, and community among women may be interpreted, like Silvia's dwindling body, against the backdrop of convent architecture and its material, gendered, and social ordering. In fact, Augusta's body, like Silvia's, dwindles during a period of intense work. Augusta may be seen in the tradition of the *pinzochere*, known also as *bizoche* and *terziare*, women of a 'Third Order' in communities of religionists.[52] Is Augusta's intermittent relationship to the 'Third Order' a way to resist the codification of women in Mussolini's 'Third Rome' (i.e., after the Caesars' and Garibaldi's halcyon seasons, a third moment of Rome's glory)? As *terziara*, a lay nun, Augusta may be seen as an intermediary between the sisters and the boarders. The sisters have invited Augusta to join their order (she has declined), and once she has become Mother Superior, Suor Lorenza even asks Augusta her advice on certain matters. In support of Augusta's status as a kind of negotiator, we remember Emanuela's observations concerning her missionary-like comportment. She finds that 'Augusta parlava come se predicasse una nuova religione' [Augusta spoke as though preaching a new religion] and imagines her 'andare per i boschi, per la campagne, come una zingara missionaria, girare per le strade provinciali in carretta, fermarsi sulle piazze dei paesi, chiamare a raccolta e parlare' [going around the countryside, like a gypsy missionary, roaming the provincial byways with her cart, stopping in the piazzas of small towns, calling the countryfolk to gather and talk] (230).

Augusta appreciates the community of women, staying on at Il Grimaldi well past the customary period of study and even during holidays. Other boarders come and go, but Augusta remains for years on end. In fact, she spends one summer holiday writing the great novel against men, which she describes in the epigraph to this section. Her work is, she tells Emanuela, 'un grande romanzo ... contro gli uomini' (181). As a treatise about the vitality of women's community, Augusta's work offers a miniature model of *Nessuno torna indietro*, and her conception of society anticipates later defintions of the feminist utopian novel. Sally Gearhart defines the feminist utopian novel as one that 'a. contrasts the present with an envisioned idealized society (separated from the present by time or space), b. offers a comprehensive critique of present values/conditions, c. sees men or male institutions as a major cause of present social ills, and d. presents women not only at least the equals of men but also as sole arbiters of their reproductive functions.'[53] *Nessuno torna indietro's mise-en-abîme* presents the possibility of a community of women from which 'l'uomo era scacciato dalla vita della donna come Lucifero dal Paradiso' [men were cast out from women's lives like Lucifer from heaven] (241). Augusta believes that without men's critical visions of women's bodies, women will re-evaluate such concepts as beauty (or ugliness), aging, or even death. Free of the presence of men

> ... nessuna di noi temerà più la vecchiaia, il disfarsi della propria bellezza. È una morte, sai? vedere a poco a poco sfiorire, afflosciarsi il proprio corpo. E tutto questo ci spaventa perchè ci sono loro, gli uomini. Quando ognuna di noi lavorerà, avrà una propria vita indipendente, di questo non si impensierirà più. Anzi, con l'avanzare degli anni che raccoglierà le maggiori soddisfazioni, che ricoprirà le cariche più elevate. È una salvezza, capsici? (241).

> [none of us will fear old age, the undoing of our beauty. It's a sort of death, you know? to see, little by little, one's body wither and sag. And all this frightens us because of them, men. When each of us works and has her own independence, we won't think about it anymore. On the contrary, with age we will achieve the greatest satisfactions and occupy the highest positions. It's a salvation, don't you see?]

Some secular women conceive of the comfort that might be had in the company of other women, united in service. Often such service has taken the form of religious communities. In this way, Augusta is comparable to Clementina in Manzini's *Tempo innamorato*, whom I referred to at the beginning of this chapter and who seeks consolation within the meditative, gender-segregated cloister.

Carceral aspects of *habitus* in *Nessuno torna indietro* enable de Céspedes to represent resistant subjects in both of the novel's communities. Like the boarders, the nuns are confined within Il Grimaldi, and like the boarders, they similarly resist dominant cultural constructions of femininity. Though once inside Il Grimaldi's compound they must conform to the regulations of the sisters' order, the young women enjoy greater freedom of movement than the nuns in society at large outside the walls. Suor Lorenza denies Vinca telephone privileges out of 'rabbia perchè lei sta chiusa qui dentro e io domattina esco' [the rage she feels because she's shut up in here and I'll get to go out tomorrow morning] (8). It is the young women and not the nuns, after all, who celebrate the joy of 'aver avuto la chiave della nostra camera, uscire, entrare all'ora che vogliamo' [having had the key to our own room, of coming and going as we please] (114). However, Il Grimaldi's walls severely diminish the freedom these keys signify; in fact, their keys are virtually useless: they do not open the entrance door, and they do not protect against the master key of the nuns, which may be used, it seems at any moment, to gain entry to the girls' rooms.[54] The young women cede freedom of movement to the sisters at the architectural conjoining of the interior with the exterior, the convent's entrance way. The entrance is an aperture into the wall of the convent that, as Lefebvre explains, is 'transitional, symbolic, and functional [and] serves to bring a space, the space of a "room," say, or of the street, to an end; and it heralds the reception to be expected in the neighboring room.'[55]

The novel signals this exchange and reception at several critical moments, and the entrance to the convent typifies the concealed incarceration that I have been describing. The entrance (*portone*), so important a descriptor that it inaugurates the novel, is clearly demarcated both architecturally and by the presence of the gatekeeper nun, who controls the exit and entrance of the boarders (though not always effectively, as Xenia's example points out). This main entrance supersedes another, unused gate to the street that is also found within the entrance way. Vinca asks Emanuela whether she has noticed it, 'a mezzo del vestibolo ... inutile dopo la vetrata d'ingresso ... È un simbolo forse; fu una cosa che mi colpì, appena arrivata, mi intimorì, addirittura' [midway through the vestibule ... useless after the glass door at the entry ... Maybe it's a symbol; it really struck me when I arrived, it actually scared me] (107). Performing no function, the second gate is a symbol that mirrors the main entrance and echoes its separation of the cloister from the piazza outside. Like Piranesi's *Carceri*, this second possible aperture is tantalizing for the exit it denotes and, at the same time, denies. The endless staircases and apertures discernible in many of Piranesi's engravings catalyze the imagination. For some, the endless staircases and multiple apertures constitute a system of perpetual containment, where one might enter through one doorway only to see another indicative of a larger containing structure. Other viewers, Vinca among them, imagine multiple exits to match the multiple apertures. The second doorway symbolizes a way out that is at once possible but not viable. No wonder Vinca finds it frightening.

Il Grimaldi's religionists, especially the 'hard-hearted Suor Lorenza,' to use Gallucci's description, seem the very embodiment of the false consciousness of black-shirted women, those female Fascists who saw in Fascism relief to women's predicament within Italian society. In this way, we might be tempted to align the nuns, particularly the ambitious Suor Lorenza, with those female masochists that Macciocchi inculpates for the Regime's foundation.[56] De Cespedes's portrayal of the Church's collusion with the Regime is bolder than Piovène's and gives literary expression not only to doctrines established by, for example, the Lateran Accord and the *Casti Connubi*, but also anticipates conventual regulations developed in the postwar period, such as the *Provida mater* and the *Sponsa christi*.

Il Grimaldi successfully constrains both communities residing within its walls. Although they serve as the boarders' guardians, the nuns themselves, in keeping with Church dictates, may not leave the convent unaccompanied.[57] A moment when both of Il Grimaldi's communities come together, the scene of the abbess's departure, exemplifies the exchange of power between the cloistered sisters and the boarders I described above:

Ragazze e monache uscirono sulla porta per salutare la badessa, s'affollarono, curiose, non volendo perdere un gesto o una parola ... Dinanzi alla porta, sulla piazza fulminata dal sole, una carrozza attendeva: il cavallo batteva sordamente uno zoccolo sulle selci. Nel rispettoso tacere delle ragazze la superiora salì, si sedette; si sparse attorno a lei la gonna viola. Accanto, nel poco spazio rimasto, s'installò una suoretta, sedendosi appena. Un minuto di silenzio impacciato, poi, alla grassa mano che s'agitava nel saluto, tanti mani risposero, innumerevoli sorrisi. Nella piazza deserta la carrozza mise alto il rotolio delle ruote. (147)

[Young women and nuns went to the entrance to say goodbye to the abbess, they gathered, curious, not wishing to miss a single gesture or word ... A carriage waited in front of the door in the piazza bathed in sunlight: the horse mutely scraped at the cobblestones with a hoof. The girls respectfully silent, the Mother Superior got into the carriage and took her seat; she spread her purple skirts around her. Next to her, in the little space that remained, a young nun took her place, barely managing to make room for herself. A moment of heavy silence and then the plump hand waved a goodbye, many hands waved in response, many mouths smiled. The wheels of the carriage raised a great sound in the deserted piazza.]

Even had the Mother Superior been well enough to travel on her own, custom (and the order's rule) would have forbidden it. The departure takes place after lunch (the piazza is in full light of the afternoon sun), which also protects the Mother Superior's modesty. The ceremony that accompanies the abbess's departure, celebrated by a reception and a gigantic cake like some 'sepulchral monument,' indicates how rare an event this is. As opposed to the boarders, who may, like Xenia, simply abscond in order to leave the convent, these nuns, it appears, must die.

The abbess's departure also marks the advent of Suor Lorenza to the position of the Mother Superior, an event she has long awaited and prepared for. Like Emanuela, Suor Lorenza is a vexing principal among the sisters. Despite the vows she has taken ensuring her isolation from the outside world, she still appears interested in worldly things. An early passage describes a kind of 'sympathy' (*simpatia*) between her and the young women that is 'inespressa, istintiva, e segreta. Non era una suora simile alle altre; alta e ancor giovane, aveva una voce modulata, mani bianche e sottili; non sembrava una vera suora: quando ella parlava le ragazze restavano a pensare; e intanto, senza volerlo, ubbidivano' [tacit, instinctive, and concealed. She was not like the other nuns; tall and still youthful, she had a lovely voice, and soft, supple hands; she didn't seem like a real nun: when she spoke the girls listened and, without wanting to, obeyed] (7–8). Such youth and comeliness recalls another sister in Italian literary history who, like Suor Lorenza, exerts great influence over the movements and destinies of non-religious women within the confines of the convent, and here I am thinking of Manzoni's Monaca di Monza, Gertrude, in *I promessi sposi*. De Céspedes provides no excursus into Suor Lorenza's life along the lines of Manzoni's, but she is the only nun whose psychology *Nessuno torna indietro* plumbs, and she appears as devious as Gertrude and just as interested in procuring power and wielding it. Although she craves community with her sisters, her prior machinations guarantee that she will be as isolated in the position of Mother Superior as she herself had isolated her predecessor.

As it does for Emanuela, her complement in Il Grimaldi's secular community, 'maternity' poses problems for Suor Lorenza within the community of the nuns and is equally divisive. We see again the problematic relation between 'mother' and 'daughter' that Piovène offers. The isolation Suor Lorenza feels once appointed Mother Superior is one she helped to create. The most senior among the nuns, she quietly appropriates administrative power, effecting changes in the abbess's name and creating around the Superior's office an aura of beatific detachment. As the registrar of applicants and newly arrived pensioners, Suor Lorenza remembers everything and everyone. I have spoken elsewhere of Macciocchi's spurious interpretation of the Duce's 'seduction' of the Italian female polity, but seduction is not an unsuitable description of Suor Lorenza's performance with the new students. In fact, Suor Lorenza embodies the potential dangers of this sort of seduction. At their first colloquy 'godeva vedendo che la nuova arrivata, ascoltandola, osservava le sue labbra, le sue mani fini, la figura alta, snella' [she took pleasure in watching the newly arrived girl listen to her, look at her lips, her fine hands, her tall, graceful figure] (37). Segregated in her room once she has been appointed the new abbess, this pleasure evaporates: Lorenza falls victim to the mystery and aura of the Mother Superior that she herself created:

This book is sent to you for review with the compliments of

University of Toronto Press

NEW TITLE PUBLISHED IN CLOTH ONLY

Prison Terms: Representing Confinement During and After Italian Fascism

TITLE

Ellen Nerenberg

AUTHOR

CLOTH: 0802035086 $45.00   EUROPE: £25.00

PAPER: EUROPE:

WORLD PUBLICATION DATE   21 July, 2001

AVAILABLE IN EUROPE BY: 21 September, 2001

OUTSIDE OF CANADA DOLLAR PRICES ARE IN US DOLLARS

UNIVERSITY OF TORONTO PRESS - HEAD OFFICE:

10 St Mary Street, Suite 700, Toronto, ON, M4Y 2W8   Fax: (416) 978-4738

CANADIAN, US, AUSTRALIAN, and R.O.W. (excluding Europe) ORDERS can be sent to:

University of Toronto Press, 5201 Dufferin Street, North York, ON, M3H 5T8
Tel: 800-565-9523 / (416) 667-7791 / Fax: 800-221-9985 / (416) 667-7832

US ORDERS can be sent to:

University of Toronto Press, 2250 Military Road, Tonawanda, NY, 14150

Tel: (716) 693-2768/Fax (716) 692-747

EUROPEAN ORDERS can be sent to:

Marston Book Services, PO Box 269, Abingdon, Oxon, OX14 4SD
Tel: (01235) 465500 / Fax: (01235) 465555

La nuova dignità impediva a suor Lorenza di scendere per prima incontro alle ragazze come usava una volta ... Nessuno veniva più a chiamare suor Lorenza ... certe volte non resisteva più, usciva fuori, domandava: 'Perchè non mi avete chiamato?' 'Non volevamo disturbarvi, Madre.' Ed ella tornava in camera senza replicare. (180)

[Her new dignity prevented Suor Lorenza from going to meet the girls as she once had ... No one came to call her any more ... sometimes, unable to stand it any longer, she came out of her room and asked, 'Why haven't you called me?' 'Because we didn't want to disturb you, Mother.' She returned to her room without a word.]

Nessuno torna indietro is hardly a condemnation of all religious women. Significantly, the nuns are implicated more by their relation to Italy and to Fascism than because they belong to a community of religious women. For de Céspedes the problem is not being Catholic, but, rather, the relation to the Italian Catholic Church. Laura Gellott and Michael Phayer have noted that Catholic women resisted the Third Reich from within the Church itself, and *Nessuno torna indietro* presents an example of such resistance in the form of the reported resistance of the Spanish nuns during the Civil War.[58] For instance, Luis's visitor reveals that the Spanish nuns actively resisted the hostile takeover announcing Franco's rise to power. As Gallucci outlines, de Céspedes makes use of Vinca Ortiz's foreignness to comment on the curtailed freedom of Italians, and another Spanish example serves to point out the failings of the Italian community of religious women. Indeed, de Céspedes's reference appears to be factually based; as Jo Ann McNamara writes, '283 nuns died among the thousands of clerical victims' in the Spanish Civil War in 1936.[59]

In contrast to Sagan's bold revision of the repressive order of the boarding-school environment in *Mädchen in Uniforme*, de Céspedes explores the subtle and complex obstacles to community among the women in *Nessuno torna indietro*. The young women succeed in coming together in a community whose location is not spatially reified by effecting a spatial practice characterized by migration and clandestinity. Solidarity is hard-won, de Céspedes says. Even when imagined, as Augusta boldly does, it may not be persuasive enough an image to recruit followers to its ranks.

Serving Time: 'Lavinia fuggita' and 'Via dell'Angelo'

Augusta and the other boarders find various ways of subverting their confinement, but securing an outlet for the imagination in confinement – the problem Anna Banti addresses in her novella 'Lavinia fuggita' – is not easily achieved.[60] Although La Pietà, the Venetian orphanage that is the material setting for Banti's novella, is less carceral than either Piovène's or de Céspedes's convents, the seventeenth-century time frame underscores more stringent social constraints of women in an earlier historical moment. In *Lettere di una novizia* and *Nessuno torna indietro*, the convents are expressly described as carceral and *prigione* (prison) recurs as an attribute. La Pietà's carceral role derives more from the story's title than from any textual reference; indeed, Banti, with her customary subtlety, uses the word 'prison' only once. Writing, as it does for those detained in other carceral analogues, figures here prominently. In this novella about the longing for unfettered creativity, Lavinia's is an attempt to escape at once the place which contains her and the historical time in which she lives.

A review of Anna Banti's bibliography shows a cluster of works that revolve around convents and nuns. From the collection of short stories *Le monache cantano* (1942) to *La monaca di Sciangai e altri racconti* (1957), Banti's choice of the convent thematizes both her interest in women's relationships and formal considerations. As Enza Biagini observes, it is with *La monaca di Sciangai* that Banti 'explicitly declares a preference for the long story, or the short novel.'[61] From her collection *Il coraggio delle donne*, 'Lavinia fuggita' dates from this period of Banti's work and attests to the double preference of the long short story set among nuns.[62]

Briefly, 'Lavinia fuggita' tells the story of a young woman who serves as the director of the choir in La Pietà, an orphanage for girls in Venice at the beginning of the seventeenth century. Lavinia, herself an orphan, has an uncommon musical talent: 'da piccola ... passò dall'uno all'altro strumento con una facilità che irritava le specialiste' [as a little girl, she passed from one instrument to another with an ease that irritated the soloists].[63] It is Lavinia's task to direct the choir and copy out the parts for Maestro Vivaldi's oratorios. But she secretly composes her own music, filling a notebook with her original *Cantate e concertini*. After the abbess and Vivaldi reprimand her on the day of the annual outing for the young charges of the Pietà, Lavinia continues to compose her music and, following a final rebuke, disappears from the orphanage, leaving Zanetta and Orsola, her friends, to their own questions about chastisement, her departure, and what it may mean for their lives.

The novella's timeless and oneiric quality leads Biagini to describe it as 'a sort of rêverie.'[64] Time – how it is marked, measured, observed, and played – is an appropriate and important matter for a musician, and the notion of 'serving' time is consonant with the carceral motif of the story and the broad lines of the present study. Not unlike Buzzati does in *Il deserto dei Tartari*, Banti plays with narrative time throughout the story, doubling such efforts (and the effect) at the story's beginning, where a jumble of tenses disarms the reader.

The present tense coincides with the reverie at the beginning of the story. The use of the present, which marks Iseppo Pomo's arrival at La Pietà, is not the actual moment in which the story is told. It is a Sunday in November and '*è* proprio la sua ... lui *compie* oggi diciott'anni ... La porta *è* trovata ... [Iseppo] *misura* collo sguardo lo spazio' [it *is* his own ... he *celebrates* his eighteenth birthday ... the door is located ... (Iseppo) *measures* the space with his gaze] (13, emphases added). Iseppo's somnolence and the oneiric quality of the story appear simultaneously. He has rowed to La Pietà to collect Orsola the day they are to be married. The island location of the orphanage stresses the spatial isolation of the convent within the city of Venice. As he waits for her in his boat, from nowhere pages fall on the water around him. It seems to him that the paper is almost like garbage, 'cartaccia,' like 'quelle che si buttano perchè non servono più' [the kind you throw away because you have no use for them anymore] (14).

The writing that Iseppo notices is 'bizarre' and he cannot recognize it: 'fasci di righi come nastri, neri, in mezzo, impigliati, certi segni come mazzetti di ciliege, ma fatti male' [bunches of lines like ribbons and suspended in the middle, certain signs, like bunches of cherries but poorly formed] (15). These are the pages of Lavinia's music, thrown out of some window from above. Iseppo gathers the pages and, with time, marries Orsola and then Zanetta.

Through the near-sleep dream-fog of the pages falling from the window above, the reader arrives at the present of Banti's story. With the turning of a page, Orsola dies and Zanetta, who has become 'madre e nonna di bambini petulanti' [mother and grandmother of petulant babies], has carefully safeguarded (Banti uses 'custodire') Lavinia's composition notebook. Lavinia's book marks the confluence of time and writing (written pages) and frames the story. It announces the story's beginning and ending, when Orsola 'voleva chieder[e] (i.e., a Zanetta) un regalo, quel loro feticcio, il quaderno strapazzato che affronta il tempo nella casa di Iseppo fornaio' [wanted to ask a favour of Zanetta, their fetish, that crazy-quilted notebook that challenges time in Iseppo the baker's house] (42). As the pages appear *ex nihilo* in the first section of the story, so do they continue to 'challenge' (*affronta*) time at story's end. Distinguishing between the past and present in Banti's novella is as problematic as discerning developments in quotidian life in the convent between, for example, the nineteenth and twentieth centuries. Indeed, Banti's merging of past and present suggests the timelessness of conventual life I observed at the beginning of this chapter.

While the best example of her transgression, Lavinia's notebook is not its only evidence. She will be pushed to confess her 'sin' of copying Vivaldi's hand and authoring 'il quaderno giallo e rosso, *il corpo del delitto confiscato*' [the red and yellow notebook, the confiscated *evidence of her crime*] (34, emphasis added). When she finally confides to Orsola that she and not Vivaldi is the author of the oratorio that the orphanage's orchestra and choir are rehearsing, she says, 'Capisci, non avevo altro mezzo, mai mi prenderebbero sul serio, mai mi permeterranno di comporre. La muscia degli altri è come un discorso rivolto a me, io devo rispondere e sentire il suono della mia voce' [You see, I didn't have any other way, they would never take me seriously, they would never let me compose. Someone else's music is like a conversation directed toward me, I have to answer and hear the sound of my own voice] (32).

Orsola encourages Lavinia to seek approval for her music and advises that she seek counsel from those at the orphanage who are in a position to help: the abbess and Vivaldi. Her eventual conversation with Vivaldi is not recorded, and, in characteristic decorum, Banti notes only Lavinia's fright prior to the conversation and her distant calm afterward. Significantly, following her interview with Vivaldi, Lavinia cloisters herself 'for Marian exercises' and thus absents herself from the annual performance for the Venetian nobility. Orsola hears that 'all'ultimo circolò la voce che una delle maestre di coro avesse deciso di prendere il velo e rimanesse perciò ritirata' [finally word travelled that one of the choir mistresses had decided to take the veil and therefore withdrew from the event] (37).

Pellico maintains that the most troubling aspect of incarceration is that the imagination roams free and, upon the return from its free reverie, awakens once more to the reality of prison and immurement.[65] 'Io facea questa riflessione ed imparava che si può rendere l'umore indipendente dal luogo. Governiamo l'immaginativa e staremo bene quasi dappertutto. Ottimo ragionamento! ma come si fa a governare l'immaginativa?' [Upon reflection I learned that the spirit can be rendered independent of the place. If we govern the imagination, we can manage almost anywhere. Great idea! But how to govern the imagination?][66]

While Pellico seeks to control the imagination, Lavinia escapes into it. Like a novice who acts upon her *vocation*, Lavinia responds to the voice that calls her into discourse and musical creation. Sometime before her disappearance, during the ferment of composition, Lavinia says she will return to the Levante, her birthplace, because 'qui non c'è posto per me, e ho bisogno di spazio. Mi vestirò da uomo, farò il pastore, sotto il sole e la luna' [there's no room here for me and I need room. I'll dress as a man, I'll be a shepherd by day and night] (40). Escape is possible for Lavinia, but costly, since she will need to forfeit her female identity. La Pietà may not provide her with the requisite space to practise her craft, but, similarly, there is no place for an unsupervised woman – in the Levante or elsewhere – and thus she will need to disguise her female identity.

Lavinia challenges time, both her own historical time and a traditional women's time. Lavinia's greatest obstacle is that the composition of music is not an ordained profession for women in the seventeenth century, at least not for orphans who must rely on benevolent institutions or on the benefaction of the patronage system.[67] The orphans at La Pietà, under the tutelage of no less a master than Vivaldi, are renowned for their musical talents, and some will find fame and success in the theatre, but as performers only, not composers.

'Via dell'Angelo,' one of Elsa Morante's first published works, exemplifies the architectural collapse of convents into prisons that I have been describing, and I will use it to conclude this exploration of conventual confinement. In this story from *Il gioco segreto*, Morante's first collection published in 1942, the confinement and enclosed spaces remarkable in the author's mature work make an early appearance. Spatial organization in some of Morante's longer prose works suggests the slippage between dystopia and utopia that 'Via dell'Angelo' focuses on. In this vein, we could consider the family home in *Menzogna e sortilegio* or the eponymous island in *Isola di Arturo*. 'Via dell'Angelo' is the name of the street where Antonia grows up in a convent, surrounded by the nuns and, outside, other convents and prisons. Morante suggests the urbanistic arrangement of Regina Coeli within Trastevere, not only by placing the convents and prisons in such proximity, but also by recalling the 'mantled' nuns – the Mantellate – of the popular song and the name of the street that bounds the prison to the north. She writes that

... in quei paraggi sorgevano numerosi e vasti monasteri, popolati da suore diverse, di alcune che portavano la ciuffa arricciata, altre il velo e alcune il mantello. Proprio di fronte si elevava l'immenso fabbricato delle prigioni, giallo e liscio e regolarmente interotto dalle sbarre delle finestre.[68]

[... numerous and vast monasteries soared up to the skyline of the neighbourhood. Of the nuns in the area, some wore brimmed wimples, others veils, still others mantles. Across the street, the imposing prison rose up, yellow and smooth, its facade interrupted at regular intervals by the bars on the windows.]

Antonia is the only child in this carceral universe. She sees other parishioners at Mass, even the prisoners from the nearby jails who, for solemn occasions, are brought to church 'con un fracasso di catene' [in a great ruckus of chains] (62). Consequently, Antonia is not surprised, several years later, to see the young man in the sacristy who 'seems to be waiting for her' (67). His youth and beauty impress her, and she asks, 'Vuoi che usciamo?' [Do you want to get out of here?] (67). As they leave, she notices that he walks 'come chi trascina un peso' [like someone dragging a weight] (68). Still unalarmed, she follows him down the Via dell'Angelo, where at random they enter a house and then undress. Only then does Antonia see the ankle restraints the young man wears. They go to bed and, as he sleeps, she undoes her braids and loops them around the young man's wrists, shackling him to her with human hair so that he cannot wake and leave her.

The window marks an important juncture in relation to architecture and signification within Morante. In terms of spatial organizations, the window here, as elsewhere, represents the limn of the carceral domain, demarcating interiors and exteriors, distinguishing confinement from liberty. In 'Via dell'Angelo,' the window symbolizes the varied degree to which analogical prisons are recognizable, which may itself result from sexual difference. The first appearance of a window occurs as Antonia waits for the young man to undress. She looks out the window of their strange room and asks innocently, 'Che cos'è quel palazzo che si vede?' È forse un cattedrale? [What's that big building? A cathedral?]. Irritated, the young man refuses to answer and, brusquely, says only,

'Non è una chiesa. Non mi parlare di *quella cosa*' [It's not a church. Do not talk to me about *that thing*] (71–2). Emphasizing the architectural equivalency of convents and prisons and their saturation of the neighbourhood, this episode also distinguishes between Antonia's confinement and the young man's. Her failure to identify the prison is linked to her response at seeing the young man's ankle restraints: though she finds both elements striking, they are, at the same time, unrecognizable. Thus, she never associates the restraints or the building she sees through the window with prison and incarceration. The young man, on the other hand, fears the unveiling of his chains and knows precisely the building's use. His refusal to name the building for Antonia (Do not talk to me about *that thing*) marks the differences in their respective confinements: his certainty throws her obliviousness into sharp relief and bespeaks the perils of the 'camouflaged' prisons I described in this and the preceding chapters.

The window's second appearance in the story underscores Antonia's ignorance and testifies to the difficulty of escape from carceral spaces, whether actual or analogical. After the young man falls asleep, Antonia 'scese in silenzio dal letto e si accostò alla finestra; e volgendo il viso per non guardare di fuori, ne chiuse ermeticamente gli sportelli' [got out of bed silently and went to the window; and turning her face so as not to look outside, she hermetically closed it] (73). Returning to bed, she takes one of her braids and as he sleeps, 'lo annodò attorno al polso' [she knotted it to his wrist]. Antonia's actions are understandable: she has been abandoned by everyone who might be expected to love her and can find no other way to keep his cherished presence close than to restrain him. But her agency also reveals the real danger of imprisonment, namely, the acquired inability to imagine any way of being in the world distinct from confinement. Familiar only with immurement, this captive becomes the captor. Antonia's naïveté, furthered by his unwillingness to educate her, leads only to their continued confinement, for they trade one kind of prison for another. The character of space, as we have seen, is determined more by practice than by appointment. Significantly, re-location, in Morante, does not guarantee freedom. The house in the Via dell'Angelo is not used as a prison, and yet prison is what it becomes.

Morante's brief, fantastic story thematizes several key concerns for the carceral matrix of convent and prison. These include implications concerning the relationship of the guard and the prisoner, an imagination exhausted by the carceral universe, an itinerary that articulates the transformation of 'free' space into confinement, the choice of confinement over liberty, the way that movement 'outside' the convent walls may still betoken the containment within them, and the way that sexuality undergirds each.

Chapter Four

Love for Sale; or, That's *Amore*: Brothels, Prison, Revision

Si dice tante volte in giro, l'ho sentito spesso, che non siamo obbligate a entrare nella vita. Non è vero: siamo peggio che obbligate. Tante volte sono dei luridi sfruttatori che costringono a darsi al prossimo, tante volte è la fame, a altre volte è il bisogno di soldi per mantenere la famiglia, o i figli, o il marito malato, eccetera.

   Ma sempre sono gli altri ad obbligarci a entrare in questi inferni ...
   [It's said – I hear it a lot – that we're not forced into the life. That's not true: it's worse than that. It's often dirty pimps who force us to go with our neighbours, it's often hunger, and it's often the need for money to support our families, children, or sick husbands, etc.

   But it's always others who force us into these hellholes ...]
                              Anonymous prostitute, 15 July 1949, in Merlin and Barberis, eds,
                                                    Lettere dalle case chiuse, p. 65

Scrivi: abolire prostituzione e tradimento ... Prostituzione intesa, si capisce, in tutti i sensi. Non solo quella della comune cortigiana ma anche di ogni ragazza che sposa per assicurarsi l'avvenire, di ogni volta, insomma, che il rapporto fisico viene a stabilirsi tra uomo e donna senza la sua necessità ... E il tradimento di ogni sua sfumatura. ... tanto la prostituzione che il tradimento vanno colpiti con la pena di morte.
[Write: abolish prostitution and betrayal ... Prostitution in all its meanings, you understand. Abolition of not only the common kind but also of every girl who gets married to secure her future, of every time, in other words, that the sexual relationship between a man and a woman happens out of

anything other than necessity [... abolish] betrayal of every type ... both prostitution and betrayal should be punishable by death.]

Elio Vittorini, Il garofano rosso, p. 221

La Repubblica riconosce a tutti i cittadini il diritto al lavoro e promuove le condizioni che rendano effettivo questo diritto.

Ogni cittadino ha il dovere di svolgere, secondo le proprie possibilità e la propria scelta, un'attività o una funzione che concorra al progresso materiale o spirituale della società.

[The Republic recognizes the rights of all citizens to work and to promote the conditions that render this right possible.

Every citizen has the right to conduct, according to her/his own possibilities and choice, an activity or a function that leads to material or spiritual progress of society.]

The Constitution of the Republic of Italy, Article 4

'Mai fidarsi delle puttane' [Never trust a whore]

When Tunin (Giancarlo Giannini), the protagonist of Lina Wertmüller's *Un film d'amore e d'anarchia* (Love and Anarchy, 1972), sleeps through his scheduled attempt on Mussolini's life, he becomes enraged and, rushing around the brothel that has served as his hiding place, shoots an officer of the carabinieri, who are there on another matter. Tunin then runs wildly from the brothel, and chaos brings up the rear. This chaos takes the form of the motley group that draws together prostitutes of all shapes and sizes, their custodians, and the carabinieri who are in Tunin's pursuit. In the brief contretemps that ends with Tunin's arrest, Wertmüller draws attention to the unacceptability of the prostitutes outside the boundaries of the brothel. The camera's frame is tightly packed with incongruities: surrounded by merchants' produce carts and the brick walls of the Roman street, the prostitutes are set in close proximity to proper matrons, their lacy peignoirs in high contrast to the starched blue uniforms of the carabinieri, and – when the prostitute Salomé starts in with her class-based harangue – the differences become even starker. Prostitution is not the cause of this public eruption but, rather, its provenance.

The discharge of the prostitutes into Rome's Via dei Fiori imitates the spillage of prostitutes into the production and articulation of ideology. As one of the clearest examples of exchange (sex for money), prostitution is often used in a metaphoric exchange to symbolize quite varied – indeed, opposing – properties. The instability of the sign of prostitution has made it available as a staging point for the study of myriad phenomena in the visual arts as well as literary and cultural criticism and in an impressive array of historical contexts.[1] Prostitution, the 'oldest' profession, seems to signify not only in a variety of historical moments, but also in the elastic sense of history itself.

In the logic of 'a whore is a whore is a whore,' prostitution engages in a diachronic dialogue, one wherein prostitutes never symbolize only prostitutes or even only prostitutes in a specific historical frame, but stand instead for prostitutes throughout history and prostitution *tout court*. When Salomé breaks faith with her fellow anarchists and decides, with Tripolina, to let Tunin sleep past the appointed hour, Wertmüller draws in for a close-up and we hear Salomé (Mariangela Melato) say beneath her breath, 'Mai fidarsi delle puttane' [never trust a whore]. Her use of the adverb 'mai' (never) indicates the durative aspect of Salomé's statement, an imperative without verbal tense that renders it virtually proverbial.[2]

Wertmüller sets *Love and Anarchy* in Rome, centre of politics and seat of the ancient empire, and seeks to advance the notion that the brothel is a sign for all of Italy itself. Whereas in her other films Wertmüller examines the dichotomous relation of Italy's North and South, her interest in *Love and Anarchy* is the peninsula entire.[3] Wertmüller achieves this by way of the actresses' myriad inflections and bowdlerizations of standard Italian: the Florentine madam, her Neapolitan assistant, the former singer from Venice, the Sicilian Tripolina, Salomé from Bologna, and so on. Their clients know no regional distinctions either: Spatoletti's Italian is boisterously Tuscan, while Tunin's bears a northern inflection. Anarchists, Fascists, and prostitutes circulate every-

where. Surely they are everywhere in the way that the forced itinerary of prostitutes in the Fascist system ensured, through their
percolation throughout Italy, a kind of cross-pollination of
accents and sexual practices. The site of the exchange of sex for
money – also the site for the mediation between sex and politics –
appears at the centre of it all.[4]

The space of the brothel and prostitutes and prostitution signals the intersection between perversion and bad politics. Both
the brothel and the convent, which I explored in the preceding
chapter, are spaces designated and set aside by law for women.
The way both places are suffused by women has led some scholars
and critics to conflate these spaces, if only satirically.[5] As we have
seen, various practices and laws helped establish the convent as a
carceral space. As the stories of actual prostitutes involved in the
Italian system of state-sanctioned prostitution show, the brothel
was clearly a place where women were often detained against
their will and by legal means. In a letter to Senator Angelina Merlin during the decade-long debates over the Merlin Law, which
called for the closing of the *case chiuse* (brothels, though literally,
'closed houses') and to which I will return in the pages that follow, one sex worker refers to herself as a prisoner in the system of
the *case chiuse*. Prostitutes are, she writes, 'simili a delinquenti, che
dura da 3 a 5 anni quando per fortuna, uscite dall'ergastolo,
vogliamo apparire in società per intraprendere un'occupazione!'
[like criminals who serve three to five years of a life sentence and
when, by chance, they get out of prison want meaningful
work!].'[6]

The brothel makes different use of architecture than do convents. In the last chapter, we saw the mutually entailing relationship of the material and discursive representations of the
convent, but the brothel yields a different perspective. In *Delayed
Space*, Fardjadi and Mostafavi caution against the erasure of
actual buildings in favour of interstices and extremities, a common methodological approach in current architectural criticism.[7] However, actual buildings do not trump interstices or
space that is imagined or theorized. Urban geography and *habitus*, the practice of space, valuably inform architecture, but, in

some cases, architectural form yields little if no information about social space. The brothel is a case in point. Attention to the discursive construction of brothels in Italy is necessary since they are not architecturally denoted: it is the practice of prostitution that creates the space of the brothel and not architecture per se. In other words, since no architectural typology applies for 'brothel,' we must turn to discursive representations in order to reconstruct it.

Da che il mondo è mondo: Shooting History's Gap

Elisa è riuscita finora a sgusciare tra le maglie, ma v'è cascata Chiccona, alla quale è stato rilasciato il foglio di via per Lucca, la sua città; v'è cascata Ada, a cui il medico delle carceri ha riscontrato una sifilide di secondo grado – e Rosetta, veterana del mestiere, recidiva specifica, che si è così assicurata per sei mesi il vitto a Santa Verdiana. Insieme ad esse, numerose altre delle venturiere. È il pogrom delle prostitute, una calamità che si abbatte ad ogni cambiamento di governo, da che il mondo è mondo. *Anch'esse come gli ebrei, sono esperte da secoli di persecuzione. Impercano appena, e non rinunciano. Giocano d'astuzia per sfuggire alla rete. Si deve pur mangiare, almeno una volta ogni ventiquattro ore, noi e chi ci sta sulle spalle! Le più giovani e presentabili si decidono al gran passo che significa perdita di libertà, catene ai piedi, ugualmente come nel carcere. È il destino a cui Olimpia si è rassegnata già da diversi mesi ...*
[Elisa had managed to slip through their nets, but Chiccona had gotten caught and had been given an exit pass to Lucca, her hometown; Ada had gotten caught, too, and the prison doctor had diagnosed her second stage syphilis; Rosetta, a veteran of the trade and a 'specific' recidivist, had thus been guaranteed six months of Santa Verdiana's cuisine. They were followed by other prostitutes too numerous to count. *It's the pogrom of the prostitutes, a calamity that accompanies every change of government since time began.* They craftily devise ways to escape the round-up. You've got to eat, at least once every twenty-four hours, you and everyone else you support! The youngest and most presentable decide on the state-run brothels, which means a loss of liberty and ankle restraints just like it would be in prison. It's the destiny Olimpia resigned herself to several months ago ...]

Vasco Pratolini, Cronache di poveri amanti, p. 903 (emphasis added)

The pogrom of the prostitutes that appears toward the end of *Cronache di poveri amanti* (1948), Vasco Pratolini's epic novel set in 1925–6 Florence, underscores their integral presence in the novel. In addition to chronicling the lives and loves of the *cornacchiai*, as he calls the inhabitants of the novel's focal Via del Corno, located just off Piazza Santa Croce, Pratolini narrativizes the transition from early to second stage Fascism. The year 1926 was pivotal in the Fascist consolidation of the state, achieved throughout the '20s by such legal processes as multi-party elections, the promulgation of the *leggi fascistissime* (the most fascist laws), and finally the arrival in 1929 of the Rocco Code, the new penal code. In an ever fascistizing Italian State filtered through memory, prostitutes are a stand-in for all Italians: some evade the clutches of the state's strong arm, the police; others flee in exile; the captured socially miscreant serve prison sentences, and while this subdues public outrage over the immorality of prostitution, the menace to public hygiene cannot be contained. (Just how many clients has Ada already infected, one wonders?) But depicting the prostitutes as a vilified and persecuted social underclass does not suffice, for Pratolini distils out of their tale that persecuted archetype, the Jew. Historical particulars, Pratolini appears to say, hardly matter: 'da che il mondo è mondo,' since time immemorial, as Pratolini states in the original Italian, when governments change, this kind of pogrom is sure to follow.[8]

'Da che il mondo è mondo' betokens historical stasis. In these pages, I address this glossing over of historical specificity and use it to reveal a curious lack of historical change or rupture in the representation of prostitution following Fascism. The lack of development for the spatial practice of prostitution and the brothel aligns with the lack of architectural change of the convent, which I discussed in the preceding chapter. Such static representation in Pratolini's novel illustrates one way in which the historical equilibrium implied by the locution 'da che il mondo è mondo' takes shape. To sketch the outlines of this problem I examine the novel's use of prostitution both in relation and contradistinction to the Merlin Law, enacted finally in 1958 but introduced some ten years earlier. Indeed, Pratolini casts back much further in history than the experience of the *ventennio* for the root of the problem of sex for sale. Whereas following the *ventennio* the male subject was free to return to the customary liberties and entitlements of civil society (suspended or deprived by Fascism), the female subject was turned back to a social order that did not seek nor guarantee her emancipation.[9] A review of *Cronache di poveri amanti* in the light of the public discourse on prostitution helps lay bare the preferential treatment of male subjects in the new republic and thus interrogates the notion of a radical rupture from Fascist practice. Pratolini uses prostitution in this 1948 novel to articulate a relationship to politics; and prostitutes, prostitution, and the places of its transaction ideate *Cronache*'s plot, character, and theme. The literary practice of neorealism and its undergirding politics are at stake in an analysis of prostitution's variable sign. By blurring historical contexts and merging different types of discourses in its portrayal of prostitution, *Cronache* – a novel written and published in the blossoming of postwar neorealism, a politico-literary practice Pratolini is thought to espouse – reveals not the disruption of juridical and discursive practices of Fascism so much as the continuation of those practices.[10]

As I described above, prostitution is both a fixed and mutable sign. Public morality has always disparaged the 'oldest profession' and has always used the concern for public hygiene as the chief reason to control or quash it. Thus, while Fascism, for example, left its particular imprint, its vilification of prostitution reveals no radical difference from the arguments against sex for sale that preceded the Regime. However, distinct from this fixed and enduring complaint, changes do develop in the public discourse concerning prostitution in Italy that correspond to the era of postwar reconstruction and which bear that historical inflection.

Pratolini figures prostitution in multiform ways. As part of the cadre of cultural practitioners active during the immediate postwar period and whose artistic expression strove toward political engagement, Pratolini acknowledges prostitution as a form of labour, and in those moments when he sees it as labour performed by women of the disenfranchised underclass, the narrative makes authorial sympathy and identification patent.[11] However, by using prostitution as the emblem of Fascist depravity, this writer also condemns it. Ugo represents a significant facet of this problem. A principal player in the novel, he overcomes the allure of the sale of sex and in so doing rejects the kind of consumer capitalism that, Pratolini seems to say, goes hand in glove with objectionable politics, which is to say, Fascism.

Da che il mondo è mondo: Ratifying the Merlin Law

One of the first legal battles to be waged in the newly formed Constitutional Republic of Italy concerned the state regulation of the sex trade. Although nearly all industrialized nations had abandoned regulationist practices after the Great War, the state-sanctioned *case chiuse* remained open for business until 1958. In fact, laws concerning the public solicitation of sex for money were among the most enforced (and transgressed) in Florence in the immediate postwar period. For example, a report ending at midnight on 21 March 1945 and submitted to the ranking Allied officer in Florence reads: 'Public safety remains good. Various offences caused the arrest of 144 persons of which 106 were prostitutes.' The same weekly report filed 4 April 1945 reads: 'The smallest number of arrests in weeks was reported this week with only 78 arrests of which 64 were prostitutes.'[12] Despite the sweeping reform of this historical moment in Italy (enfranchisement granted regardless of sex, a new form of government decided by national referendum in 1946, a newly drafted Constitution), the plight of Italian prostitutes shows that women were still bound up in the exaggeratedly patriarchal discourse characteristic of, but not limited to, Fascism.[13]

During its twenty-year tenure, the Fascist government considered and acted upon the social problem of prostitution three times: in 1923, 1931, and again in 1940. Of primary concern during the first campaign was public hygiene and the risk the (male) citizen incurred by frequenting prostitutes. The state promulgated several laws during the historical period in which Pratolini sets his novel. For instance, the *Regio decreto* (law) n. 846 of March

1923 required of all prostitutes proof – documented and certified by a physician – that they were free of all contagious venereal diseases.[14] The machinery surrounding the integrity of public health gathered steam during the '20s, as the Regime consolidated its power, until finally, with the promulgation of the new penal code in 1929, the 'knowing transmission of a venereal disease' was transformed from a misdemeanour offence into a crime 'against the race.'[15] Significantly, the June 1931 Public Safety Law against Prostitution offers another meaningful transformation; this law did not change but, rather, reconfirmed the regulationist stance of the Cavour and Nicotera Laws (of 1860 and 1905 respectively), endorsing the brothels already tolerated (and administrated) by the state.[16]

Practices and attitudes codified by the 1931 law did not wither away in the face of Fascism's collapse. Indeed, Article 16 of the section on 'Rapporti civili' of the Constitution approved by the Assemblea Costituente in December 1947 stipulates that 'ogni cittadino può circolare ... liberamente' [all citizens are free to travel], but specifically circumscribes prostitutes' movements out of respect for 'motivi di sanità' [reasons concerning public health].[17] Gibson concludes her excellent study of prostitution in Italy between 1860 and 1915 by commenting on the absence of change in the public debates concerning the Merlin Law and the proposed end of state-regulated prostitution. 'The parliamentary debates over the Merlin [L]aw,' she observes, 'rehashed for the most part the same positions assumed by regulationists and abolitionists almost a century earlier.'[18] The protracted and difficult fight for the abolition of the *case chiuse* began in August 1948 and continued until the Merlin Law was ratified in February 1958. As one of the first tasks of the Italian Republic, the abolition of the *case chiuse* resounds with meaning: the formative period of the actual Italian State and the Merlin Law precisely and significantly coincide.[19] Lina Merlin, an intrepid socialist senator from the Veneto, wrote and introduced this hotly contested legislation. She sought to abolish the state-run brothels, rehabilitate and relocate the some 4,000 prostitute residents, render criminal any act of pandering, create a special branch of the police dedicated to the enforcement of the law and composed solely of women, and restore fundamental and constitutional rights to prostitutes. In Merlin's vision, prostitutes *alone* would not *solely* safeguard public hygiene; rather, clients, too, would be compelled toward both a heightened sense of civic duty and examination and treatment. It was a too-tall order and, over the ten years required to quilt together the requisite multilateral support, the Merlin Bill lost its original focus and force. What emerged from the debate was a vitiated version of what had been proposed a decade earlier: gone was the presumption of equality between men and women, and in its place was a moralistic and paternalistic (Pitch goes so far as to say Lombrosian) tone.[20] The focus of the law ratified in 1958 became *prostitution*, not the abolition of the *case chiuse*, a significant shift that runs counter to the general *Zeitgeist* of liberation, resistance, and reconstruction that neorealist cultural practices helped shore up. The shift also served to drag the discourse on prostitution back to its previous register composed of issues concerning public hygiene and morality. The Merlin Law travels a trajectory that reaches from a committed and progressive (perhaps even radical) starting point to a dulled and condemning terminus. And the representation of prostitution in *Cronache* takes a similar path.

Da che le demimonde è demimonde; or, Looking for Love in All the Wrong Places

The Albergo Cervia is the second-class hotel in Via del Corno to which the prostitutes bring their clients. The dispassionate description dominating the initial characterization of the hotel and of prostitution offers what is generally considered quintessential neorealism.[21] This sort of characterization cedes to a stylized, lurid, and sensational portrayal that belies its patent (explicit and avowed) political aesthetic, namely, to show things for what and as they were with no spectacular mythologizing. This progression, from a nude, neorealist narrative mode to a highly stylized one, signals Pratolini's ambivalent position. The author's initial detailing of the prostitutes' expenses (how much they pay

Ristori, the proprietor, how much they charge their clients, how many clients they service each day, how many times they change linens, how large their rooms are and what they are like, and so forth) likens them to the other subsistence-level residents of Via del Corno for whom prostitution is simply another way of keeping body and soul together. The prostitutes

> non possono dire comunque che via del Corno le giudichi e le rimproveri. All'occasione esse ricevono saluti cortesi e sguardi di solidarietà. *I poveri e i lavoratori hanno imparato a proprie spese che la vita si suda in tanti modi, e quella è in fondo la maniera più disgraziata e umiliante.* La stessa Clorinda, che fra le donne di chiesa è la più bacchettona, non trova da ridire: le prostitute le danno indubbiamente meno fastidio dei martelli di Maciste e dello Staderini. (emphasis added)[22]

> [can't say that Via del Corno judges or criticizes them. When there is occasion for it they receive courteous greetings and looks of solidarity. *The poor and the working class have already learned at their own expense that life is lived in many ways and that particular one might be the most unfortunate and humiliating.* The very same Clorinda, the most bigoted of the churchgoers, can't find anything bad to say: the prostitutes doubtless bother her less than Maciste's and Staderini's hammering.]

Initially we see how the prostitutes resemble their proletarian neighbours.[23] However, the egalitarian tone soon changes key; from prostitution as 'women's work' and therefore worthy of recognition as labour, Pratolini manipulates it into an example of Fascist handiwork, achieved at the Cervia.[24]

Were it not for the Albergo Cervia there would be no direct conflict between Fascist and anti-Fascist factions in Via del Corno, a microcosm of Florence, itself a regionalized, miniature Italy. Osvaldo and Ugo are exiled from both home and political party, and find new lodgings and society at the Cervia, where they naturally have more extensive social contacts than their previous circumstances would have yielded. Ristori, the hotelier, notices their newfound fraternity and says to Ugo, 'Vedo vi siete affiatati, anche se le vostre idee non collimano a perfezione' [I see you've gotten to know each other even if your ideas don't perfectly mesh] (741).[25] The Cervia provides the politically uncharged territory where, with liquor and women, they transcend ideological differences.

The Cervia epitomizes Ugo's descent into depravity, Fascism, and petty capitalism; when he leaves the company of Fascists and whores and finds the love of a 'respectable' woman, he regains his political purity and proletarian consciousness. When he lived at the Caressis,' he was thrifty and did a day's honest work, frequented Party meetings with Maciste, and kept company with the residents of Via del Corno. Conversely, as a Cervia resident,

> Ugo ha tolto la confidenza a via del Corno. Pare serbar rancore non a Maciste soltanto, ma alla strada intera. Rientra in albergo quando è già buio e la mattina sgattaiola furtiva. Se qualcuno lo incontra e lo saluta, egli risponde portandosi due dita alla visiera del beretto comperato da poco ... Ora tiene alle sue dipendenze un garzone a cui affida un secondo carretto di frutta e verdura e lo indirizza nei Quartieri opposti a quelli che batte lui. Compensa il garzone con dieci lire al giorno; personalmente ricava un utile al disopra del doppio. È quanto ogni sera regala ad Olimpia. 'La succursale l'ho aperta per te,' aggiunse. 'Ti verserò quanto il secondo barroccio mi rende, se tu mi resterai fedele ogni sera, dalle dieci in là.' Ugo è persuaso, in cuor suo, di avere un'amante che non gli costa un soldo, se non un 'ammortizzamento di capitale.' (792)

[Ugo has withdrawn from Via del Corno. It seems as though he's angry not only with Maciste, but with the entire street. He returns to the hotel when it's dark and he scurries furtively away in the early morning hours. If someone sees him and waves, he responds by bringing two fingers up to the visor of his beret which he acquired a short time ago ... Now he has two carts and entrusts the one selling fruit and vegetables to a young boy, directing him into the neighbourhoods distant from the ones he covers. He pays the boy ten lire a day; personally, he makes a little more than twice what he gives the boy. This is what he gives to Olimpia every evening. 'I opened the second cart for you,' he says. 'I'll give you everything I make from the second cart if you'll stay free every evening from ten on.' Ugo is persuaded, in his heart of hearts, that he has a lover who doesn't cost him anything, only a 'reduction of capital.']

Freedom of circulation distinguishes Ugo and his enterprise, and creates structural correspondences to Osvaldo and the Cervia prostitutes. In the main, the actions of the *cornacchiai* (save the ones just mentioned) are geographically circumscribed by the Via del Corno cosmos, and the choral effect of the narrative derives from their cheek-by-jowl proximity. (Carlo Lizzani's 1954 film of the novel also makes this proximity patent.)[26]

In the preceding quotation, we see Ugo 'scurry' away from Via del Corno in search of capital. The free movement of his push-cart through Florence suggests the free circulation of capital and its drive toward cluster or accumulation. Although he later expresses regret over the transformation of his labour, Ugo's work in travelling sales, unlike that of the craftsmen whose work-shops line the ground level of the buildings on the street, is not geographically ordained. He ranges freely so that he might sell; the success of his ambulatory commerce implies regular consumption of his goods, most likely by women of the different neighbourhoods he travels, among whose tasks is to buy and prepare food.

Ugo is a bounder. Significantly, as he falls further from socio-political grace, he unroots socially and 'takes off' economically. When his goal becomes profit, for example, it happens that he moves from his fixed address to the Cervia, a hotel for transients: tourists, travelling salesmen, and the clients of prostitutes. Even though he might leave Via del Corno altogether, he chooses the Cervia instead, a hotel marking the permanence of the temporary. In a correspondingly convenient and 'temporary' arrangement, he invests his profits in a 'lover who costs him only "a loss of capital"': a prostitute.[27]

The sexual alliance during prostitution is fiscal and temporary

(it is fiscal *because* it is temporary, temporary *because* it is fiscal).
While hotels are obviously interstitial spaces (like closets, alleys or
small streets, vestibules, landings, spaces within other spaces, to
name just several examples), the *habitus* of transience makes
them marginal in the way of interstices. The *case chiuse* were typically converted *pensioni* or hotels, as Wertmüller makes visible in
Love and Anarchy or as is the Albergo Cervia in *Cronache di poveri
amanti*. The connection between hotels and prostitution is outlined by one of the prostitutes. In an undated letter to Senator
Merlin that reveals no location, she writes that the proprietors
of the brothels 'corrompono tutti. Adesso tutti vogliono fare
alberghi, pensioni, così fanno peggio di prima. Date le case alla
povera gente che qui ce n'è 24 locali da 4, 5 piani occupati per
quel lavoro' [corrupt everyone. Now they want to set up hotels
and *pensioni* and they'll be worse than before. Give these houses
to the poor; (throughout town) there are about 24 brothels that
take up 4 to 5 floors of each building reserved for sex work].[28]

Were Ugo simply to dissociate himself from his previous household and political comrades in order to devote himself to Olimpia, one of the cadre prostitutes at the Cervia, the development
would say little about the way Pratolini deploys prostitution as cor-
rupt and capitalistic. Instead, by showing that it drives Ugo's motivation for expanding his base of economic operations, Pratolini
flags sex work as a chief contributing factor in the downfall of a
good ('red') man.

The kind of entrepreneurial capitalism Ugo engages in to
secure Olimpia's time is the very sort he will disparage after
Maciste's murder and his politico-spiritual conversion. Ugo's
speech to Gesuina (the embodiment of, Gesù!, true consciousness) reveals the operant system of binaries: good woman / bad
woman (one could easily say Madonna/Maddalena), good politics / bad politics, etc. He tells her:

> Io che mi batto per la causa dei lavoratori, che mi riempio la testa, e
> la riempio agli altri, di proletariato, di capitalismo, di sfruttati e
> sfruttatori, come privato cittadino che sono? Un commerciante!
> Uno che, sia pure in piccolo, vive di ciò che gli rende il suo denaro.

Uno che aspetta in piazza il contadino per comperargli la roba che
questi ha maturato col suo sudore ... Che razza di lavoratore sono?
Cosa produco? Io che avevo un mestiere fra le mani, l'ho abbando-
nato ... (957)

[Me who knocks myself out for the workers' cause, who fills my
head and others' with talk about the proletariat, about capitalism,
about the exploited and exploiters, as a private citizen what am I? A
businessman! Someone who, even if it's only in a small way, lives off
of what gives me my money. I wait in the piazza for the farmer and I
buy the produce he has grown with his own sweat. What kind of
worker am I? What do I produce? I had a trade and I let it slip
through my fingers ...]

Ugo's progress from Olimpia and the Albergo Cervia to Gesuina
and a domestic apartment space exemplifies the shift in Pratolini's evaluation of prostitution and shows how Ugo's female companions function as agents of his social and ideological bias.
Ugo's petty entrepreneurship subtends his political disavowal: he
abandons political principle for the opportunity of greater earnings with which he can secure a lover who costs him no emotional
expenditure, merely 'a loss of capital.' Although saying Pratolini
equates petty entrepreneurship with Fascism is too reductive, it is
clear that it paves the way for bad politics and false consciousness.

The events leading up to the Night of the Apocalypse show
Ugo the error of his ways. The nocturnal trip through Florence
on Maciste's motorcycle during the Night of the Apocalypse
provides him with his purifying journey. When he learns of the
Fascists' plot to execute several high-ranking Communist Party
members, Ugo overcomes and subdues Osvaldo and, with Olimpia's help, keeps him prisoner in her room (which concretely
illustrates the intersection of opposed political ideologies).[29] Ugo
declines Osvaldo's offer to 'fashion himself a new virginity'
(rifarti una nuova verginità [810]) with the Fascists, choosing
instead a new virginity (which is to say, a new beginning) with his
communist comrade, Maciste. Together they leave Via del Corno
behind and, when Ugo returns to the street, wounded from the

foray, it is into Gesuina's and not Olimpia's care that he enters. He tries to explain this renewal to Gesuina while he recuperates from his wounds at the Signora's. She at first retreats, observing that Ugo 'non ha avuto un pensiero per Olimpia!' [hasn't had a thought for Olimpia!] (862). But Olimpia does not worry him for

> è una donna che si sa cavare dagl'impicci da sola ... Era una donna con cui avevo dei rapporti, da tre mesi. Lo dico senza intenzione di offenderla. Tra di noi c'era una specie di contratto: io ti do tanto, tu altrettanto ... Ora, dopo quello che è successo, il contratto è scaduto. E Olimpia l'avrà capito fino dal primo momento ... Olimpia avrà capito che quanto è successo mi ha fatto ridiventare l'Ugo di prima. ... Quello che ero prima non avrebbe accettato di fare contratto con una donna che batte il marciapiede. (862–3)

> [she's a woman who knows how to get out of scrapes on her own ... She was a woman I had a relationship with, for three months. I don't mean to offend you by saying it. Between us there was a kind of contract: I'll give you this much and you'll give me that ... Now, after what's happened, the contract is over. And Olimpia will have understood that from the first ... Olimpia will have understood that what's happened has made me become the Ugo I used to be ... The man I was at first would never have accepted a contractual relationship with a streetwalker.]

Significantly, Gesuina, 'una ragazza ingenua' [an innocent girl] (863), cannot grasp Ugo's meaning. As if the economic discourse of the use-exchange value relation is simply over her head, he adds, 'Dovrei usare delle parole difficili per spiegarmi' [I'd need to use big words to explain myself] (863). Thus, at the moment Ugo purges himself of false political consciousness and the habit of prostitution, he similarly disengages from the language of economics: the overt contractual language that Olimpia traffics in and understands ('io ti do tanto, tu altrettanto') cannot be spoken with Gesuina. Significantly, the narrative makes a diegetic feint, withdrawing into as much description of Ugo and Gesuina's discussion as mimetic presentation of it.[30] Gesuina is not immediately won over, but Ugo is politically born anew and needs a 'good' woman to complement his regained political righteousness. The narrative then fills with conventionally romantic tics: moonlight, hushed voices, heartfelt exchange. Rather than the language of commerce and economics, Ugo now speaks the language of 'free' love: 'Parlarono a lungo entrambi, col cuore sulle labbra' [They spoke at length, their hearts on their lips] (866). Ugo's and Gesuina's is a meeting of souls; no bartering or contracts would be appropriate, and their first night together, occurring several nights later, is characterized by metaphors of newness and youth.[31]

Pratolini builds into the narrative parallels between Ugo and Osvaldo that grow increasingly apparent: both are travelling salesmen, both live in the Albergo Cervia, both seek the sham domesticity of sex for hire, and the politics of both, during the course of *Cronache*, are in an uncertain state of becoming. Ugo's progress in the novel, like some puritan's allegorical journey, helps him to purge heroically these defects, whereas Osvaldo shows what happens when he cannot.

Pratolini does not merely invert Ugo to create Osvaldo's character. In addition to the shared characteristics enumerated, both men have also fledgling politics. Pratolini's deliberate vagueness concerning political affiliation suggests the 'dumbing down' of simple economics to which Ugo resorts for Gesuina's sake. Rather than name Carlino and Osvaldo as PNF (National Fascist Party) members, or label Maciste and Ugo 'Communists,' he is satisfied by the simple 'black' and 'red.' Though indeterminacy will produce additional consequences, it more immediately fuels the nostalgia of the novel. Pratolini's reluctance to name precisely the politics involved evokes a kind of impreciseness attendant on the adolescence so characteristic of a certain vintage neorealism (Vittorini of *Il garofano rosso* and *Erica e i suoi fratelli*, Calvino of *Il sentiero dei nidi del ragno*, Pavese of *La luna e i falò*, and so forth); like adolescents, Ugo and Osvaldo seek definition, but not necessarily one that sharply distinguishes them from their cohort.[32]

Like Ugo, Osvaldo has fallen from a previous state of political engagement, only from the other side of the spectrum. When he refuses to join the *squadristi* (young PNF thugs) in the attack on Alfredo, Carlino evicts him and, politically, casts him out. Like Ugo, rather than leave Via del Corno, he takes up residence at the Cervia. Like Ugo, Osvaldo is a travelling salesman (with Alfredo, in fact, for a client), though he appears to sell to his clients his image as a dutiful Fascist as much as his paper products. Osvaldo's lapel pin signs his political allegiance and currency, and his commercial success seems owed in equal parts to youthful entrepreneurial exuberance and his demonstrated political conformity:

> Simile a Colombo, egli ha toccato terra felicemente, scoprendo clienti nuovi e caricandoli di partite con l'audacia che un giovane deve avere, ed anche un po,' sì, in virtù del dischetto che porta all'occhiello della giacca e che in provincia accresce di giorno in giorno il suo ascendente. Il distintivo è a forma d'uovo ... con il bianco-il-rosso-e-il-verde smaltati in verticale: un fascio in mezzo ... Osvaldo non fa nulla per ricordare ai suoi clienti di essere un fascista: porta il distintivo perchè lo ritiene suo dovere. (723)

> [Like Columbus he had landed happily, uncovering new clients and talking to them about sports matches with the kind of confidence that a young man ought to have and also, it's true, by dint of the pin he wore in the buttonhole of his jacket and that, in the outskirts of town, gained importance almost everyday. The pin was egg-shaped with red-white-and-green enamelled in vertical stripes: a fasces at center ... Osvaldo doesn't do anything to remind his clients that he's a Fascist: he wears his pin because he thinks of it as his duty.]

We find prostitution, finally, at the end of this laundry list of shared attributes and structural similarities: resembling Ugo's arrangement with Olimpia, Osvaldo contracts to spend each night with another of the Cervia prostitutes, Elisa.

Here, however, similarities end; as soon as reflection on prostitution is required, Ugo and Osvaldo separate. Ugo clearly understands that his relationship with Olimpia is fiscal and impermanent; indeed, he has pursued her precisely so as to avoid any involvement beyond a commercial one. Although Osvaldo recognizes the firm (and paid for) distinctions between 'free' love and its prostituted version, he lulls himself into either believing or wishing it were otherwise. The following quotation reveals Osvaldo's inability or unwillingness to distinguish between the sex of prostitution and conjugal intimacy. Osvaldo is drawn into the spectacle of prostitution as a voyeur, and the complacency so characteristic of the scene of prostitution becomes a kind of conjugal intimacy of fantasy, one that would certainly inhibit a good Fascist marriage, if indeed such a thing existed. Osvaldo and Elisa spend every night together, and

> ogni mattina egli si desta allorchè Elisa lascia cautamente il letto, ma continua a fingersi addormentato. Socchiude un occhio: la vede adattarsi il vestito, infilarsi le calze seduta sulla sedia, la vede prendere in mano le scarpe e andarsene in punta di piedi. Elisa è bella, docile, averla accanto gli dà un senso di completezza, di fiducia. Le batte precipitosamente il cuore nei momenti più belli, ed anche questa è una cosa che ad Osvaldo garba. Tutto di Elisa gli garba: vorrebbe richiamarla, vorrebbe ch'ella uscisse dopo di lui, vorrebbe lasciarla in letto magari rimboccarle i lenzuoli. *È ad una pace coniugale ch'egli aspira. E ciò gli costerebbe appena qualche lira di più.* Ma appunto per questo non la trattiene. Egli si rende conto, adesso, svaniti i fumi dell'ubriacatura, che ogni gesto di Elisa è una finzione. Nell'aggiustarsi il vestito, non sapendosi spiata, Elisa ha un'espressione spaventosa, fatta di stanchezza e di disgusto: un ghigno che la sfigura. (795, emphasis added)[33]

[each morning he wakes up just as Elisa quietly leaves the bed, but he pretends to still be asleep. He closes his eyes halfway: he watches her put on her dress, and, seated, her stockings; he watches her take her shoes and leave on tiptoe. Elisa is pretty, docile, and having her next to him gives him a sense of completion and trust. Her heart beats quickly in their most beautiful moments together and this, too, is something Osvaldo likes. He likes everything about Elisa: he'd like to call her back to bed, he'd like for her to leave after he does, he'd like to leave her in bed and maybe even tuck the sheets in around her. *He wishes for conjugal peace. And this would only cost him just a few lire more.* But it's just for this reason that he doesn't detain her. He's aware, now that the fumes of alcohol are leaving him, that Elisa's every gesture is a fiction. When she puts on her dress, unaware that he spies on her, Elisa wears a frightening expression made up of weariness and disgust: a smirk disfigures her.]

In contrast to Ugo, Osvaldo would like to change the terms of his contract with Elisa. He desires, not the spectacle of their relationship, its fiction ('ogni gesto di Elisa è una finzione'), so much as 'una pace coniugale.' An undetected Osvaldo observes Elisa, who believes herself alone and thus, unafraid of censure (or worse, a consequent loss of capital), discloses her 'true' feelings: disgust. Disgust for Osvaldo, for her work, perhaps for herself. Such an expression would understandably frighten Osvaldo: if her disgust proves great enough, perhaps she will spurn him and he would lose that sense of 'completion and trust' their relationship gives him. Finally, Osvaldo sees Elisa as disfigured because that smirk mars the beautiful face he has paid for. As the young Marx wrote, 'Money's properties are my properties and essential powers ... I am *ugly* but I can buy for myself the most *beautiful* of women.'[34] Osvaldo expects Elisa to play a part – he is even certain he could engage her to play-act marital bliss for 'qualche lira di più' [just a few lire more].

When Osvaldo does not distinguish between the real and the fantastic, he actually offers an almost hilarious instantiation of the evil of prostitution according to Richard Korherr. Victoria de Grazia observes that 'only by segregating illicit sex from public view and by drawing a sharp line between bad women and good ones might the state preserve the site and purpose of legitimate sex, namely in marriage, at the initiative of the man and for the purposes of procreation.'[35]

The spectacle Osvaldo succumbs to suggests a blurring of historical contexts and discourses. Osvaldo capitulates not only to the routine spectacle of prostitution but also to what would have been the contemporary public discourse on prostitution. In other words, Osvaldo's 'seduction' may well correspond to the way that Fascism sought to entice the Italian polity through a variety of spectacular practices, including the staging of sundry veritable spectacles and parades. Theatrics and the spectacular practices of advertising during Fascism, recent scholarship has argued, served to ratify the State through the creation of the mass spectator.[36] Although the degree to which the State succeeded in creating mass spectators varied, the attractiveness of spectacle for a State such as Italy during Fascism is unquestionable; equally indisputable is the fact that the State sought to capitalize on the power of spectacle.

Although Osvaldo is capable of recognizing the difference between the 'finzione' of his relationship with Elisa and, say, sexual intimacy in marriage (which is to say, a scene of non-prostituted sex), he prefers not to. The *show* of a 'pace coniugale' is preferable to the real-life version for all the same hackneyed reasons that sex contracted for in prostitution may be preferable to its extra-prostituted equivalent: because it is less complicated. The spectacle of prostitution poses danger in and of itself.[37] The ultimate hazard of prostitution is its lotus-eaters' seduction, the ease with which, as a young Marx observed, a modicum of desire is satisfied by the exchange of a few lire. (And, if we read the letters prostitutes wrote to Senator Merlin during the time of the debates over the Bill, it was never much money, anyway.)[38]

Spectacle is integral for the transaction of prostitution in *Cronache*, which begins as a pantomime and ends in charade. *Prostituere*, in Latin, means to place before, *expose publicly*, offer for sale. As Staderini observes, however, 'cotesto commercio non conosce crisi!'[there's no depression for this here merchandise!] (732). *Cronache's* prostitutes perform their pantomime of seduction 'in piazza Signoria, Orsanmichele, e le Logge del Porcellino, ove fattori e sensali tengono i crocchi delle contratazioni' [in Piazza Signoria, Orsanmichele, the Logge del Porcellino, where farmers and brokers keep track of their deals] (735), in the local markets not far from the Santa Croce neighbourhood. The prostitutes silently lure their clients with the display of their available bodies from these open air markets down the several short streets to the Cervia:

> Le prostitute si trascinano dietro l'uomo con lo sguardo, poi con il muovere delle spalle e del sedere. Il fattore le segue abbacinato, tumido in viso più del naturale. Se incontra un conoscente sarà il primo a salutarlo ed a accompagnarsi con lui per non destargli il minimo sospetto. Ammaestrate da ciò, le prostitute controllano il loro uomo con la coda dell'occhio, nel timore di perderlo lungo la strada; cercano vie traverse, per metterlo a suo agio. Davanti a via del Corno, avviene l'ultima scena della pantomima. La donna ha già infilato il portone dell'albergo, e riparata dietro la soglia spia le mosse del fattore. Lo vede guarda di qua e di là, che si ferma sulla cantonata, che imbocca la strada e poi si arresta, torna sui suoi passi e sbircia di nuovo l'occidente, quindi sfila lungo il muro e con tutta l'elasticità di cui è capace raggiunge di un salto l'androne. (735)

[The prostitutes drag their man behind them with a come-hither look and then with the movement of their shoulders and behinds. The customer follows them blindly, more red in the face than usual. If he meets someone he knows in the street, he'll be the first to extend a greeting and accompany him so as not to raise the slightest suspicion as to what he was about. Apprised of this, the prostitutes check on their man out of the corner of their eyes, for fear of losing him along the way; they take out of the way streets to put him at his ease. The last scene in the pantomime takes place at the foot of Via del Corno. The woman has already crossed the threshold of the hotel and from there spies on her customer's actions. From here and there she watches him hesitate along the outside of a building, come into the street and then stop short, turn back and glance quickly around, then file along the wall and with all his acrobatic skill leap through the hotel doorway.]

Cronache is rife with theatrical elements and devices, such as this pantomime of prostitute and client.[39] Ruggero Jaccobi believes that the spectacular component corresponds to the author's political engagement. In the two books he writes within the span of a year (*Cronaca familiare* and *Cronache di poveri amanti*), Pratolini achieves quite different stylistic ends. In the first, Jac-cobi asserts, 'he draws Florence close to him with a jerk, and in the other he detaches himself by way of an "epic operation," to use the drammaturgical term coined by Brecht.'[40] Further, some critics believe that the representational immediacy Pratolini reaches for in *Cronache* (excepting, of course, the diegetic lapse of the sort discussed above) correlates to the kind of engagement Brecht's epic theatre sought to achieve. In 'Per un saggio' from 1949, Pratolini emphasized the affinity of the epic novel (the 'novel-as-chronicle') and cinema. He believed, as Lucia Re observes, that film 'could provide the "unadorned chronicle" of the quotidian but is endowed with direct spatiotemporal immediacy that the novel could achieve only indirectly, through the mediation of words and the "complicity" of the reader.'[41] The socio-aesthetic aim, however, may not hit its mark. The clearest instance of Pratolini's use of the spectacle of prostitution is found in the *serata nera*, the most explicit example of how Pratolini talks through prostitution and uses it to signify Fascism.

The 'serata' especially illustrates the symbolization of Fascism's debasement. It also offers a real spectacle: a show that the prostitutes put on for their guests, replete with costumes and 'live acts.' All five cadre prostitutes are present: Olimpia, the 'hostess' and Osvaldo's date; Elisa, who is escorted by Ugo; the indecorous Rosetta; Ada; and Chiccona. The depravity escalates as the scene develops:

Ada e Chiccona strapparono un applauso a scena aperta: si svelò finalmente il perchè della loro intimità. Rosetta aveva preso a nolo un tutù dal vestiarista teatrale di via della Pergola: era un bebè macabro e ridicolo. Olimpia indossava una 'rete' rimastale dall'epoca che ella chiamava delle *maisons d'amour.* Elisa era sfacciatamente nuda, e nello stesso tempo pudica come dentro un saio: si convenne ch'era la più bella delle cinque ... a un certo momento Rosetta si era finta una neonata, e Chiccona l'aveva presa sulle ginocchie per allattarla. Ada, eccitata dal vino, aveva assalito Ugo a morsi e baci. Respinta, era caduta in convulsioni. (793)

[Ada and Chiccona drew terrific applause as the scene opened: the reason for their friendship was finally revealed. Rosetta had rented a tutu from a costume shop in Via della Pergola: she was a ridiculous and macabre baby. Olimpia had on a 'fishnet' left over from her time in what she called the *maisons d'amour*. Elisa was boldly nude and, at the same time, seemed as virtuous as if she wore a nun's habit: it was agreed that she was the prettiest of the five ... at one point Rosetta pretended to be a newborn and Chiccona took her on her lap to nurse her. Ada, excited by the wine, had leapt on Ugo, covering him with kisses and lovebites. She collapsed in convulsions when he rebuffed her.]

The perversion in the scene assumes Pasolinian proportions, beginning with Rosetta's 'macabre' impersonation of a baby, extending to the peculiar (and suggestive) onset of Ada's convulsions, and culminating with Chiccona urinating on Osvaldo's head. Ada's convulsions suggest illness, more precisely, epilepsy. This fit also recalls Lombroso's taxonomy of female deviance, which he begins setting in motion in the 1880s. Ultimately, it is Osvaldo who solidifies the connection between depraved behaviour and Fascism when he instructs Chiccona to continue, saying, 'Non me la sono mica presa a male! Almeno Chiccona ha inteso farmi complimento! *I camerati, invece, me lo fecero per spregio!*' [I didn't take it wrong! At least Chiccona meant to pay me a compliment! *The camerati just did it out of disdain*] (794, emphasis in original).

The complicated negotiation of sex, ideology, and prostitution is not limited to Pratolini's novel alone; rather, prostitution and the places for its enactment figure in this period and in subsequent revisions as the analogue for perversion and, therefore, the most readily available symbol for Fascism. Vittorini's *Il garofano rosso* offers similar problematics of the politics of the exchange of sex for money, and the place of love in an ideological context. Like *Cronache*, *Il garofano rosso* involves an operation of mediated memory. Both novels fix the frame of reference in the mid-1920s, but *Il garofano rosso* offers greater complication still in that it first appeared, in instalments, in the Florentine journal *Solaria*, beginning in 1933. Censorship stayed its continued publication, however, and, beginning with the third instalment, the balance of the work remained unpublished until it appeared in book form with a new, lengthy Preface in 1947. Thus, the events the author imagines taking place in Syracuse in 1924 are filtered through a remembrance of the events a decade later, and ultimately twenty-three additional years later. At the end of *Il garofano rosso,* a group of young men (high school students, for the most part) discuss the relative demerits of the practice of prostitution and decide that it must be abolished. As they do in *Cronache*, prostitution and its venue have figured prominently in this short novel about six months in the life of Alessio Mainardi, the protagonist. I have used this passage as an epigraph for this chapter, as well. The group of young dissidents calls for the abolition of prostitution as a requirement of the new society: 'Scrivi: abolire prostituzione e tradimento ... Prostituzione intesa, si capisce, in tutti i sensi.'[42] In what is by now the familiar ahistorical representation of the sale of sex, prostitution does not experience any change in Vittorini's novelistic use of it.[43] The novel begins in June 1924, shortly after Matteotti's assassination in Rome, thus barely more than a year after the Regime's first legislation concerning prostitution. Its ambivalence and lability are even more clear in this novel than in Pratolini's, for what appears as a gathering of young revolutionaries at the novel's end actually exemplifies rather than impugns Fascism's vilification of prostitution.

The brothel as the place for the convergence of opposing ideologies figures elsewhere in prose narrative of the period. Consider, for example, Alberto Moravia's 1947 novel *La romana* (Woman of Rome), where the exchange of sex for money makes possible the substitution of anti-fascism with fascism.[44] Moravia's novel proffers the obverse to Ugo's trajectory in *Cronache*. Giacomo (Mino) is a student committed to anti-fascist activities, but, once he takes up with Adriana, he not only abandons these principles but contradicts them, and actually denounces his former comrades to Astarita, Adriana's client high in the ranks of the Fascist Secret Police.[45] The alliance of 'bad' politics and what is considered prurient sexuality – stock in trade for the portrayal of Fascism in Italian cinema – also finds its beginning around 1946–7.[46] The scenes of prostitution that take place with Astarita are somehow perverted – simulated rape scenes, displays of violence against Adriana and her wishes, basic sadomasochist exchanges of dominance and submission. Like many clients, Astarita enjoys being a submissive, catering to Adriana's needs in a way only a submissive would.[47]

Returning to Pratolini, Ada's convulsions and the presence of Olimpia from the *maisons d'amour* in the performance at the Albergo Cervia in *Cronache* suggest both the timelessness of prostitution and the enduring predictability of female criminal behaviour, which appeared well before the advent of Fascism and will last well after. With the name Olimpia, Pratolini evokes the rich literary, spectacular, and iconographic history of the representation of prostitutes.[48] Olimpia's history as prostitute-icon operates in tandem with Ada's seizure. The problem with prostitution is the threat it poses to public health; Pratolini reminds us that in the pogrom of the prostitutes, Ada is diagnosed with secondary syphilis (whose symptomology does not include seizures or convulsive episodes). But Ada's convulsions recall, too, one of Lombroso's first studies on epileptic pathology, which remained influential in Italian criminology until well after the Second World War. In *Una donna nelle carceri fasciste*, Cesira Fiori ascribes the poor treatment of epileptic inmates to a pervasive suspiciousness that they were 'born criminals' of the sort that Lombroso tried to categorize. In Fiori's opinion, Fascism's greatest crime was to have arrested or thwarted the development of scientific inquiry in the educational system so that methodologies that had long since been debunked (viz., Lombrosianism) flourished in the absence of competition.[49] Tamar Pitch observes that Lombroso's biologistic and essentializing categories of women in general and prostitutes in particular persisted through the 1960s. As I observed above, Lombrosian moralism coloured the final version of the Merlin Bill.[50] This moralism is operant in *Cronache di poveri amanti* and illustrated by the banal representation of the 'sickness' of Olimpia and Ada, and of Elisa's 'cuore malato.'[51]

Elisa with her heart 'diseased' by prostitution and Ada with her prostitutes' malady (not venereal disease, but epilepsy) are the preparation for the truly invalided whore in Via del Corno, the Signora. She is centrally situated in nearly every aspect of the novel; the Signora is so pivotal, in fact, that at a certain point she becomes the proprietor of Via del Corno, threatening to evict everyone and erect a sign that reads 'strada privata.' She also engineers Aurora's elopement, Nesi's downfall, and even, in a way, Gesuina and Ugo's meeting. The Signora, however, is propelled into a downward spiral of degeneration that is better understood in light of her prostituted past.

The Signora is a retired prostitute who lives in immense wealth and semi-infirmity. She gives great sums to the *Fascio*, but only because it is the political power of the day. As Ugo tells Gesuina, whom the Signora has adopted, 'E riguardo alla politica ... per la Signora rossi e neri sono la stessa zuppa' [As for politics ... to the Signora red and blacks are all the same] (864). Giulio warns Liliana of the Signora saying, 'Chissà dove mira! Non devi dimenticarti che è una vecchia *maîtresse*' [Who knows what she's aiming at! Never forget she's an old *maîtresse*] (610). In her dotage, however, the Signora becomes a kind of patron saint of Via del Corno, though she is not all that she appears. In fact, Pratolini's transformation of her into the Duce consolidates the correlation between prostitution's wickedness and the evil of Fascism's uncomplicated 'seduction.'[52] If the depravity of the Albergo Cervia is the metaphoric rendering of Fascist baseness, then the analogy of the Signora (the *maîtresse*, or Madam, and thus director of the brothel) to Mussolini (the titular head of the Fascist State) is a logical one. The Signora is the acme of depravity, 'un essere sensitivo, una creatura che ha posto se stessa al centro dell' Universo, un Dittatore che somiglia assai, nei suoi moti fisici ed intellettuali, a Colui che regge la Nazione' [a sensitive soul, a creature who has placed herself at the centre of the universe, she resembles a dictator who, in his physical and intellectual actions, rules the nation] (938).[53]

Writing on *Cronache* in 1958, critic Alberto Asor Rosa is candidly nonplussed by the Signora and misreads several of her most significant characteristics. 'Il personaggio' of the Signora is for him intentionally 'enigmatico e oscuro: lascia sospettare che dietro di esso ci siano dei simboli, dei profondi significati da svelare, che restano però nascosti, incerti' [dark and enigmatic: one suspects it symbolizes something and that there are deep meanings to uncover that nevertheless remain ambiguous].[54] But if the Signora perplexes, it is most likely owed to something critics would call a heterosexual imperative, or the blind spot of what poet-critic Adrienne Rich has termed compulsive heterosexuality. For Asor Rosa, who himself played no small role in the shaping of public reception of the 'engagement' of postwar literature and writers, the Signora has one dominant valence only, that of 'il simbolo ... di un Male che affonda le radici negli abissi più oscuri e ributtanti dell'istinto umano pervertito' [the symbol ... of an evil that puts down roots in the darkest and most repellent recesses of a perverted human spirit].[55] Surely what is truly perverted about the Signora, and what 'remains to be unveiled,' is what the critic cannot bring himself to name, to wit: her lesbianism and her sexual voracity, both of which, according to forensic and thus legal and public discourse, derive from her past in prostitution. Such criticism is unsurprising if what the critic has been listening to is Lombrosian moralism filtered through both Pratolini and the public debates on the Merlin Law, which, as I mentioned, grew more and more condemning of the prostitutes and not prostitution as such. Failing to acknowledge fundamental attributes of the Signora makes her final appearances in the novel seem unmotivated, dramatic but vacuous, perhaps titillating. Pandering, as it were.

The Signora loves no one, or, put another way, her lesbian love is seen as 'perverted' (from *pervertere*), turned away from its 'true' object choice. The Rocco Code, as I mentioned, interdicted homosexual acts. Robin Pickering-Iazzi reminds us that 'the representation of lesbianism as perversion, or disease, could avail itself of an existing discursive apparatus' shaped by physicians who treated venereal disease in the prostitute population from the 1880s onward.[56] As Gibson observes, lesbianism was widespread in the clinics where venereal disease was treated. Thus the study of sexual love between women and that of prostitution are historically twinned, born of the same historical moment.[57]

Da che il mondo è mondo: History, Politics, and Prostitution

In immediate postwar Florence, history meets itself coming and going. When Pratolini begins his trilogy, 'Una storia italiana,' with *Metello* in 1952 (published in 1955),[58] he will telescope back only so far as the middle of the nineteenth century to look for the germ of what became the episode of Fascism during 1922–43. But in his investigation of the root of Fascism in *Cronache,* he casts back much further.

The notion of the 'chronicle' provided Pratolini and others a much wider historical frame in which to place the phenomenon of Fascism. The chronicle, Fernand Braudel asserted in 1949, was able to capture 'a history of gentle rhythms, of groups and groupings,' instead of the 'surface disturbance, the waves stirred up by the powerful movement of the tides' of history's grand events.[59] In 1947, Pratolini himself writes three chronicles, each referring to Dino Compagni's late-thirteenth-century *Cronica,* and not with regard to genre alone.[60]

In 'Cronache fiorentine xx secolo,' which Asor Rosa believes appeared concurrently with *Cronache,* Pratolini declares that in the recent military engagement 'non era più Nazifascismo e Nazioni Unite che si battevano; *erano fiorentini di due opposte fazioni che si ritrovavano ad uno dei tanti appunti nella storia*' [it was no longer Nazism and the United Nations locked in combat but Florentines of opposing factions that faced each other as they had on numerous occasions throughout history].[61] Moreover, in the same article: '*A Firenze il fascismo s'impose allo stesso modo che si imposero i Guelfi*' [In Florence, Fascism took power in the same way the Guelfs had].[62] Perhaps the author has avoided identifying his 'red' and 'black' blocs in *Cronache* precisely because he believes they conform to an established set of opposing political forces, reaching down from the time of Compagni: the Guelfs against the Ghibellines, the Black Guelfs against the Whites, the Republicans against supporters of the Medici, competing factions that continue to the ones of Pratolini's own time, Fascists against Anti-Fascists, Christian Democrats against Communists, Monarchists against Republicans.

But Pratolini's journalistic chronicle offers a corrective to such 'antico sangue.' Evidently, love helps save Florence from its own internecine strife. As he states: '*C'è anche amore in questa città: un grande amarsi col cuore e col sesso che compensa l'odio che ha imperversato lungo i secoli*' [There's also love in this city: a great love with heart and sex that compensates for the hatred that has dominated for centuries].[63] A concern for love stylistically consolidates Pratolini's chronicle-novel and satisfies ideological aims. In a more felicitous passage of his study, Asor Rosa observes that love is not limited to the lovers of the title but governs all the characters. But love, he writes,

> ... (the capacity to survive and save oneself during times of poverty and oppression) belongs to other characters as well, like Maciste, like Ugo, who, at times, it would otherwise be difficult to understand. Because for them the Communism that they believe in, the sacrifice that they give themselves up to, is in reality nothing more than Love, a great Love for suffering humanity, for the oppressed, for the impoverished, for all those that are crushed underfoot.[64]

For Asor Rosa, it is simple: in *Cronache,* love is communism. Pratolini, despite rumours of his militancy, eschews such political classification; love, for him, is a balm for the factionalism found in Florence 'da che il mondo è mondo.' If love can correct ages-old dissension, then, as *Cronache* makes clear, it should be sought out and revered, not deformed, as happens in its sale during the transaction of prostitution and, quite literally, during its enactment.

Love is what stands at the heart of the 'problem' of prostitution. Love, the argument goes, should not be paid for or coerced. For Gayle Rubin, the difference between giving something freely and giving something in exchange for money lies in the complex system of feelings attendant on the act of giving. Glossing Marcel Mauss's influential essay on the anthropological importance of giving gifts, she observes that 'gift giving confers upon its participants a special relationship of trust, solidarity, and mutual aid. One can solicit a friendly relationship in the offer of a gift, acceptance implies a willingness to return a gift and a confirmation of the relationship.'[65]

The interpretants of prostitution's unstable sign may change, but one thing regularly resurfaces: its censure and the 'pogrom' of the prostitutes deriving therefrom. Training specifically on the historical moment in which it appears, Pratolini's ambivalent portrayal of prostitution in *Cronache di poveri amanti*, as women's work and Fascist machination, offers an analogy for the public discourse on prostitution that emerged following Fascism. Like the discussions in Parliament concerning the Merlin Law, Pratolini's representation of prostitution advances from politically engaged and aware to predictable and banal, from, as Asor Rosa would have it, 'Communism' to the equivalent of Fascism. Prostitution in *Cronache* is equated with Fascism: through prostitution's spectacular enactment of it, love is deformed; it is perverted (as we see in the Signora's lesbianism and nymphomania) and commodified.

But Pratolini's argument against and manipulation of prostitution in *Cronache* reveals an evaluation of it informed not so much by Fascism or social issues following Fascism's fall as by the lessons offered by Florentine chroniclers who have come before him. Pratolini's blending of different discourses on prostitution shows how little different his 'neorealist' treatment of it is from, say, the complaint about prostitution dating from a century before, and even earlier. The incongruous and ahistorical manoeuvrings in *Cronache's* portrayal of prostitution shed light on the author's understanding of history and of Fascism, no isolated or unusual event or even a phenomenon limited to the twentieth century. Written in 1946 but set in a Florence twenty years earlier, *Cronache* brings together elements pertaining to the discourse on prostitution belonging to these two precise historical moments and beyond: to Lombroso's taxonomy of female criminality dating from the 1880s, to nineteenth-century French painting, to the association of prostitution and the theatre, to a political problem plaguing Florence and Italy 'da secoli ... da che il mondo è mondo.'

Chapter Five

House Arrest

How often do women awake
in the prison of marriage,
of solitary motherhood
  alone and forgotten.

Erika Huggins, 'I Wake in Middle-of-the-Night Terror,'
Off Our Backs 2:8 (April 1972), 17

La mamma, rimasta vedova, s'è risposata con un garzone giovane. E lui s'è preso
mia sorella, più grande, e poi anche me, il porco! mamma, accecata di lui l'ha
lasciato fare per non perderlo ... ma poi ha scacciato via me ... Ed io ho, qui a
Perugia, fatto la p[uttana] e ci sono rimasta incastrata e sono andata dalla
levatrice ... Cocchina mia! Tutte e due ci hanno beccato, per aborto, quattro anni,
sai?
[My mother had been widowed and (then) married a younger man. And he
took up with my older sister and then with me, the swine! My mother,
blinded by her love or need for him, let him do what he wanted so as not to
lose him ... but then she kicked me out ... Me, I turned to p(rostitution)
here in Perugia and then I got in trouble and went to the midwife ... Dearie!
Both of us got pinched for abortion: four years, each, y'know?]

Anonymous woman in a fascist-era prison, quoted in Cesira Fiori,
Una donna nelle carceri fasciste, p. 76

Gli ho sparato negli occhi.
[I shot him between the eyes.]

Natalia Ginzburg, *È stato così*, p. 3

Houses and Homes: The Dystopic Dyad

Alessandra's failure to exonerate herself for the murder of her husband in Alba de Céspedes's 1949 novel *Dalla parte di lei* (The Best of Husbands) gives exemplary literary expression to the captivity of women in postwar Italy. The male-public, female-private dichotomy is impelled to its dramatic conclusion in this novel, where the female subject is rendered criminal by male juridical prerogative. Detained for Francesco's murder, Alessandra tells her story from prison and in the form of a lengthy confession. She does not proffer the gender-neutral prisoner Simone Weil describes in a 1951 entry in her *Cahiers*, that 'human being' (être humain) 'where lives a prisoner with all the world' (où habite un prisonnier avec tout l'univers).[1] Like Alessandra, the anonymous female narrator of Natalia Ginzburg's 1947 novel, *È stato così* (The Dry Heart), and the cast of female characters in Ugo Betti's 1950 drama, *L'isola delle capre* [Crime on Goat Island], respond violently and criminally to their carceral domesticity: as the passage that stands as one of the epigraphs to this chapter indicates, Ginzburg's narrator kills her husband by shooting him at point-blank range, and Betti's isolated women check the temptation of the male interloper by chasing him down the well (where, presumably, they will leave him to perish). In the prisonhouse of marriage, in their carceral homes, these characters allegorize the Italian Everywoman; they emblazon female subalternity in postwar, newly post-Fascist Italy, a subalternity guaranteed by juridical and architectural constructs, in turn shored up by the tactics of domestic space.[2]

These characters are both victims and perpetrators, a contradiction indicative of a fundamental ambivalence surrounding the notion of 'home.' Prostitutes are not the lone female offenders during the period in question. Drawn (or forced) into criminality by their respective domestic situations, these homemakers unveil the home not only as the place for the confinement of women but also as the place where women are induced into criminality. In a contemporary but nevertheless relevant context, Biddy Martin and Chandra Mohanty note this ambivalence, asserting that home locates the contestation between 'being home' and 'not being home.'[3]

Ambivalence is the concomitance of two opposed notions and, as such, summons up some of the binaries I explored in chapter 1: the relation between Fascism and post-Fascism in Italy, between actual prisons and their cultural analogues, between prisoners' representations of imprisonment and its representation by authors who are not themselves detained by the State. It is not accidental that 'home' is the etymological and epistemological provenance of the uncanny (*Heim-Unheimlich*), where something is at once itself and its double.[4] As Freud describes it, *'heimlich* is a word the meaning of which develops in the direction of ambivalence, until it finally coincides with its opposite, *unheimlich.*' Like the uncanny, utopia is also a notion that is doubled and ambivalent. For example, Thomas More presents a work in two parts (a political treatise and a fable); utopia is both the location of happiness (*eú-topos*) and no location at all (*oú-topos*, or no-place); and – the central paradox deriving from this bit of homophonic play – the utopians seek pleasure and delight, but their lives are highly ordered and tightly controlled.[5] Thus the difference between utopia and its obverse, dystopia, is not substantive but, rather, a matter of degree.

The embedding of dystopic oppression in utopic protectiveness shapes the theme of this chapter, which addresses the way notions of home incarcerate and criminalize women during and after Fascism. In Italian, the phoneme *casa* signifies both house, as in constructed dwelling, and home, with all homelike notions accruing to it. In the preceding chapter, I discussed the absence of an architectural denotation of the 'brothel' and the consequent need to explore its discursive formations, and the home presents a similar problematic. As Douglas reminds us, home 'is located in space, but it is not necessarily fixed in space ... For a home neither the space nor its appurtenances have to be fixed, but there has to be something regular about the appearance and reappearance of its furnishings.'[6] To examine the carceral formations of 'home' between 1930 and 1960, I focus on the ways several disciplinary discourses work together to articulate 'home's' ambivalence: I will explore the mutually informing discourses of architectural design, urban planning, criminology, and literary representation in the fifteen years following Fascism's official fall from power.

An ambivalent sign and the location of crime, home is the primary trope of Carlo Emilio Gadda's *Quer pasticciaccio brutto de via Merulana* (That Awful Mess on Via Merulana). Like the works of de Céspedes, Ginzburg, and (we are left to assume) Betti, Gadda's novel also features a brutal murder within the ostensibly protective confines of the home. Unlike her counterparts in Ginzburg, de Céspedes, and Betti, however, the victim in Gadda's novel takes no part in criminal activity; this notwithstanding, her very femaleness implicates her in the murder of which she herself is victim.

Quer pasticciaccio manifests strong interest in the spatialization of gender, dominance, and subversion. This interest expresses itself in the novel's substance as well as its form, and geography plays a role for both. Female dangerousness is studied within the Roman domicile and, pulled taut along the lines of a grotesque female reproductive system writ large, spreads onto the metropolitan periphery and the countryside surrounding Rome. Gadda's delineation of women, of female delinquency, and of maternity are riddled –or rattled – by ambivalence: Inspector Ingravallo has sympathy for Liliana Balducci's barrenness but believes that female biology or, rather, endocrinology, makes women hysterical and (following Lombroso) predisposed toward delinquency. As a result, although Ingravallo is horrified by Liliana's murder, he also believes that she must be partially responsible for it, providing for a version of the 'blaming the victim' scenario often associated with violence against women, especially rape.[7]

Formally, this ambivalence toward women is demonstrated by the simultaneous adherence to and rupture with the properties of the detective story genre.[8] Such textual and subtextual ambivalence makes the time frame of the novel's composition even more suggestive. Like the period required for the ratification of the Merlin Law, *Quer pasticciaccio* was written and rewritten in the ten-year period beginning in 1946 and ending with its publication by

Garzanti in 1957. The struggle of women to achieve parity before the law is understood in a context in which the judiciary, as we have seen, revealed its inability to assist Italian society in the process of defascistization. The Merlin Law tells part of the story of this struggle, and the *Pasticciaccio* tells another. However laborious its progress, and whatever accommodations Senator Merlin and her supporters made, the Merlin Law inched women's legal status into uncharted territory and greater equality. The predictability of women's criminal dangerousness, as Gadda's metaphysical detective novel attests, moves in the opposite direction from the one signalled by the Merlin Law. Comparison of the 1947 and 1957 variants of the *Pasticciaccio* reveals Gadda's withdrawal from a formal resolution of crime and his retreat into ambiguity and the familiar representation of the innate delinquency of women.[9]

During the *ventennio*, the ideas of home and family were freighted with Fascist demographic philosophy, declared most baldly by Mussolini in the May 1927 proclamation known as 'Il discorso dell'Ascensione' (The Speech about Population Growth): 'We must be vigilant in safekeeping the destiny of our race ... we must safeguard the race and we must start with mothers and children.'[10] Women stood at the crossroads of neo-imperialism and economic autarky; women's role was that of the 'sposa e madre esemplare,' the exemplary wife and mother, and her place was the home. I do not mean to suggest in the following pages that women did not find myriad ways to resist such misogynist constructions as those reified during the Regime, something that would disavow the convincing findings of recent scholarship exploring women under Fascism; rather, I mean to draw attention to the ways in which those constructions, steeped in gendered hierarchy that clearly antedated the Regime, survived Fascism's demise. Moroever, the continued containment of women during the postwar period called for continued struggle and resistance. As Dolores Hayden writes, for women, the body, the home, and the street have all been arenas of conflict. Examining them as political territories – bounded spaces with some form of enforcement of the boundaries – helps us to analyse the spatial dimensions of 'woman's sphere' at any given time.[11]

Although Fascism confirmed that women's place was in the home, the home was itself opening onto the public. Emblematic of this opening is corporative family life, assisted and affected by the various agencies and movements that reached into the home as well as the kinds of leisure activities organized, not according to family structure, but, rather, along generational and gender lines. Such programs and agencies included the Sabato fascista (Fascist Saturday programs), the ONMI (Opera nazionale per la maternità e l'infanzia [national organization for mothers and children]) for pregnant women and new mothers, the Dopola-voro (afterwork programs), or any of the Fascist organizations for youth, including Gioventù littorio, the Ballila, etc.[12] Thus, the home experienced a paradoxical development: outward toward programs intended to nurture nationalist zeal and, simulta-neously, inward to reconstitute the conventional family. But 'home' lost its private valence through the State's transformation of it into the site for state-sanctioned sex and procreation.

House of Glass: Transparency, Surveillance, and Public Housing

... the Mussolinian concept that fascism [sic] is a glass house into which all can look gives rise to this interpretation ... no encumbrance, no barrier, no obstacle between the political leaders and the people.
Giuseppe Terragni, 'La construzione della Casa del Fascio di Como,'
quoted in Dennis Doordan, *Building Modern Italy*, p. 137

Seeking to domesticate its public presence, Fascism constructed its own 'homes,' the *case del fascio* (Fascist centres), throughout the Peninsula during the '20s and '30s, which exemplify this con-tradictory notion of the 'open' home. Customarily, the design called for office space for various affiliate agencies, a conference room, a reading room, an assembly hall, and various meeting rooms. Awarded to architects on the basis of national competi-tions, the various *case del fascio* were 'the architectural presence [of official Fascism] in countless cities, towns, and villages.'[13]

Giuseppe Terragni's Casa del Fascio, built between 1932 and 1936 in Como, typifies the tendencies of Rationalist architecture, which was regnant throughout Italy in the '30s and enjoyed stylistic continuity in Northern Italy following the Second World War.[14] Terragni's Casa del Fascio features two conspicuous elements: its synthetic character and its transparency. With its synthesis of both traditional and contemporary forms, the Casa enacts a cardinal operating principle of Fascism. Fascism works by splitting apart logical connections and quilting together what Barbara Spackman terms 'seemingly incompatible elements and polarities: [Fascism's] ideological specificity therefore lies not in the elements it gathers together but in the binding mechanism itself.'[15]

Terragni's synthesis of style and form betokens this binding mechanism, and the Casa del Fascio endeavours to suture the temporal gap between Italy's contemporary and ancient achievements.[16] Formally, Terragni's building offers a synthesis of epic space and national grandeur. In the context of 1930s Rome, for example, the desire for synthesis is quite clear in another building designed for state purposes, the Palace of Italian Civilization (now the Department of Labour), located in EUR, designed by the team of Guerrini, La Padula, and Romano, and built between 1938 and '39. The synthetic aim of this building is obvious from the series of arched windows, which were clearly meant to recall the exterior of the Colosseum. The arches were designed for the display of statues commemorating heroes from the history of Italian civilization. Terragni's design for the Casa del Fascio in Como creates synthesis by establishing a host of oppositions, including, for example, a traditional as opposed to a modern tectonic conception (the mural surface over against the grid frame), artificial as opposed to natural light (admitted by the open bays on the top floor), and the alternation of strip and sash windows.[17] The configuration of the windows and natural illumination of the building yield the salient point concerning the transparency of the 'benign' Regime.

That Fascism's 'house' was made of glass and open to plain view from all exposures argues for the 'opening' of the house/home I described above. Marla Stone reminds us of the 'clean, functional lines' that hark back to de Stijl, Le Corbusier, and a similarly impeccable modernist genealogy and she describes the Casa del Fascio as an 'open container,' about which I will say more presently.[18] The glass doors on the ground level and the many windows on all sides of the building provided saturated vision from within and without. Significantly, one could see as easily into the assembly space of the central hall (where the rank and file convened) as one could into the Office of the Federale. A useful illustration of surveillance, the unobstructed vision into the 'rankless' casa is, of course, completely disingenuous: Fascism's political mechanisms, presented as visible and, therefore, guileless, were in reality somewhat more inscrutable.

The glass house that Terragni built defies explicit tenets of surveillance, developed and popularized by Jeremy Bentham for his eighteenth-century panopticon. Discipline, for Bentham (and later, for Foucault), was contingent on readily available surveillance and on the self-disciplining of the criminals. The watchtower positioned at the centre of the panoptical structure may or may not have housed an observant guard, but the inmates would never know when or whether the guard was present. Placing the *gerarchi* in perpetual visibility from both within and without, the Como Casa del Fascio strikes an effect contrary to the Benthamite panopticon. Yet the surveillance of Terragni's glass house, in which even ranking Fascists were subject to perpetual scrutiny, seems all the more sinister: although we may freely regard Fascism's casa and the manoeuvres within it, the *gerarchi*, with the stealth and power of cobras, stare back.[19]

In the dismantling of the Regime, surveillance (particularly surveillance of the home) is recuperated. As Rossellini makes clear in *Open City* (1946), Fascism does not monopolize surveillance as a tactic of social control. From Nazi headquarters in via Tasso, Bergmann controls Rome from a windowless room that seems ably to analogize Bentham's notions of surveillance; he monitors the activities of known and suspected anti-Fascists in the Eternal City during the Occupation with help from the artificial means of photographs and maps. Opposed to such denatured surveillance, Rossellini offers an organic (and salutary) version that the resistance workers, his protagonists, carry out among themselves and in their apartment complexes.[20] Critics have pointed out that while the Nazis consistently occupy the horizontal axis of the frame in *Open City*, the resistance workers dominate entrance to the vertical coordinates.[21] What results are many high-angle, exterior shots from the resistance workers' point of view, revealing their quite literally superior vision of Rome, of its internal movements, and of its residents. Similarly, the working-class protagonists keep careful and protective watch over each other, and Rossellini uses with great success the interior stairwell of the public-housing building to just that end.

Like writers and film-makers of the period clustering in the capital, Rossellini acclaimed among them, architects during the immediate postwar period sought to do away with Fascism's monumentalist grammar.[22] The newly elected editor of *Domus*, distinguished architect Ernesto Nathan Rogers, put it well in his inaugural editor's column from 1946: 'The problem is one of forging a taste, a technique, a morality, as different manifestations of the same problem: the problem of building a society.'[23] In what Vittorio Gregotti calls the 'striving toward reality,' the so-called 'organic' school calibrated its efforts bearing in mind a more human scale. On the development of a more 'organic' style of architecture and design, Bruno Zevi wrote:

> Organic architecture is at once a socio-technical activity and an artistic activity directed towards creating the environment for a new democratic civilization: it is aimed at the architecture for the human being, shaped to the human scale, and following the spiritual, psychological, and contemporary needs of man as a part of society. Organic architecture is therefore the antithesis of the monumental architecture used to create official myths.[24]

No mere handmaiden to social reality, postwar literature and cinema created for the organicists their grammar and syntax. The politically engaged architects of the APAO (Associazione per l'Architettura Organica, or the Association for Organic Architecture) derived their precepts for public housing from literature, cinema, and, it is doubtless, the other arts.[25]

However, if architects envisioned a non-monumentalist revolution in design, it took place within the context of urban planning and policy that had changed very little since the *ventennio*. The continuity of state apparatuses from the Fascist Regime into the era of reconstruction affected many state agencies, including housing and town planning. Rather than reconfigure policy or agencies, the structure and aim of the housing industry remained curiously intact since the 1942 town-planning law, which, Ginsborg informs, 'safeguarded the rights of landowners, made no attempt to tax profits deriving from land speculation, and abandoned the idea of any serious government intervention.'[26] Private interest therefore dictated the appointment and the construction of housing, which increased its numbers: 73,400 houses built in 1950, 273,000 in 1957, 450,000 in 1964. Although interests of the private sector dominated in this period (only 16 per cent of total investment in the construction of houses derived from public schemes), this is not to suggest that public initiative was lacking entirely. On the contrary, such state agencies as the INA-Casa (Istituto Nazionale Abitazioni, or the National Institute for the Housing Industry), the GESCAL (Gestione Casa Lavoratori, or the Agency for Public Housing, literally workers' housing), as well as the IACP (the Istituto Autonomo Case Popolari, or the Independent Institute for Public Housing) did effect some differences.[27]

Mario Ridolfi's reconstruction-era projects thematize surveillance and control, and concisely synthesize some of the continuing effects of the para-state agencies associated with the Regime. Two housing projects in Rome, one in Viale Etiopia and the other in the Tiburtino area, and the new prison in Nuoro (Sardegna) are of interest for what they impart about about the postwar housing industry, urban planning, and residential design.[28] Although these homologous structures share few typological similarities, their common urbanistic locations elaborate on the themes of isolation, captivity, and surveillance. As we shall see, the question of containment establishes the primary connection between Ridolfi's postwar projects and Gadda's *Pasticciaccio*, which predicates on the division between within and without Rome, a division Gadda makes explicitly gendered.

A word about the construction of new prisons clarifies the problem of isolation within the urban landscape. Before the 1970s, Italy seldom built new prisons. Rather than construct new places for the confinement of criminals, the Italian State (unified only in 1870, we remember) exploited extant spaces for their carceral usage.[29] As we have seen, prisons were adapted from former ecclesiastical buildings (monasteries and convents) in central urban locations. Prisoners detained, for example, in Rome's Regina Coeli, the complex of the Murate (including Santa Verdiana) adjacent to Florence's Santa Croce neighbourhood, or San Vittore in Milan, were attached to the life of the neighbourhoods located just outside the prison walls. From these and others of the older prison types, inmates could see the buildings of the surrounding neighbourhoods and, significantly, could hear the life of their non-imprisoned neighbours emanating from outside the walls.[30] For prisons constructed in the twentieth century, this was never the case. Pushed to the outskirts of town and out of public view, prisons lose their relationship to the urban environment, and punishment, as Foucault outlined, becomes an intangible – and invisible – threat.[31] This is the circumstance for both prisons Ridolfi constructed during the period 1953–5.[32] The problem of isolation, as we will see, similarly affects the apartment complexes in Via Tiburtina.

From the exterior, the prison in Nuoro is seen as part of a barren and remote landscape. Ridolfi's design displays a triangular complex, including administrative buildings, barracks for the penitentiary police, and a small entrance. Enclosed by a rectangular wall that would be visible to the inmates only from the windows of their cells, the design displays a forceful geometry. The plan reveals four large rectangular cell blocks for men and one rather smallish and square cell block for women, adjacent to the church. (The number of cell blocks corresponds to the percentage of men and and women in the prison's population.) Because of the rather low security of the ring wall, prisoners exercised, walked, and took air within the almond-shaped courtyard, though women may have had greater access to the other courtyard areas. (Typically they did in other prisons.)

Surveillance, enclosure, and confinement are anticipated features of prison architecture; they are less expected, however, in
housing design.[33] The apartment complexes that Ridolfi built in
Rome during the same time share with his designs for the prisons
a similar remoteness of location and the possibility of surveillance. This is especially characteristic of the public housing
designed for Via Tiburtina that Ridolfi built with his colleague
Ludovico Quaroni during 1950–4. The Tiburtino, as the area was
known, was the first project administrated by the INA-Casa and
marked the first competitions for public housing in the postwar
period.[34] Sharply critical of the urbanistic location of the housing
project, Tafuri remarked: 'Exiled from the city, the Tiburtino
scornfully turns its back on it.'[35]

And exiled the residents of the Tiburtino were. Tafuri describes
the complex as 'an affirmation of both rage and hope, even if the
mythologies that sustained it made its rage impotent and its hope
ambiguous.'[36] The wished-for oasis in the city proved a chimera.
Far from any tramlines that might easily conduce residents to
work in more close-lying areas, the Tiburtino strove for self-sufficiency but never overcame its geographical appointment. The
design of the Tiburtino was also cause for complaint: Ridolfi's
critics dwelled on the 'baroque' aspects of his pastiche, calling
the Tiburtino a 'slap in the face of good taste' and, in some cases,
grotesque. The Tiburtino design was informal, and Ridolfi hoped
that the use of certain materials, namely the Roman roof tiles and
the wrought iron for the balconies, would offset the feeling of
alienation stemming from its urbanistic appointment.

In a post-Fascist context, these public-housing structures dis-
pensed with Fascist-era 'monumentalism' and, at the same time,
reclaimed and restored a benign side to surveillance. The
sequences of balconies and external staircases furnished the possibility for the sort of community-minded surveillance I have
been describing. We may, for example, consider the possible
monitoring of entrance and exit to the buildings and the relief
some residents may have felt at conducting their own surveillance. Critics believed Ridolfi's design established 'communication' between the buildings, and we might compare it to the

contemporary 'neighbourhood watch' in urban and suburban centres, where residents practise protective surveillance.

Despite the friendly and neighbourly intentions of communication and vigil, however, women did not necessarily fare well in these new communities located far outside the city centre. As Ginsborg notes, the kind of idealized confinement 'of women to the home in the [1950s] and 1960s, served to enclose them in a purely private dimension, and to remove them even more than previously from the political and public life of the nation.'[37] The amenities of the new apartment complexes in previously sparsely occupied sections of the city, in concert with the increase in the domestic production of new domestic appliances, were intended to improve the home economics of housewives in the urban capital. Although in the early years of reconstruction the domestic appliances firms that were to become household names were still 'artisan concerns,' the rise in production is easily traced in the decade that followed the war. In 1947 Candy produced one washing machine per day, Ignis had less than 100 workers, and Zanussi employees numbered only 250. In 1951 Italy produced 18,500 refrigerators; by 1957 it was producing 370,000 annually, and a decade later, 3,200,000. By this time, Italy had also become the chief producer worldwide of washing machines and dishwashers.[38] The postwar domestic imperative differed little from the theories of home economists and Taylorists concerning the efficient running of the household that had been so impressed upon middle-class Italian women of the late 1920s and early 1930s.[39] Although these appliances were certainly labour-saving, they nevertheless can be seen as producing the less desirable effect of depriving women of reasons to leave the domestic sphere. Alberto Moravia comments on the containment of domesticity at the metropolitan periphery in his 1947 novel *La romana* (Woman of Rome). Moravia at once anticipates the postwar flurry of construction and mirrors the sense of fascist surveillance I have outlined; the split between the novel's historical setting (late 1930s Rome) and its date of publication (1947) mirrors the divide between Fascism and its immediate aftermath.[40] When the protagonist Adriana pays a visit to her friend Gisella in Via Casablanca, 'strada nuova in un quartiere nuovo' [a new street in a new neighbourhood], Moravia gives literary expression to Rome's sprawl, where the new residential neighbourhoods are far removed from the urban centre:

> Via via che il taxi correva, ci allontanavamo dal centro della città e dalle sue case vecchie, allineate in strade anguste, addossate le une alle altre. Le strade si allargavano, biforcandosi, confluendo in piazze e diventando sempre più larghe, le case erano nuove e tra le case ogni tanto si intravedeva la striscia verde della campagna.[41]

> [As the taxi flew through the streets, we retreated from the centre of town and the old houses that lined the narrow streets, one on top of the other. The streets grew broader and then divided, emptying into piazzas and growing ever wider, the houses were new and between them every so often one glimpsed a bit of the green countryside.]

Adriana's trip through Rome's urbanizing periphery is significant in two related ways. First, her taxi ride provides the opportunity to distinguish between Gisella's past poverty and newer wealth. Second, it shows that distance from the centre does not guarantee diminished scrutiny or surveillance, a theme I explored in detail in chapter 2. Adriana finds her friend in a building noticeable for the recent construction that has left in its wake 'certe botti, travi, e vanghe accatastaste nel piccolo giardino brullo' [barrels, beams, and shovels in a heap in the small, forlorn garden] and where 'schizzi di calce ... macchiavano le sbarre del cancello' [whitewash speckled the bars of the gate] (305). Gisella is far from the slatternly room where Adriana was accustomed to visiting her deep in the heart of Rome. With the help (and money) of her new boyfriend, she now occupies an ultra-modern and comfortable new domicile on the outskirts of town. And yet even in such an ostensibly remote location, potential surveillance reappears. It only takes Adriana a moment, as she waits for her friend and hostess to appear, to notice the 'ampia vetrata che pareva occupare tutta la parete di fronte alla porta' [the pic-

ture window that seemed to fill the entire wall opposite the door]
(307).

Big House: Home and Via Merulana

*... un fascino, un imperio tutto latino e sabellico, per cui gli andavano insieme i
nomi antichi, d'antiche vergini guerriere e latine e di mogli non reluttanti già
tolte a forza ne la sagra lupercale, con l'idea dei colli e delle vigne e degli scabri
palazzi, e con le sagre e col Papa in carrozza, e coi bei moccoloni di Sant'Agnese
in Agone e di Santa Maria in Porta Paradisi a la candelora, a la benedizione dei
ceri: un senso d'aria dei giorni sereni e lontani tra frascatano e tiburtino, soffiata
a le ragazze del Pinelli tra le rovine del Piranesi ...*
[... a fascination, a completely Latin and Sabine bearing, which summoned
up the names of the ancients, of ancient virgin warriors of Rome, of not
unwilling wives already taken by force during the festival of Pan, with the
idea of hills and vines and scabrous palaces, and with festivals and the Pope
in his carriage, and with the lovely votives in Sant'Agnese in Agone and
Santa Maria in Porta Paradisi or the feast of Candlemas and the benediction
of the candles: a sense of the air of serene and distant days between Frascati
and the land of the Tiber, stirred by Pinelli's subjects, girls amid the ruins of
Piranesi ...]

Carlo Emilio Gadda, Quer pasticciaccio brutto de via Merulana, p. 8

The concomitance of Ridolfi's housing and prison projects is
symptomatic of the carceral homologue of the home. To examine
the discursive creation of the carceral space, I now return to more
sustained analysis of its literary representation, more precisely, to
its representation in detective literature during the period, more
precisely still, to Carlo Emilio Gadda's *Quer pasticciaccio brutto de
via Merulana*.

The choice of the detective genre has formal significance for
Gadda and relates to the thematic of homes and houses. Home in
the detective story is the thing invaded and plundered; it is the
secure place that may be 'effectively breached' by the impinging
world outside the ostensibly protective shell of the home.[42] Detective fiction, as Walter Benjamin reminds us, derives from
nineteenth-century bourgeois materialism, the greatest example

of which is the bourgeois home. Expanding on Marx's belief that the bourgeoisie achieved its goals by way of the July Revolution, Benjamin writes that

> for the private citizen the space in which he lives enters for the first time into contrast with the one of daily work. The first becomes the *interieur*, the office is its complement. The private citizen, who keeps account of reality in the office, demands that his *interieur* entertain him in his illusions ... The *interieur* is the refuge of art ... *The* interieur *is also the container of the private citizen.* To inhabit means to leave traces which acquire, in the *interieur*, a particular importance. A profusion of covers and cases, sheaths and boxes where objects of everyday use impress their traces. Even the traces of the inhabitant impress themselves upon the *interieur* and from them is born the detective story, which goes after these traces.[43]

The detective story itself registers the latent fear of change that may subvert law and order, and the reading of detective fiction is a kind of modelling of that fear.

In August of 1941, the Bolognese journal *Assalto* reported that the Ministero della Cultura Popolare (the Ministry of Popular Culture, known as the Minculpop) had ruled that 'for reasons concerning their moral character [that] ... the publication of detective novels, both in periodical and serialized form, shall be brought under its protective authorization.'[44] In addition to censoring the future publication of *gialli* (as the yellow-jacketed detective novels were popularly known), the Minculpop called for the removal from circulation 'detective novels already published and which are judged harmful to Italy's youth.'[45] This fiat heralded the end of Mondadori's enormously popular series *I volumetti gialli*. The series, ushered in with such verve in September 1929, helped cultivate interest in the detective story, which dominated Italy in the '30s. As Rambelli observes, 'the hard-boiled detective novel was all the rage in Italy during the 30s.'[46] It is suitably ironic, Rambelli further notes, that a police state could not tolerate novels that revolved around police action and police investigation. The novels in and of themselves were not considered *nocivi* (harmful): true harm – and sedition – lay in the method of investigation that could be discerned in their pages. Although the overwhelming popularity of the *giallo* seemed to guarantee its censorship, more suggestive still is the last title in the cancelled series: Ezio D'Errico's *La casa inabitabile* (The Uninhabitable House).

The home gives crime a home. As Martin and Mohanty assert, home does not necessarily produce feelings of 'being at home'; rather, the notion of home produces a feeling of cognitive dissonance symptomatic of the psychological itinerary of the *Unheimlich*. As Freud describes it, the *Unheimlich* is the jarring misrecognition of a place so 'like' home (Heim) that one feels 'at home' (*Heimlich*). This misrecognition is followed quickly by an 'uncanny' (*Unheimlich*) sensation of feeling at home in a place that is not home.[47] William Spanos is less concerned with psychoanalysis than with the ontological importance of the *Unheimlich* in detective literature. 'To put it in Heidegger's terms,' he writes, 'it has been the process of discovering that the at-home of the modern world has in fact become the realm of the not-at-home.'[48]

The ambivalence of the home and women's place within it is fundamental to the detective story, whose formal conventions Gadda seriously violates. Briefly, *Quer pasticciaccio* tells the story of Don Ciccio Ingravallo's investigation of two crimes that occur, within several days of each other, at the large apartment house at 219 Via Merulana. The negligible aspect of the first crime, the theft of the Venetian Signora Menecacci's jewels (probably paste, Ingravallo intimates), is more than compensated for by the second, the horrifying murder of Roman matron Liliana Balducci. First, there is the curious absence of interest in, or pursuit of, physical evidence. In a genre that must keep current of technological innovations in the field (or have its readers guess the outcome too easily or too soon), it is significant that Don Ciccio eschews any technological advances in forensic anthropology and pathology that might assist him in solving the crimes and that could bring him up-to-date of his fictional counterparts.

Already, by 1927, the year in which the novel takes place, Don

Ciccio would have had at his disposal sophisticated methods for the forensic analysis of criminal evidence. Ingravallo could easily have called for laboratory work that would have established an authentic linkage between the two crimes at 219 Via Merulana, including fingerprint dusting and analysis, combing for trace blood at Signora Menecacci's apartment that could have been compared by serological analyses with blood samples found at the Balducci crime scene, fabric analysis of the scarf to determine if fibres were present at the Balducci homicide, etc.[49] Significantly, Gadda deploys none of these methods.

For comparison, we can look at the contemporary development of forensic science and its uses in a detective novel of the period. Two cases important to the advancement of forensic analysis took place in Italy: the one concerned Renzo Girardi and the other Giulio Canella. The first involved the contributions made in 1915 to the field of forensic serology by Dr Leone Lattes, lecturer at Turin's Institute of Forensic Medicine. The Canella case, which took place in Turin a dozen years later, is a significant benchmark in the history of fingerprinting.[50] Detective literature of the same period is also revealing of the state of forensic investigation. In her 1926 bestseller *The Murder of Roger Ackroyd*, Agatha Christie makes Inspector Poirot avoid serological analyses, even though the practice is by then common enough for one of the suspects to suggest that he do so.[51]

Logic takes the place of accepted forensic practice, and Don Ciccio's *logica docens* is Gadda's second rupture of the detective story paradigm. Abductory induction is the conventional logical mode of the literary detective and, evidently, Don Ciccio's method.[52] During the investigation of the murder scene, he stands in the Balduccis' living-room and

> si studiò radunare l'evidenze, così disgiunte: avvicinare i momenti, i logori momenti della consecuzione, del tempo lacero, morto. Anzitutto: le due 'birbonate' erano da connettere, o no? La incredibile rapina ai danni di quela povera cocorita de la Menegazzi, 'e chilla femmena ...' nguacchiata 'e sugo 'e spinaci: e questo

orrore, mo. Lo stesso palazzo, 'o stesso piano. Tuttavia ... possibile?
A tre giorni di distanza?

La ragione gli diceva che i due delitti non avevano nulla in comune
... La ragione gli diceva di studiare separatamente i due casi, di 'pal-
parli' a fondo, ma ognuno per sè. L'ambo non esce poi così di rado
alla ruota di Napoli, o di Bari, o di Roma pure, che anche lì a via
de' Merli, a quel migragnoso falanstero del duecentodiciannove
imbottito d'oro non potesse uscirgli fora il suo bravo ambo anche a
lui. L'ambo non auspicato del delitto. Tac, tac. Senz'altra connes-
sione che la topica, cioè la causa esterna 'e chella gran fama dei
pescicani pesci: e del loro oro del diavolo. Fama ubiqua oramai, pe
tutto San Giovanni.[53]

[he watched the gathering of disparate evidence: the drawing near
of moments, the worn-out moments of the sequence, of dead, lac-
erated time. Above all: were the two crimes to be connected or not?
The incredible theft to the damnation of that poor parakeet, la
Menegazzi, that broad spotted with spinach and gravy: and now this
horror. The same apartment house, the same floor ... Is it possible?
Three days apart?

Reason told him that the two crimes had nothing to do with each
other ... Reason told him to study the two cases separately, to 'pal-
pate them' in depth, but each one individually. The double zero
doesn't come up so rarely in the Naples or Bari lotteries, or even in
the Rome lottery for that matter; maybe there, in Crow's Alley, in
that great headache of a phalanstery of 219, padded with gold,
maybe the double zero could come up for him, too. The inauspi-
cious double zero of the crime. Bada bing. Without a doubt the
connection that draws it all together, that is, the external cause, is
dat great hullabaloo about the sharks and their goddamn money.
Common knowledge, by now, in all of San Giovanni.]

Reason opposes the conjoining of both crimes at 219 Via Merulana. Gadda's slippage between linguistic registers (a prevailing

technique in the novel) signals change in point of view.[54] The fractured perspective is regularly marked by different patterns that can be thought of as the discrepancies between thought and enunciation, between Standard Italian and dialect (of various regions and cities), between the protagonist and the narrator or, alternatively, between the protagonist's varying linguistic competencies. In this example, Don Ciccio's linguistically littered perspective controls the first paragraph and hypothesizes a connection between Signora Balducci's murder and the theft of Signora Menecacci's jewelry. Characterized by Roman/Molisan overtones ('quela povera cocorita de la Menegazzi, 'e chilla femmena ... e questo orrore, mo'), Don Ciccio's point of view slips to one less infused by regional richness, an evidently more 'objective' perspective, cleansed of both dialect and regional intuition. This second perspective represents another voice, a further remove within Don Ciccio's psyche, or, possibly, the voice of Reason, embodied and active (e.g., 'Reason told him').

When Gadda unseats logic and turns instead to the aleatory, he fractures the genre of the detective story a third time. Instead of the familiar and time-honoured tradition of the brilliant detective-logician, or any rigorous logical method, we have chance, the lottery, speculation. The rhetorical slippage in this passage enacts the negotiation between logic and chance. In the first sentence of the second paragraph, Reason speaks and advises against connecting the murder to the theft. The next sentence, rather longer than the first, slides toward a return to Don Ciccio's point of view that is delicately calibrated with 'Reason' in the form of Logic's law of averages: 'L'ambo non esce poi così di rado alla ruota di Napoli, o di Bari, o di Roma pure, che anche lì a via de' Merli ... non potesse uscirgli fora il suo bravo ambo anche a lui.' By paragraph's end, spoken idiom returns ('e chella gran fama dei pescicani pesci') and the dominant point of view is that of Don Ciccio, who, now despite logic, will pursue a metaphysical line of investigation: the physical home of both crimes, 219 Via Merulana.

The lucky 'ambo' epitomizes the *Unheimlich* notion of 'home.' In the first section of 'The Uncanny,' Freud indulges in a rather lengthy etymology that makes its ambivalent nature clear: pertaining to the home and therefore something familiar and known, and at the same time something unfamiliar, frightening, and occultish. When he elaborates on the etymological model, Freud alludes to the role of chance in creating an atmosphere of the uncanny: the chance juxtaposition of otherwise unrelated events creates the illusion of connection:

> For instance, we naturally attach no importance to the event when we hand in an overcoat and get a cloakroom ticket with the number, let us say, 62; or when we find that our cabin on a ship bears that number. But the impression is altered if two such events, each in itself indifferent, happen close together – if we come across the number 62 several times in a single day, or when we begin to notice that everything that has a number – addresses, hotel rooms, compartments in railway trains – invariably has the same one, or at all events, one which contains the same figures.[55]

In this case, it is the number 219 that recurs 'a tre giorni di distanza' [within a three-day period], and Don Ciccio's pursuit of a criminal common to both crimes is brought into existence in an analogical fashion akin to one of Freud's descriptions of the uncanny.

'The horror, the horror': Blood, Crime, and 'la donna delinquente' [the delinquent woman]

Il furto nei magazzini viene commesso dalle donne di Parigi specialmente dell' epoca dei mestrui: su 56 di tali ladre, studiate da Legrand e de Saulle, 35 erano nell'epoca mestruale, e dieci avevano passato l'epoca critica; ... quando le isteriche giovani rubano bibelots, profumeries, ecc., è quasi sempre nell'epoca mestruale. Un'altra quota si raccoglie in quelle in cui si stablisce la funzione, il che si collega con quell'intossicazione che, come vedemmo sopra, pare accompagnarsi lo state mestruale.
[Theft in Parisian department stores was committed by women particularly during the period of menstruation: out of 56 female thieves, as studied by Legrand and Saulle, 35 were in their menstrual periods, and ten had passed

the critical moment; ... when hysterical women steal bibelots, perfumes, and so forth, it is almost always during their menstrual period. Another group [of thieves] is composed of those women for whom, as we have already seen, the menstrual state is accompanied by a kind of intoxication.]

Cesare Lombroso and G. Ferrero, La donna delinquente, p. 225

As both its creator and victim, Woman stands at both ends of the *pasticcio* [mess] in this eponymous novel.[56] Women of the *Pasticciaccio* are locked up or locked out: whether within the walls of the apartment building in Via Merulana or outside city walls, women cleave to Fascist codes of maternity and femininity. Indeed, the mere fact of being 'Woman' razes almost every individuating trait between the female characters, forming a rallying point for *Quer pasticciaccio*'s ambivalent representation of criminal women.

Far from Zamira's coven, within the walls of Rome itself, and enclosed within the walls of the Roman apartment house (the latter-day palace), lives Liliana Balducci in her 'gineceo,' her gynaeceum, the room in Roman houses reserved for women. Like Janus, the two-faced Roman household god, the Liliana-Zamira diptych embodies the ambivalent relation between the *Heimlich* and *Unheimlich*. If we remember one of the etymologies Freud tracks in his essay, we see that the *Unheimlich* terminates in magic and the occult.[57] Aligning Liliana with the *Heim* (the home) and Zamira with *Unheimlich* (the occultish) reveals Gadda's structuring of the uncanny. Like the etymological relation between the two terms, they are parallel in development yet divergent. Liliana's gynaeceum is a 'sororale sforzata' [forced sisterhood] that consists of 'the forgotten of God,' like Liliana, who 'accarezza e bacia nel sogno il ventre fecondo delle consorelle. Guarda tra i fiori de' giardini i bambini delle altre: e piange. Si rivolge alle monache e agli orfanotrofi pur di avere la "sua" creatura, pur di fare anche lei il suo bambino' [in her dream kisses and caresses the fecund womb of her sisters. She looks through the flowers of gardens at the children of other women: and cries. She turns to nuns and to orphanages so that she, too, might have 'her' little one, so that she, too, can give birth to her child] (122). Liliana's gynaeceum is founded, not on strength, but on the collective weakness of its members, susceptible as they are to a rhetoric that reduced women to reproductive vessels, which flourished during the *ventennio* but was hardly limited to it. Indeed, the 'family values' rhetoric that imbued the Christian Democrats' campaigns during the strategically consequential 1948 election season compare to formations of the family during the *ventennio*.[58]

Liliana's gynaeceum of barren women and surrogate daughters is a temporary arrangement: once their maternal potential is realized, these women will leave the unwelcome reminder of their failure behind. This contrived sisterhood is victim to what Ingravallo calls the 'omoerotia sublimata' [sublimated homoeroticism] characteristic of all such sororities. According to Fascist schemata, Liliana's childless household and Liliana herself are national failures.[59] Although Gadda seems to divide the guilt over their childlessness evenly between the Balducci spouses, eventually Liliana bears the burden alone. 'Il marito,' Ingravallo thinks, 'era pure un marito; un pezzaccio di marito. Se un bambino non era venuto fuori, peggio pe lui ... Nun ce ne avevano colpa gli uomini' [The husband is nevertheless a husband, a big brute of a husband. If a child hadn't materialized, too bad for him ... It ain't us guys' fault] (140). Liliana's maternal mania is best explained through internalized Fascist objectification. Juridical measures (e.g., legal interdiction of abortion and contraception) and generalized social control transform Liliana into the *instrumentum regni* Gadda eventually lampoons in *Eros e Priapo*. Yet the bitter irony of this later text is not present in the *Pasticciaccio*, which objectifies Liliana's body at least as much as Fascist constructions of gender. The murder of Liliana is not a latter-day example of Lucrezia, whose rape by Tarquin gave rise to an outrage that enabled the founding of the first Republic. Nowhere is Liliana's objectification clearer than in the scene where Don Ciccio views her dead body, 'tramutata ora nella immobilità di un oggetto o come d'uno sfigurato manichino' [now transformed into the immobility of an object or like some disfigured manequin] (58).[60]

Don Ciccio's examination of Liliana's body symbolically fuses a series of 'homes': the Balducci house, Liliana's 'home of all human beings,' and – as the novel's use of geography will reveal –

Italy itself. Although this scene could be read as yet another illustration of the uncanny, I would like to draw attention to the pulsation between 'horror' and wonder, and how this exemplifies the rhythm of the abject.[61] The positioning of Liliana's body on the floor of the dining-room is reported minutely, and Don Ciccio alternates fetishistically between horror and fascination in the pulsation of the abject I just described. Worse than the horrific mother Julia Kristeva describes in the process of abjection, Liliana's absent, fervently wished-for motherhood transforms her into 'horror' itself.[62]

Childless Liliana's *Heim*, as we are shown, is untouched, but the *pasticcio* (mess), the horror ('questo orrore, mo'' [now this horror]) of her wound transfixes the inspector. The visual pull between Liliana's *Heim* and her wound is more suggestive still. Her purity and modesty approach virginal; indeed, *Virgin*ia, one of the Balduccis' 'nieces,' tells her, 'Sora mia bella Liliana, voi site "a Madonna pe mme!"' [My beautiful Signora Liliana, you're like the Madonna for me!]. Although the homophonic relationship between *Heim* and hymen functions only in English, the relationship in Italian between 'imène' (hymen) and 'immane' (monstrous) leads us to a consideration of the monstrous mother and the abject. Liliana's *Heim* is visible because of the position of her body, 'infame' with her skirt and slip 'buttate all'indietro' [thrown up over her head]. Don Ciccio first scrutinizes the thighs, the underwear, the garters, the stockings; all that was denied to him in life and now open to him legitimately as the investigator on the case:

Il corpo della povera signora giaceva in una posizione infame, supino, con la gonna di lana grigia e una sottogonna bianca buttate all'indietro, fin quasi al petto: come se qualcuno avesse voluto scoprire il candore affascinante di quel dessous, o indagarne lo stato di nettezza. Aveva mutande bianche, di maglia a punto gentile, sottilissimo, che terminava a metà coscia in una delicata orlatura. Tra l'orlature e le caze, c'erano in un lieve luce di seta, denudò se stessa la bianchezza estrema della carne, d'un pallore da clorosi: quelle due cosce un po' aperte, che i due elastici – in un tono di

lilla – parevano distinguere in grado, avevano perduto il loro
tepido senso ...

Le giarrettiere tese, ondulate appena agli orli, d'una ondu-
lazione chiara di lattuga: l'elastico di seta lilla, in quel tono che
pareva un profumo, significava a momenti la frale gentilezza della
donna e del ceto, l'eleganza spenta degli indumenti, degli atti, il
secreto modo della sommissione, tramutata ora nella immobilità di
un oggetto o come d'uno sfigurato manichino. (58)

[The body of the poor signora lay in an infamous position, supine,
with her gray wool skirt and white slip thrown back, nearly to her
chest; almost as if someone had wanted to uncover the fascinating
whiteness of that *dessous*, or probe the state of its cleanliness. Her
white underwear was of a soft knit and delicate, and reached down
to about mid-thigh where it ended in soft ribbing. Between the ribbing and the stockings, the extreme whiteness of the skin bared
itself in the soft light of silk, were the two slightly parted thighs
(which the elastic straps – in a shade of lilac – deemed worthy) that
were stiffening ...

The taut garters, rippling slightly at the edges, like the slight
curling of lettuce leaves: the elastic strap of lilac silk, in that shade
that seemed almost like a perfume, signified now the frailty of the
woman, now of her social class, the spent elegance of her undergar-
ments, of the acts, the secret way of submission, she was now transformed into the immobility of an object or some disfigured
manequin.]

Don Ciccio's eyes travel to the victim's face and, finally, to the
gaping wound at the neck. Although the face, neck, and torso are
bloodied by the jagged knife wound (no clean cut of the razor
here, the crime scene analyst intones), the underwear have
remained untouched, we could say, 'virginal.' A kind of *displatio*,
all the blood present at the scene of the murder is located above
the waist, at the neck.[63] Significantly, the attack on Liliana is not
sexualized: the genitals are closer to the ground and, thus, to
things of this earth, and the head is not a particularly sexualized
locus. The sexlessness of Liliana's murder could lead us to con-

sider the attack on her body as directed toward the embour-
geoised home; after all, Gadda conflates Liliana's womanly frailty
with that of her class ('frale gentilezza della donna e del ceto'). In
this regard, Kipnis's thoughts on pornography, which concern a
different context, are nevertheless relevant. Studying the photo-
graphically sexual American magazine *Hustler*, Kipnis equates the
lower body with the lower socio-economic class and locations
higher on the body with a correspondingly elevated social class.[64]

The displacement of blood serves another function. Like a col-
ophon, the blood from Liliana's wound directs (Don Ciccio's, the
reader's) attention away from the bloodless skin of the legs or the
unstained underwear visible from between 'quelle due cosce un
po' aperte' [those two slightly parted thighs]. Liliana's immacu-
late underwear reminds the reader of her fragility, certainly, and
of her childlessness. Yet the *displatio* points to a displacement on a
still larger scale, as the absent ovulation and menstruation – an
indisputable index of reproductive capability – is displaced from
Liliana onto greater metropolitan Rome.

Gadda explicitly maps the female reproductive system onto
Rome and surrounding Lazio. The author's virtuoso mixage of
linguistic register returns in this passage, where Don Ciccio rumi-
nates on the 'nieces' Liliana takes into her home in Via Merulana
as domestic servants and surrogate daughters:

> Per lei, dal Tevere in giù, là, là dietro i diroccati castelli e dopo le
> bionde vigne, c'era, sui colli e sui monti e nelle breve piane d'Italia,
> come un grande ventre fecondo, due salpinge grasse, zigrinate
> d'una dovizia di granuli, granuloso e untuoso, il felice caviale delle
> gente. Di quando in quando dal grande Ovario follicoli maturati
> si aprivano, come ciche d'una melagrana: e rossi chicchi, pazzi
> d'un'amorosa certezza, ne discendevano ad urbe, a incontrare
> l'afflatto maschile, l'impulso vitalizzante, quell'aura spermatica di
> cui favoleggiavano gli ovaristi del Settecento. E a via Merulana 219,
> scala A, piano terzo, ci rifioriva la nipote, nel meglio grumolo, pro-
> pio, del palazzo dell'Oro. (13)

[For her, from the Tiber onward, there, there behind the crumbling castles and the blonde vines, there was, on the hills and mountains and in the shallow plains of Italy, like a great and fertile womb, two fat salpinguses, chock full of a store of granules, grainy and oily, the happy roe of the *Volk*. From time to time, from the great Ovary, follicles matured and opened, like the seeds of a pomegranate: and red seeds, crazed by amorous certainty, travelled southward to the Urbs, to encounter the male organ, the vitalizing impulse, that spermatic aura that the eigtheenth-century ovarists talked about. And there in Via Merulana 219, stairway A, fourth floor, the 'niece' flowered in the best of wombs, right within the Palace of Gold.]

Women and this feminized Rome proliferate good fascists. The sprinkling of medical terms (salpingus, ovary, follicle) in a more homespun lexicon (womb, roe), itself rendered curiously poetic in tone and register, creates an ironic distance between the advent of the Balduccis' 'nieces' and Liliana's unrealized maternity. The anatomical and endocrinological language reporting on the arrival of the young women recalls Margherita Sarfatti's description of the family's relation to the state. Mussolini's collaborator and lover wrote in 1933 that, 'the family is the first cell, elementary and insufficient but nonetheless fundamental for the State.'[65] The happy ovum (the surrogate) travels down the Fallopian tube (the Tiber) to the procreant womb (the Balduccis' apartment house in Via Merulana) in the direction of the Urbs, a kind of *vagina mundi*, where it will encounter the male member, which furnishes the required catalyst, sperm. Liliana Balducci is in this 'grumulo' (womb) the ersatz matriarch. This meditation on the menstrual cycle foreshadows a similar description in *Eros e Priapo* (1967), where Gadda writes that during the ventennio 'tutto era, allora, maschio ... insino le femmine ... e le trombe di Falloppio e la vagina' [everything was male then ... even the females ... and the Fallopian tubes and the vagina].[66]

Gadda frames the question of surrogacy quite differently in the version of the *Pasticciaccio* that appeared in instalments in the literary magazine *Letteratura* in 1947 and in the final version published by Garzanti ten years later. These differences are highly significant, given that they convey different conclusions. Surrogacy is missing from the book-length version, and in the Fascist order of things, it takes on new meaning. With public and private distinctions blurred, the state seeks to make of itself a surrogate for the family, the Duce both surrogate father and husband.[67] As de Grazia outlines, the bourgeois family in pre–First World War Italy was protected by the Pisanelli civil statutes, Church dogma, as well as cultural practice.[68] The new Fascist state advantageously exploited the collapse of the liberal government for political gain, but ratified, when convenient, 'liberal' statutes that infantalized and discriminated against women.

The changes between editions of the manuscript include specifically changes in Don Corpi's testimony about Virginia and an additional scene between Liliana and Virginia, which Signor Balducci reports, both of which warrant re-presentation. In his testimony, Don Corpi relates that

un'altra vorta, na domenica, mentre che staveno ad affetta' er rosbiffe freddo p'un po' de cena, in cucina, che la Rita nun c'era, perchè la domenica annava a spasso ... lei, la Virginia, aveva sbottato a rise'tutt'in una volta, d'un riso convulsivo, che le strideva su dalla gola traverso i denti a triangolo: con un lampo nero senza misericordia che ciaveva negli occhi, de sardegnola vendicativa ... 'er cortello de cucina se sa che tajja: è fatt'apposta' ... aveva detto: 'si nun me regalate l'ori che m'avete promesso ... ve lo pianto ner core ...' E l'aveva baciata sulla bocca, pe'fforza, stringendole er capo dietro, co l'artra mano, dentro tutti quei capelli, come Liliana fosse er suo amante, invece ... ma in tanto ciaveva sempre in mano er cortello ... lei, Liliana, povera fijja ... a quel bacio aveva inorridito: forze lei si era spalancato davati il portone de l'Inferno, tutt'a un colpo: *aperient peccata portas Inferi.* Un'altra volta all'usci' der bagno: la Virginia aveva spalancato er portone de l'accapatoio, coi capelli ch'erano come tanti aspidi co'la coda in un braciere le due pupille due gridi della tenebra: sottovoce viso contro viso: 'Er pupo ve lo fo io, cor mio ventre, vedete che ventre che cio': e lo aveva sporto in fuora, da basso, piantata là che facevano come un cinto, come a spremerne fuori una serpe ... Piantata là sulla soglia der bagno, a

gambe larghe spaccata, contro luce ... 'Dateme vostro marito: ve lo
faccio ... nun sono na smorfiosa come voi ... In manco dieci mesi
v'oo faccio io co 'sto ventre mio rosso ...' Aveva rugghiato sottovoce: 'Vostro marito ha da lavorare con me, si volete er pupo ...'[69]

[another time, a Sunday, while they were in the kitchen getting
ready to slice up a little cold roast beef for dinner – Rita wasn't
there because she had Sundays off – she, Virginia, burst out laugh-
ing all of a sudden, in a kind of spastic way, the laughter coming
out of her throat in little shrieks, up past her triangular teeth: with
a black, merciless flash in her eyes, like a vindictive *sardegnola* ...
'The kitchen knife cuts good, it's made just right ...' she had said:
'If you don't treat me well, do you see? do you see this?' The point
glinted in the air: 'If you don't give me that money you promised
me ... I'll stick it in your heart ...' And then she kissed her on the
mouth, forcing her head back with her other hand, in all that hair,
as if Liliana were her lover ... She had the knife in her hand the
whole time ... She, Liliana, poor child ... was horrified by that kiss:
maybe the door to Hell opened for her all of a sudden: *aperient peccata portas Inferi.* Another time, at the bathroom door: Virginia had
opened her bathrobe, her hair like so many asps with their tails in
the fire, her pupils two wails in the darkness: sottovoce, face to face:
'I'll have the kid for you, with my belly, see the gut I've got': and
she thrust it out from below, planted there on her big legs, swad-
dling it, clasping it with her hands like a vise, as if ready to squeeze
a snake out of it ... Planted there on the threshold of the bathroom
against the light, big legs split, ... 'Give me your husband: I'll do it
... I'm not a simpering flirt like you ... I'll do it for you in less than
ten months ... with this red belly of mine ...' She had brayed in
a whisper: 'Your husband's got business with me, if you want the
brat ...']

Here the ambivalent and contradictory attitudes of the Fascist
State's family design become manifest. Between Liliana's and Virginia's acts of surrogacy, the difference is one of degree. Because
she cannot have children of her own, Liliana's roles as surrogate
aunt and mother are acceptable, even Christian. Virginia carries

surrogacy to an extreme: she is not in service to the State, but she will help Liliana refashion herself as a mother. The cost, however, is the privacy of the family, the sacrament of marriage.

This is a momentous scene for a reading of a gendered context for *Quer pasticciaccio*, particularly for the way it reveals Gadda's interest in the spatialization of power and sexuality within the domestic sphere. The first reported exchange between Liliana and Virginia takes place in the kitchen, a place within the house where both would have equal access, Liliana as the homeowner and employer, Virginia as the domestic servant. The second scene occurs in a passageway, where Virginia perches, significantly, on the threshold of the bathroom, a place marked by privacy for any occupant, employer or servant. The scene functions in symmetry to the Zamira sequence, which I address presently, and is further evidence of how fundamental are women's relationships in the novel. Liliana's desperation for 'er pupo' is brought to full flower here. The young woman whom she has 'adopted' as a substitute child would willingly act as some kind of corporeal and mythical surrogate for Liliana and her husband, Remo. Virginia is at once child (symbol of the Balducci union), potential mother, lover (to both husband and wife Balducci), and virgin (a Latin Sabine, *Virginia*). And she is also Liliana's killer. Both killer and solution are patent in the *Letteratura* version of the story, from 1947, as Dombroski has detailed.[70] The excised scenes contain the motivation for the ostensibly digressive (ultimately frustrating) plot changes, which include leaving Rome for the outskirts, and abandoning the search for Liliana's murderer to look for the jewel thief.

Virginia's threat is clear: upon entering the Balducci home, she is bent on destroying it. Medusan ('coi capelli ch'erano come tanti aspidi co'la coda in un braciere'), Virginia's display of her 'red belly' also recalls another like figure deployed to great discursive significance in the preparatory stage before the accession of the Regime, Caterina Sforza. As Spackman observes, Caterina's reappearance in D'Annunzio's Fiuman tract, *Il Sudore del sangue* (1919), has particular resonances within the Regime and its construction of sexuality. Like Caterina, who, in defiance of her captors in Renaissance Forlì, hoisted her skirts and dared them to put her children to death for 'Qui, n'ho il conio' [I've got the mint right here], Virginia boldly flaunts her 'mint.' In another scene excised from the 1957 version, Virginia pushes the model of surrogacy too far, threatening to kill Liliana and usurp her place in the Balducci household.

During his interrogation, Remo Balducci describes the threatening scene:

'Nun potrò mai scordarme finchè campo ... l'occhicata che mi diede ...' soggiunse il Balducci, '... nè quell'artra che je furminò a Liliana in dell'usci' ... Era pallida: bianca de rabbia che pareva ce volesse ammazza' tutt' e due ... "So vvenuta come na fijja," disse: "ma stateve sicura che ce tornerò da padrona" ... "Che vuol di'?" fece Liliana. "Annamo, ritirate, basta, non dajje retta," je feci ... "Er pupo sta que," disse quella. Se battè na mano sulla panza. Nun era vero un corno. De ffa' er pupo, nun dico era capacissima ... Un pupo te può usci' de fallo anche a nun volello ... ma de fallo pe ddispetto! Per quanto ... Co' quell'idea de Liliana de vole n pupo a tutti i costi ... che nne so? Chi ce capisce è bravo ... Speravo forse de prennece in trappola. Ma p'un verso, Liliana per quell'artro ...' Alzò le spalle, tentennò il capo perplesso: 'Li pupi erano questi.' Stropicciò il pollice sull'indice.[71]

['I can never forget as long as I live ... that look she gave me ...' Mr Balducci added, 'nor the one she shot at Liliana, either, from the doorway ... She was pale, white with rage and it seemed like she wanted to kill the pair of us ... "I came here as a daughter," she said: "but rest assured I'll be back as lady of the house" ... "What does that mean?" Liliana said. "Let's go, you get out of here, that's enough, don't pay any attention to her," I said to her ... "The brat's right here," the girl said. She patted her belly. It wasn't true at all. I'm not saying she wasn't completely capable of producing a kid ... A kid can appear even without you wanting it to ... But to have one out of spite? As much as ... With that idea of Liliana's to have a kid no matter what it cost ... how should I know? Whoever understands it is a genius ... Maybe she hoped to trip us up. On the other hand,

Liliana ...' He hunched up his shoulders, shook his head, per-
plexed. 'Kids were these.' And he rubbed his thumb and forefinger
together.]

Gadda's earlier excursus describes the ovum, stimulated by follicles within the ovary, and travelling the Fallopian tubes. The
maturation of the ovum, which is imagined here concluding in
conception, happens regularly; indeed, such a process takes place
monthly in the menstrual cycle. As a metaphor of women's same-
ness, blood (specifically menses) links the novel's disparate communities of women. The communities of women constituted
around Zamira and Liliana seem completely different. Zamira is
awful, grotesque with her missing eight front teeth, and known to
everyone in the area between Marino and Ariccia as a 'maga
antica in sacerdozio d'abominevoli sortilegi' [an ancient witch in
a priesthood of abominable sorceries] (176).[72] Liliana is her foil,
the Madonna to her Alban nieces, the latter-day Sabines come to
the city centre as Liliana's surrogate children. Gadda's dyadic representation of women in the novel can be seen not so much as the
hackneyed opposition between the Madonna and the whore as
between the Madonna and the witch.[73]

Zamira is the witch whose midwifery skills are feared and
sought after. Zamira is the neighbourhood hag, a crone beyond
child-bearing years who takes under her protective wing the still
fertile younger women of the area. She is a clairvoyant, a reader
of cards, an exorcist capable of casting or lifting spells, a necro-
mancer able to conjure love potions and repellents, and a kind of
veterinary abortionist. The *Malleus mallificarum* (The hammer of
female malefactors), a late-fifteenth-century treatise on demonol-
ogy and witchcraft, comments extensively on midwives' abortafa-
cient technology. Innocent VII, after a long list of the harms that
derive from intercourse with demons, incubi, and succubi, finished his 1484 Bull by writing that 'these demons suffocate, extin-
guish and cause to perish births of women ... so that men beget
not ... nor women conceive; and they impede the conjugal action
of men and women.'[74] It is Zamira who rectifies the situation
when 'fermava er mese a quarche regazza, o per nervosità o *per*

altro sturbo' [some girl's period stopped, either out of nerves or *for some other disturbance*] (176) (emphasis added).

Pestalozzi, during his interview with Zamira, is baffled by the woman's preoccupation with blood as it manifests itself in the menstrual cycle of the young women who work at her bar, I Due Santi. Indeed, Pestalozzi's journey to Marino along the Appian Way might be seen to echo the one taken by the 'happy ovum,' the surrogate niece of the Balduccis. In one of her digressions during the interview, Zamira says that '"m'immagino che ce lo sa pure, lei ... che noi donne ... dal momento che semo donne ... ci avemo pure li fastidi nostri. Er mal di testa, noi donne, ce l'abbiamo qua." E si toccò il buzzino, quasi carrezzandolo' ['I guess you know too, sir, don't you, that we women, from the time we become women, have our little aggravations. Us women have our headaches here.' And she touched her belly, almost caressing it] (247). The image of the woman who caresses her presently empty womb returns significantly in Don Ciccio's description of Liliana's gynaeceum and in the 'completed' 1947 version of *Quer pasticciaccio*. When asked whether she remembers the whereabouts of Camilla, one of the employees at I Due Santi on the day of the crimes at 219 Via Merulana, Zamira responds that 'sarà stato er mese scorso, prima di questo. Mo che ce penzo, semo appena a luna nova ... Che posso ave a mente? le lune di tutte le regazze' [that would have been last month, before this one. Now that I think about it we're just at the new moon. What the matter with you? You think I can remember the periods of all the girls who work here?] (248).

Blood in Zamira's community is a measure of time and its passing. The witch marks time not so much by the calendar as by the waxing and waning of the moon. In her book concerning women's communities as a topos in literature, Nina Auerbach remarks that the Graie, a mythic community of women, are located outside of Time.[75] Like other communities of women (e.g., the Amazons, the Sirens, the Sabines, etc.), I Due Santi is situated outside of the sphere of social control, conceptually and literally. It virtually skirts the edge of Rome, and, more figuratively, the community stands outside the Law, as represented by the carabineri sergeant, Pestalozzi. Zamira and her community stand outside of time, as well, as her conversation with Pestalozzi reveals: her gynocentric notion of time cannot be made compatible with the officer's.[76]

Zamira's preoccupation with blood is clearly transgressive of the backgrounded Regime. The year 1927, the setting for the *Pasticciaccio*, sees the launching of Mussolini's demographic design: Il discorso dell'Ascensione, to which I referred at the beginning of the chapter, was given in May of that year. Zamira is not simply a woman able and willing to control the reproductive fertility of other women, something the Fascists were already accomplishing; rather, she is a woman other women enlist in order to control their own reproductive activity. Had the novel been set two years later, however, Zamira's acts as abortionist would not only have been transgressive, they would have been felonious.

As I outlined earlier, the Rocco Code of 1929 reckoned abortion as tantamount to treason. In a communiqué to the king, Alfredo Rocco himelf likened the interruption of pregnancy to an act of sedition: 'Induced abortion, as concerns maternity as the unquenchable source of life of both individuals and the race, constitutes in reality an offense against life itself and, consequently, an offense against the Nation and the State.'[77] Not repealed until 1978, these interdictions are very much a part of the world of the *Pasticciaccio*, whether of 1947 or the decade that followed.

Zamira is the location of Gadda's ambivalent representation of women in the novel. Read in anti-fascist key, she is contrary, anomic, a-topic, wayward, and unruly. But, ambivalence prevailing, she is also one more participant in the pageant of criminal women that paves the way for anomie and lawlessness. Denied subjective status, she is but a synecdoche, another criminal woman, reduced to the anarchic mass.

'Woman' follows hard upon the heels of method of investigation in Don Ciccio's description of 'la causale.' The admixture of the metaphysical (pseudo-scientific, quasi-philosophical characterization of 'method') and the physical (the presence of desire for the inevitable woman) adds to the spuriousness of Ingravallo's summary of his *logica docens*:

La causale apparente, la causale principe, era sì, una. Ma il fattaccio era l'effetto di tutta una rosa di causali che gli erano soffiate adosso a molinello (come i sedici venti della rosa dei venti quando s'avviluppano a tromba una depressione ciclonica) e avevano finito per strizzare nel vortice del delitto la debilitata 'ragione del mondo.' (3)

[The apparent motive, the principal cause was, to be sure, single. But the dirty deed was the culmination of an entire ensemble of causes, blown its way by squall (like the sixteen winds that merge in a cyclonic depression in a hurricane) and had finally extinguished the debilitated 'reason of the world' in its vortex.]

Yet Don Ciccio dismisses such a scientific 'method' and, like any good amateur, embraces his (Latin) intuition instead. Gadda writes:

E poi soleva dire, ma questo un po' stancamente, 'ch'i femmene se retroveno addo' n'i' vuo' truva'.' Una tarda riedizione italica del vieto 'cherchez la femme.' E poi pareva pentirsi, come d'aver calunniato 'e femmene, e voleva mutar idea ... Sicchè taceva pensieroso, come temendo di aver detto troppo. Voleva significare che un certo momento affettivo, un tanto o, direste oggi, un quanto di affettività, un certo 'quanto di erotia,' si mescolava anche ai 'casi d'interesse,' ai delitti apparentemente più lontani dalle tempeste d'amore. (4)

[And then he used to say, but this a little wearily, 'that you find dames just where you don't want to.' A late Italian version of the much vaunted 'cherchez la femme.' And then he appeared to regret it, as if he had calumnied the dames and he wanted to change his tune. ... So that he grew quiet and pensive, as if fearing he had said too much. He wanted to say that a certain affective moment, a little or – you'd say today – a 'quantum' of affect, a certain 'quantum of eros,' became blended into his 'interesting cases,' to the crimes apparently the farthest from love interests.]

The female body is the alpha and omega of the *pasticcio*; the *pasticcio* is at once the crime and its victim. Out of the alembic of the female body, Gadda the alchemist distils his bogus meta/physical 'method.' Don Ciccio's method, misconceived in the way that an abortion is mis-conception, emplots the narrative.

Gadda's 'terminologia da medico di matti' [the terminology of a doctor for crazy people] flags the novel's other pastiche: for he has haphazardly combined cultural attributes of the '20s (dominant Crocean idealism, the advent of Fascism, malingering Lombrosian positivism) with postwar *mentalité* (the delayed arrival of psychoanalysis in Italy as an intellectual and cultural enterprise, a climate of revisionism tolerant of invective against the Regime). Critics have culled Freudian referents from Gadda's oeuvre, but I would like to turn to his alternative model, Cesare Lombroso.[78] Don Ciccio, with his vocabulary culled from 'doctors for crazy people,' with his 'bernoccoli metafisici' [metaphysical cranial bumps], and with his perspective of 'e femmene,' and especially of the female complaint (namely, the menstrual cycle) and its indispensable role in the predictability of the dangerous criminal type, returns us to Lombroso.[79]

Unlike the interpolated Freudianisms, Gadda's use of Lombroso's typology of criminal, 'delinquent' women is not anachronistic. The notion of the 'criminal woman' was introduced with late-nineteenth-century developments in the fields of forensic anthropology and psychiatry and remained a current and practicable framework well into the 1940s and beyond. Historian of psychiatry Michel David mentions that Lombrosianism was alive and well in Italy ('redignified') as late as 1965.[80] Moreover, positivism reigned in Fascist criminology, appearing in the pages of penal publications during the *ventennio*.[81] Lombrosian methodology continued to flourish even though anthropologists outside of Italy dismissed the 'science' of craniology or andropometry. By 1899, for example, Franz Boas had dismissed Lombroso's 'cranial index by showing that it varied widely among adults of a single group and within the life of an individual.'[82] In Italy, however, Lombroso's methodology persisted as the dominant conceptual framework, championed by such educators as Maria Montessori, who blithely ignored the salient epistemological differences between a system like Lombroso's and her own.[83]

More directly applicable to the case of maternity, Fascism employed Lombrosian method to identify 'proliferous females' in the '20s. Anticipating the 1931 World Population Conference, which took place in Rome, the physician Nicola Pende was charged with documenting 'the physiological factors which led people to have big families.'[84] Government researchers tallied the correlations between 'family size and morphological features such as pelvis size, body fat, height, hormonal secretions, and hirsute upper lips.'[85] Proliferous females were thought to be shorter, broad through their hips, and 'slovenly.' And even though some contemporary sceptics pointed to non-physiological factors (among them socio-economics, regional factors, etc.), as de Grazia reports, the emphasis was quite clearly on the selection of the physical characteristics to provide for the creation of a 'profile.'

In his 1893 study, *La donna delinquente, la prostituta e la donna normale*, Cesare Lombroso demarcates the field of female criminality by promoting basic positivist principles of empirical evidence: andropometry, phrenology, the presumed relation between the somatic manifestation of such diseases as epilepsy and pellagra and madness, the physiological characteristics of 'born' criminals, and so forth. While delinquency must be charted for both sexes, Lombroso is compelled to outline 'normalcy' for women only.

Perhaps the most notorious of Lombroso's contributions to the field of forensic psychiatry concern the tenuous connection he draws between the menstrual cycle and the predictability of female dangerousness. Reviewing Lombroso's findings shows defiantly misconstrued statistics. In words reminiscent of Pestalozzi's interview of Zamira, Lombroso begins the section 'Biologia e psicologia delle criminali e delle prostitute' [Biology and psychology of criminal women and of prostitutes] by saying

'Mestruazione. – Essendo la funzione più specialmente femminile dovremmo su questa alquanto fermarci' [Menstruation. Being the most feminine of biological functions, we should pause to examine this topic].[86] However, Lombroso does not appear to find any representative pattern in the statistics gathered: evidently menarche (the onset of menses) is 'precocious' among prostitutes but also 'irregular'; among murderesses, menarche is 'retarded.' From the information given, it seems that if a woman is already of a criminal nature, thievery is actually induced by menstruation.

Women are criminal by their very womanliness. The connection between theft and menstruation is clear in the *Letteratura* version, just as the crime is resolved.[87] Virginia and her lover, Enea, rob the Countess of her jewels and return to the same apartment complex, different stairway, to do in Virginia's foster mother as well.[88] Perhaps the most significant fact about the production of the two endings and the novel's missing solution is Gadda's interpretation of readers' and critics' confusion. Gadda insisted that the Garzanti edition (1957) is complete and there is, moreover, an identifiable killer and, further, that Ingravallo knows who the killer is. In an interview with Dacia Maraini, Gadda declared that he considered the novel 'finito.' Maraini asks him if he means 'literarily' complete. 'Sì, letterariamente concluso. Il poliziotto capisce chi è l'assassino e questo basta' [Yes, literarily complete. The detective understands who the killer is and this is sufficient].[89] Since the evidence in the novel does not support this claim to 'conclusiveness,' it is Gadda's interpolation of the two versions, not his intention, that is significant.

Quer pasticciaccio, the history of its production, its genre, and its representation of women are all clearly ambivalent: damning and supportive, sympathetic and resistant, confirming and challenging. *Quer Pasticciaccio* is a perpetual spinning out of 'Woman' who somehow never appears to be just what she is but is always and already the symbol of something else, in this case, Italy and Rome. Gadda's aborted detective novel presents the last of the carceral analogues in this study. That Italian Fascism sought to confine women by way of myriad measures of social control is not surprising. Nor is it surprising that Gadda, like Pratolini, uses the representation of women and female sexuality to emblematize the depraved Fascist state and, in so doing, reveals the absence of escape for the female subject in the system of gendered domination, whether during Fascism or after.

Demarcating space, as Michael Keith and Steve Pile remind us, is a political act.[90] Politics and its supercategory, ideology, therefore visit the multiple articulations and practices of 'enclosing.' We see the manifestation of politics and ideology at various junctures: in a strictly geographical sense, for example, in the surveying expedition in *Il deserto dei tartari* (in chapter 2), in the practice of architecture (e.g., the convent, as we saw in chapter 3), or in the representation of space and spatial relations.[91] Its privacy plundered by Fascist policy and practice, the domestic sphere, like its public counterpart, sought equilibrium in the postwar era of reconstruction. This equilibrium, as we saw in the case of the Merlin Law, was established on the restitution of pre-Fascist civil rights and liberties. A return to the law, order, and the status quo of the pre-Fascist era was not precisely what women in Italy, instructed and politicized as many had been by their active involvement in the Resistance, desired.[92] It is not surprising that bitterness and disappointment should erupt in postwar representations of the domestic sphere, nor that such eruption should take the shape of murderous reprisal, a recognizable symbol of the inherent deadliness of the space called home.

Notes

All translations are my own. Available published translations of Italian and other foreign-language texts are listed in the Bibliography.

1. Introduction: Prisons and Their Analogues

1 In the following pages, I will distinguish between Fascism, the political movement in Italy during the years 1919–43, and fascism, the historically delimited political phenomenon.

2 See *Il razionalismo e l'architettura in Italia durante il fascismo*, ed. Silvia Danesi and Luciano Panetta (Venice: Edizioni La Biennale di Venezia, 1976); *La costruzione dell'utopia: Architetti e urbanisti nell'Italia fascista*, ed. Guilio Ernesti (Rome: Edizioni lavoro, 1988); Diane Ghirardo, *Building New Comunities: New Deal America and Fascist Italy* (Princeton, NJ: Princeton UP, 1989); Giorgio Ciucci, *Gli architetti e il fascismo* (Turin: Einaudi, 1989); Richard Etlin, *Modernism in Italian Architecture 1890–1940* (Cambridge: MIT P, 1991); Andrew Hewitt, 'Fascist Modernism, Futurism, and "Post-Modernity,"' in *Fascism, Aesthetics, and Culture*, ed. Richard Golsan (Hanover, NH: University P of New England, 1992), 38–55; Marla Stone, *Patron State: Culture and Politics in Fascist Italy* (Princeton, NJ: Princeton UP, 1998); and Emily Braun, *Mario Sironi and Italian Modernism: Art and Politics under Fascism* (Cambridge: Cambridge UP, 2000). It is worth noting the way Mussolini stressed hand-labour rather than mechanized means of construction in order to employ large numbers of otherwise perpetually underemployed men. I thank Joseph Siry for this observation.

3 Barbara Spackman, *Fascist Virilities: Rhetoric, Ideology, and Social Fantasy in Italy* (Minneapolis: U of Minnesota P, 1996), 52.

4 Autarky meant complete economic as well as cultural self-sufficiency. Concerning the cultural aspect of this policy, see Giuseppe Carlo Marino, *L'autarchia della cultura: Intellettuali e fascismo negli anni trenta* (Rome: Riuniti, 1983).

5 Historiography and its practitioners have usually periodized Fascism according to Renzo De Felice's schema: the years of the Regime's consolidation of power, and the years in which it sought the Italian polity's 'consensus,' roughly 1922–9 and 1930–43 respectively. For a critique of De Felice's influence on Italian historiography, see Emilio Gentile, 'Renzo de Felice: A Tribute,' *Journal of Contemporary History* 32 (1997), 139–51; and Borden Painter, 'Renzo de Felice and the Historiography of Italian Fascism,' *American Historical Review* 95 (April 1990), 391–405.

6 Michel de Certeau, *The Practice of Everyday Life*, tr. Steven Rendall (Berkeley: U of California P, 1988), 117.

7 Elizabeth Grosz, *Space, Time, and Perversion* (London and New York: Routledge, 1995), 123.

8 Henri Lefebvre, *The Production of Space*, tr. Donald Nicholson-Smith (Oxford: Blackwell, 1991), 286.

9 Pierre Bourdieu, *Outline of a Theory of Practice* (Cambridge: Cambridge UP, 1977), 72 and 95.

10 See Roberta Gilchrist, *Gender and Material Culture: The Archaeology of Religious Women* (London and New York: Routledge, 1994), 168. Like Bourdieu, Foucault, as we will learn, does not explicitly consider women within his theory of power and space. I will speak of this in greater detail below.

11 Among others, see Emiliana Noether, 'Italian Women under Fascism: A Reevaluation,' *Italian Quarterly* 32:90 (Fall 1982), 69–80; *When Biology Becomes Destiny: Women in Weimar and Nazi Germany*, ed. R. Bridenthal, A. Grossmann, and M. Kaplan (New York: Monthly Review, 1984); *Becoming Visible: Women in European History*, ed. R. Bridenthal and C. Koonz (Boston: Houghton Mifflin, 1986); Miriam Mafai, *Pane nero: Donne e vita quotidiana nella Seconda guerra mondiale* (Milan: Mondadori, 1987); Luisa Passerini, *Fascism and Popular Memory: The Cultural Experience of the Turin Working Class*, tr. R. Lumley and J. Bloomfield (Cambridge: Cambridge UP, 1987); Elisabetta Mondello, *La nuova italiana: La donna nella stampa e nella cultura del ventennio* (Rome: Riuniti, 1987); *La corporazione delle donne*, ed. Marina Addis Saba (Florence: Vallechi, 1988); Victoria de Grazia, *How Fascism Ruled Women, Italy 1922–45* (Berkeley: U of California P, 1992); Giovanni De Luna, *Donne in oggetto: L'antifascismo nella società italiana 1922–39* (Turin: Bollati Boringhieri, 1995); the essays collected in *Mothers of Invention: Women, Italian Fascism, and Culture*, ed. Robin Pickering-Iazzi (Minneapolis: U of Minnesota P, 1995); Jane Slaughter, *Women and the Italian Resistance* (Denver, CO: Arden P, 1997); and

Robin Pickering-Iazzi, *Politics of the Visible: Writing Women, Culture, and Fascism* (Minneapolis: U of Minnesota P, 1997).

12 Mabel Berezin, *Making the Fascist Self* (Ithaca: Cornell UP, 1997), 7. See also Emilio Gentile's early 'Alcune considerazioni sull'ideologia fascista,' *Storia contemporanea* (January 1974). Other recent investigations of the cultural articulations of Fascist ideology include Jeffrey Schnapp, *Staging Fascism: 18BL and the Theatre of Masses for Masses* (Stanford: Stanford UP, 1996); Jonathan Petropoulos, *Art as Politics in the Third Reich* (Chapel Hill: U of North Carolina P, 1996); the essays Günther Berghaus collects in *Fascism and Theater* (Providence: Berghahn Books, 1997); Stone, *Patron State*; and Braun, *Mario Sironi.*

13 Marie Antonietta Macciocchi, *La donna 'nera': 'Consenso' femminile e fascismo* (Milan: Feltrinelli, 1976).

14 Spackman, *Fascist Virilities*, 27.

15 See Zeev Sternhell, *Neither Right nor Left: Fascist Ideology in France*, tr. David Maisel (Berkeley: U of California P, 1986); and Zeev Sternhell, Mario Sznajder, and Maia Asheri, *The Birth of Fascist Ideology*, tr. David Maisel (Princeton: Princeton UP, 1994). See also Robert Wohl, 'French Fascism: Both Right and Left: Reflections on the Sternhell Controversy,' *Journal of Modern History* 63:1 (1991), 91–8. The first wave of Marxist challenge comes from Ernesto Laclau, 'Fascism and Ideology,' in *Politics and Ideology in Marxist Theory: Capitalism, Fascism, and Populism* (London: Verso, 1977); and Louis Althusser, *Lenin and Philosophy and Other Essays*, tr. Ben Brewster (New York and London: Monthly Review, 1971), esp. 164 and 175, where Althusser explains his notion of the ideological 'interpellation' of the subject. A subsequent and important wave of critique, following Laclau and Althusser, issues from Alice Yeager Kaplan, *The Reproduction of Banality: Fascism, Literature and French Intellectual Life* (Minneapolis: U of Minnesota P, 1986), and from Spackman.

16 Quoted in Gillian Rose, *Feminism and Geography: The Limits of Geographical Knowledge* (London and New York: Routledge, 1993), 4.

17 See Isidore Abramowitz, *The Great Prisoners: The First Anthology of Literature Written in Prison* (New York: Dutton, 1946); Ioan Davies, *Writers in Prison* (Oxford: Blackwell, 1990); *Wall Tappings: An Anthology of Writing by Women Prisoners*, ed. Judith Scheffler (Boston: Northeastern UP, 1986); Charles Klopp, *Sentences: The Memoirs and Letters of Italian Political Prisoners from Bevenuto Cellini to Aldo Moro* (Toronto: U of Toronto P, 1999); Adriano Sofri, *Memoria* (Palermo: Sellerio, 1990), and his *Le prigioni degli altri* (Palermo: Sellerio, 1993). This rubric also accommodates Elaine Scarry's investigation of the detained and tortured body. See her *The Body in Pain: The Making and Unmaking of the World* (New York: Oxford UP, 1985).

18 W.B. Carnochan, 'The Literature of Confinement,' in *The Oxford History of Prison* (Oxford and London: Oxford UP, 1995), 427. This grouping also features such works as Victor Brombert, *The Romantic Prison* (Princeton: Princeton UP, 1978); Mary Ann Witt, *Existential Prisons: Captivity in Mid-Twentieth Century French Literature* (Durham: Duke UP, 1985); and Martha Duncan, *Romantic Outlaws, Beloved Prisons: The Unconscious Meanings of Crime and Punishment* (New York: New York UP, 1996).

19 John Bender, *Imagining the Penitentiary: Fiction and the Architecture of the Mind in Eighteenth-Century England* (Chicago: U of Chicago P, 1987).

20 See Klopp, *Sentences*. I study in greater detail the architectural superimposition of the prison onto the convent in chapter 3.

21 Cf. Dolores Hayden, *The Power of Place* (Cambridge: MIT P, 1995), 22. For the New Towns, see Ghirardo, *Building New Communities*. For the 1932 Mostra, see Jeffrey Schnapp, 'Epic Demonstrations: Fascist Modernity and the 1932 Exhibition of Fascist Culture,' in Golsan, ed., *Fascism, Aesthetics, and Culture*, 1–37; and Braun, *Mario Sironi*.

22 Concerning *domicilio coatto* (internment), the nineteenth-century precursor to Fascism's practice of the *confino* (internal exile) of political subversives, see John Davis, *Conflict and Control: Law and Order in Nineteenth-Century Italy* (Atlantic Highlands, NJ: Humanities International P, 1988), esp. 326–39. During the Regime, see Benito Mussolini, *Opera omnia*, ed. Edoardo and Duilio Susmel (Florence: La Fenice, 1951), 40; quoted in Dennis Mack Smith, *Mussolini* (New York: Knopf, 1982), 147–8.

23 See Ghirardo, *Building New Communities*, for the role Italian colonies in Africa played with regard to the Fascist spatial scheme. For too long, historiography of the 'kinder, gentler' National Socialism, as Italian Fascism has often been characterized, disavowed extermination camps within Italian Peninsular confines. On the camps, specifically Fossoli, see Susan Zuccotti, *The Italians and the Holocaust: Persecution, Rescue, and Survival* (New York: Basic Books, 1987). .

24 On the fate of Italian Jews during the Regime, see Meir Michaelis, *Mussolini and the Jews: German-Italian Relations and the Jewish Question in Italy, 1922–45* (Oxford: Clarendon P, 1978); Susan Zuccotti, *The Italians and the Holocaust*, and her recent *Under His Very Windows* (New Haven: Yale UP, 2000); Renzo De Felice, *Storia degli ebrei sotto il fascismo* (Turin: Einaudi, 1988); Etlin, *Modernism in Italian Architecture 1890–1940*, esp. 569–98; Philip V. Cannistraro and Brian Sullivan, *Il Duce's Other Woman* (New York: William Morrow, 1993); Alexander Stille, *Benevolence and Betrayal: Five Italian Jewish Families under Fascism* (New York: Pengiun, 1993); Georges Passeleqc and Bernard Suchecky,

The Hidden Encyclical of Pius xi (New York: Harcourt Brace, 1997); and Furio Jesi, *La cultura di destra* (Milan: Garzanti, 1979), esp. 50–60. On Italian racial policy in North Africa, see Alberto Sbacchi, *Ethiopia under Mussolini: Fascism and the Colonial Experience* (London: Zed Books, 1985).

25 The formulation of the 'lexical' prison is Mary Ann Witt's. See her *Existential Prisons.*

26 Carnochan, 'The Literature of Confinement,' 428.

27 Michael Keith and Steve Pile, 'Conclusion: Towards New Radical Geographies,' in *Place and the Politics of Identity,* ed. Michael Keith and Steve Pile (New York and London: Routledge, 1993), 222.

28 See *La costituzione della repubblica italiana,* ed. Vincenzo Carullo (Bologna: Zuffi, 1950); and Piero Calamandrei, *La costituzione inattuata, L'Attualità* 9 (May 1956) (special supplement).

29 Carolyn Heilbrun and Judith Resnick, 'Convergences: Law, Literature, and Feminism,' *Yale Law Review* 99 (1989–90), 1914.

30 Claudio Pavone, 'The Continuity of the State and the Legacy of Fascism,' in *After the War: Violence, Justice, Continuity and Renewal in Italian Society,* ed. Jonathan Dunnage (Leicester: Troubador, 1999), 17.

31 Giuseppe Di Palma, 'Italy: Is There a Legacy and Is It Fascist?' in *Transitional Justice, ii,* ed. Neil Kritz (Washington, DC: United States Institute of Peace P, 1995), 162.

32 Juan Linz, *The Breakdown of Democratic Regimes: Crisis, Breakdown, and Reequilibration* (Baltimore: Johns Hopkins UP, 1978), 35. For an examination of the role of the Action Party in the call for *epurazione,* see David Ward, *Antifascisms* (Cranbury, NJ: Fairleigh-Dickinson UP, 1997), 132–3. See also Lamberto Mercuri, *L'epurazione in Italia 1943–1948* (Cuneo: L'Arciere, 1988); and Hans Woller, *I conti con il fascismo: L'epurazione in Italia. 1943–48* (Bologna: Il Mulino, 1997).

33 Quoted in Di Palma, 162 n. 47. See also Claudio Pavone, *Alle origini della Repubblica: Scritti sul fascismo, antifascismo, e continuità dello Stato* (Turin: Bollati Boringhieri, 1995), 244.

34 Cf. Roy Palmer Domenico, *Italian Fascists on Trial, 1943–48* (Chapel Hill: U of North Carolina P, 1991). The received understanding of partisans as lawless hoodlums finds its way into Cesare Pavese's 1950 novel *La luna e i falò,* where mistrust of the former partisans seems particularly acute and embittering.

35 For the lack of change in the judiciary between Fascism and post-Fascism, see Guido Neppi Modona, 'La magistratura e il fascismo,' in *Fascismo e società italiana,* ed. Guido Quazza (Turin: Einaudi, 1973), 125–81.

36 The notion of the continuity of the Regime into the aftermath of the Second

World War and the founding of the Republic has attracted the attention of scholars in recent years and concerns the general revision of Italian historiography. I address this topic in greater detail in the chapters that follow. On the notion of 'continuity,' see, among others, *Le origini della Repubblica*, ed. Enzo Piscitelli (Turin: Giappichelli, 1974); Guido Quazza, *Resistenza e storia d'Italia: Problemi e ipotesi di ricerca* (Milan: Feltrinelli, 1976); *Scritti storici in memoria di Enzo Piscitelli*, ed. Renzo Paci (Padua: Antenore, 1982); Claudio Pavone, *Una guerra civile: Saggio storico sulla moralità nella Resistenza* (Turin: Bollati Boringhieri, 1991), as well as *Alle origini della Repubblica;* Paul Ginsborg, 'Resistenza e riforma in Francia e Italia, 1943–48,' *Ventesimo secolo* 2:5–6 (1992), 297–319; and Kritz, ed., *Transitional Justice*, esp. 153–204.

37 For the enfranchisement of women, see Chiara Saraceno, 'La struttura di genere della cittadinanza,' *Democrazia e diritto* 28:1 (Jan.–Feb. 1988), 273–95; and Anna Rossi Doria, *Diventare cittadine: Il voto alle donne in Italia nel 1945* (Florence: Giunti, 1996).

38 Paul Ginsborg, *A History of Contemporary Italy: Society and Politics 1943–88* (London: Penguin, 1990), 145–53. See also C. Rodotà, *La corte costituzionale* (Rome: 1986); Maria Virgilio, 'La donna nel Codice Rocco,' in *Diritto e rovescio: Studi sulle donne e il controllo sociale*, ed. Tamar Pitch (Naples: Edizioni scientifiche italiane, 1987), 39–75. For other court cases in the postwar period, see Laura Balbo, *Stato di famiglia* (Milan: Garzanti, 1976); and Michaela De Giorgio, *Le italiane dall'Unità a oggi: Modelli culturali e comportamenti sociali* (Rome-Bari: Laterza, 1992).

39 See Pitch, ed., *Diritto e rovescio;* and Alisa Del Re, 'Politiche demografiche e controllo in Francia, Italia, e Germania negli anni '30,' in *Stato e rapporti sociali di sesso*, ed. A. Del Re (Milan: Franco Angeli, 1989).

40 Quoted in Mary McLeod, '"Other Spaces" and "Others",' in *The Sex of Architecture*, ed. Diana Agrest, Patricia Conway, and Leslie Kanes Weisman (New York: Harry N. Abrams, 1996), 25n5. Following Lefebvre, Sharon Marcus points out that Foucault was reluctant to invest space with 'intentional agency.' See her *Apartment Stories: City and Home in Nineteenth-Century Paris and London* (Berkeley: U of California P, 1999), 203n17. However, Foucault's hesitancy at investing space with any sort of agency (it is 'the practise of liberty' and not the space where that liberty is practised, as he noted in the interview 'Space, Knowledge, and Power,' collected in *The Foucault Reader,* ed. Paul Rabinow [New York: Pantheon, 1984], 239–56) is a manoeuvre related to his assessment of 'power' and leads us to see, with Hartsock, the limitations of his theorization. I say more of Hartsock directly.

41 See McLeod, '"Other Spaces" and "Others."'

42 Davies's well-documented account of imprisoned writers does not address women writing from prison. Klopp's contributions on the prison writings of

Enrichetta Caracciolo and Anna Kulisciof may be seen as a gesture toward redressing this lacuna. Studies taking this neglect under consideration include Elissa Gelfand, 'Imprisoned Women: Toward a Socio-Literary Feminist Analysis,' *Yale French Studies* 62 (1981), 185–203, and her *Imagination in Confinement: Women's Writings from French Prisons* (Ithaca and London: Cornell UP, 1983); and Scheffler, ed., *Wall Tappings*. In social sciences literature, see also Meda Chesney-Lind, *The Female Offender: Girls, Women, and Crime* (Thousand Oaks: Sage Publications, 1995); Coramae Richey Mann, *Female Crime and Delinquency* (Birmingham: U of Alabama P, 1984); Carol Smart, *Women, Crime, and Criminality: A Feminist Critique* (London and Boston: Routledge and Kegan Paul, 1977).

43 The potential in Foucault's theory for feminists has been the subject of at least three recent collections of essays, including *Feminist Interpretations of Michel Foucault*, ed. Susan Hekman (University Park: Pennsylvania State UP, 1996); *Up against Foucault: Explorations of Some Tensions between Foucault and Feminism*, ed. Caroline Ramazanoglu (London: Routledge, 1993); and *Feminism and Foucault: Reflections on Resistance*, ed. Irene Diamond and Lee Quinby (Boston: Northeastern UP, 1988). See also Meaghan Morris, 'The Pirate's Fiancée: Feminists and Philosophers; or, Maybe Tonight It'll Happen,' in *Michel Foucault: Power, Truth, Strategy*, ed. Meaghan Morris and Paul Patton (Sydney: Feral Publications, 1979), 148–68; Edith Kurzweil, 'Michel Foucault's History of Sexuality as Interpreted by Feminists and Marxists,' *Social Research* 53:4 (1986), 647–66; Nancy Hartsock and Peggy Kamuf, 'Replacing Feminist Criticism,' in *Conflicts in Feminism*, ed. Marianne Hirsch and Evelyn Fox Keller (New York and London: Routledge, 1990), 105–11; and Judith Still, '"What Foucault Fails to Acknowledge ...": Feminists and the History of Sexuality,' *History of the Human Sciences* 7:2 (1994), 150–7.

44 For Foucault's explanation of heterotopia, see 'Of Other Spaces: Utopias and Heterotopias,' in *Architecture Culture 1943–68: A Documentary Anthology*, ed. Joan Ockham (New York: Rizzoli, 1993), 420–6. In addition to McLeod, on the problematics of this alternative social ordering see Kevin Heatherington's useful *The Badlands of Modernity: Heterotopia and Social Ordering* (London and New York: Routledge, 1997), esp. 20–38.

45 Michel Foucault, *Discipline and Punish*, tr. Alan Sheridan (New York: Viking, 1979), 231.

46 Nancy Hartsock, 'Foucault: A Theory of Power for Women?' in *Feminism and Postmodernism*, ed. Linda Nicholson (New York and London: Routledge, 1990), 170.

47 See, for example, Mark Wigley's analysis of Leon Battista Alberti's Renaissance treatise on domestic economy and the spatialization of the family, *Della famiglia*, in 'Untitled: The Housing of Gender,' in *Sexuality and Space*,

ed. Beatriz Colamina (Princeton: Princeton Architectural Papers, 1992), 327–90.

48 Frances Bartkowski, 'Epistemic Drift in Foucault,' in Diamond and Quinby, eds., *Feminism and Foucault*, 45.

49 Judith Butler, 'Variations on Gender: Beauvoir, Wittig, and Foucault,' *Praxis International* 5 (1985/86), 507. See also Iris Marion Young, 'Throwing like a Girl: Phenomenology of Feminine Body Comportment, Motility, and Spatiality,' in *The Thinking Muse: Feminism and Modern French Philosophy*, ed. Jeffner Allen and Iris Marion Young (Bloomington: Indiana UP, 1979), 51–70.

50 The formulation of 'hostile' space is Gaston Bachelard's. See his *The Poetics of Space*, tr. Maria Jolas (Boston: Beacon, 1958).

51 Klopp makes excellent progress toward addressing this critical oversight. The historical frame for *Sentences* – from Cellini to Moro – means that the complete history of the writings of Fascism's prisoners has yet to be written. For more published letters of the prisoners, especially prisoners of war, see *Prigionia, C'ero anch'io*, 2 vols (Milan: Mursia, 1990); and *Lettere di antifascisti dal carcere e dal confino*, 2 vols (Rome: Riuniti, 1962).

52 We could compare this distinction between grades and types of imprisonments to the one Hélène Cixous draws in her essay 'We Who Are Free, Are We Free?' in *Freedom and Interpretation: The Oxford Amnesty International Lectures, 1992*, ed. Barbara Johnson (New York: HarperCollins, 1993). Homologies should be avoided as an interpretive model, Jameson warns, because of the false commonalities they establish and their tendency to encourage 'intellectual dishonesty [that, for example,] assimilates the production of texts to the production of goods by factory workers.' See his *The Political Unconscious: Narrative as a Socially Symbolic Act* (Ithaca and London: Cornell UP, 1981), 43–6.

53 See, for example, *Rethinking Italian Fascism: Capitalism, Populism, and Culture*, ed. David Forgacs (Atlantic Highlands, NJ: Humanities International P, 1986); de Grazia; Passerini; Pavone; Quazza; Piscitelli; and Paci.

54 See Robert Dombroski, *L'esistenza ubbidiente: Letterati italiani sotto il fascismo* (Naples: Guida, 1984); Paul Corner, 'Liberalism, Pre-Fascism, and Fascism,' in Forgacs, ed., *Rethinking Italian Fascism*, 11–20; Andrew Hewitt, *Fascist Modernism: Aesthetics, Politics, and the Avant-garde* (Stanford: Stanford UP, 1993); and Spackman, *Fascist Virilities*.

55 See *Futurismo, cultura, e politica*, ed. Renzo de Felice (Turin: Edizioni della Fondazione Giovanni Agnelli, 1988); Claudia Salaris, *Artecrazia: L'avanguardia futurista negli anni del fascismo* (Florence: La Nuova Italia, 1988); the special volume of *Modernism and Modernity* (1:3) dedicated to Futurism (Sept. 1994); and *Modernism and Modernity*'s two special volumes on fascism

and culture, 2:3 (Sept. 1995) and 3:1 (Jan. 1996). See also the special volume on fascism and culture from the *Stanford Italian Review* (1990).

56 Roger Griffin, 'Staging the Nation's Rebirth: The Politics and Aesthetics of Performance in the Context of Fascist Studies,' in Berghaus, ed., *Fascism and Theater.*

57 The expression 'explosion of orality' is Lucia Re's. See her *Calvino and the Age of Neorealism: Fables of Estrangement* (Stanford: Stanford UP, 1990). For a critique of the received periodization of neorealism, see Romano Luperini, *Il Novecento*, 2 vols (Turin: Loescher, 1981); and Ruth Ben-Ghiat, 'Neorealism in Italy 1930–50: From Fascism to Resistance,' *Romance Languages Annual* 3 (1991), 155–9.

58 Mark Mazower, 'Introduction,' in Dunnager, ed., *After the War: Violence, Justice, Continuity and Renewal in Italian Society*, 3. See also Fabio Levi, 'Italian Society and Jews after the Second World War: Between Silence and Reparation,' in *After the War*, 21–31.

59 See Marco Belpoliti, 'Introduzione,' in Levi's *La ricerca delle radici* (Turin: Einaudi, 1997).

60 Luperini, *Il Novecento*, 406–7. See also Re, *Calvino and the Age of Neorealism.*

61 On realism in the period, see Ben-Ghiat, 'Neorealism in Italy 1930–50,' and additionally her 'The Politics of Neorealism: *Corrente di Vita Giovanile* and the Youth Culture of the 1930s,' *Stanford Italian Review* 8:1–2 (1990), 139–64; Pasquale Voza, 'Il problema del neorealismo negli anni Trenta: *Il Saggiatore, Il Cantiere,*' *Lavoro critico* 21–2 (1981), 65–105; Re, *Calvino and the Age of Neorealism*; and Bruno Falcetto, *Storia della narrativa neorealista* (Milan: Mursia, 1992).

62 Cf. Klopp, *Sentences*; Carnochan, 'The Literature of Confinement'; Davies, *Writers in Prison*; Abramowitz, *The Great Prisoners*; and H. Stuart Hughes, *Prisoners of Hope: The Silver Age of Italian Jews, 1924–74* (Cambridge: Harvard UP, 1983). This is not to suggest that prisoners do not make use of other genres. See, for example, Maria Ponce de Léon, 'Meccanismi di sopravvivenza: Letteratura carceraria contemporanea in Italia. Poesia, narrativa, teatro 1970–97' (Ph.D. diss., Northwestern University, 1998). It is worth noting that prose narrative has also served as the focus for inquiries of the spatiality of literature. See, among others, Bachelard, *The Poetics of Space*; Michel Butor, 'The Space of the Novel,' in *Inventory*, ed. Richard Howard (New York: Simon and Schuster, 1968), 31–8; Riccardo Gúllon, 'On Space and Time in the Novel,' *Critical Inquiry* 2 (1975), 11–28; Joseph Frank, 'Spatial Form: An Answer to Critics,' *Critical Inquiry* 4 (1977), 126–34; Joseph Kestner, *The Spatiality of the Novel* (Detroit: Wayne State UP, 1978); *Spatial Form in Narrative*, ed. Jeffrey Smitten and Ann Daghistany (Ithaca: Cornell UP, 1981).

63 Risa Sodi, 'An Interview with Primo Levi,' *Partisan Review* 54:3 (Summer 1987), 356.

64 As Levi writes in *I sommersi e i salvati* (The Drowned and the Saved), political prisoners were the historians of the Lager largely because the conditions of their material lives were tolerable and better than the rank and file *Häftlinge*. These conditions, Levi writes, 'permitted them, for example, to write and preserve notes, an unthinkable luxury for Jews and a possibility of no interest to criminals.' See Primo Levi, *The Drowned and the Saved*, tr. Raymond Rosenthal (New York: Vintage Books, 1989), 18–19. Cf. Levi's story 'Il giocaliere' (The Juggler), in the collection *Lilìt e altri racconti*, [collected in *Racconti*, [Turin: Einaudi, 1996], where he describes the specific interdiction against Lager writing.

65 Antonio Gramsci, *Lettere dal carcere*, ed. Sergio Caprioglio and Elsa Fubini (Turin: Einaudi, 1975).

66 See Gelfand, 'Imprisoned Women: Toward a Socio-Literary Feminist Analysis,' and her *Imagination in Confinement*. See also Scheffler, ed., *Wall Tappings*. For the comparison between Jews and women, it is worth remembering Otto Weininger's collapse of the two categories in his notorious study from 1903, *Sex and Character* (London and New York: AMS, 1975). For the contribution Weininger's theorizing later made to racial policy in both the Third Reich and Fascist Italy, see *Jews and Gender: Responses to Otto Weininger*, ed. Nancy Harrowitz and Barbara Hyams (Philadelphia: Temple UP, 1995).

67 See Gelfand, 'Imprisoned Women.'

68 In addition to Lefebvre, Heatherington, de Certeau, Grosz, Hayden, and Keith and Pile, see the essays collected in Colamina, ed., *Sexuality and Space*; Louis Marin, *Utopics: The Semiological Play of Textual Spaces*, tr. Robert Vollrath (Atlantic Highlands, NJ: Humanities International Press, 1990); Edward Soja, *Postmodern Geographies: The Reassertion of Space in Critical Social Theory* (London and New York: Verso, 1989); Gilles Deleuze, *Cinema I: The Movement-Image* (Minneapolis: U of Minnesota P, 1986), and *Dialogues* (New York: Columbia UP, 1987); Gilles Deleuze and Félix Guattari, 'City/State,' *Zone* 1:2 (1986); Yi-Fu Tuan, *Space and Place: The Perspective of Experience* (Minneapolis: U of Minnesota P, 1977).

69 Cf. Spackman, *Fascist Virilities*; Bruno Wanrooij, *Storia del pudore: La question sessuale in Italia* (Venice: Marsilio, 1990); and Tracy Koon, *Believe, Obey, Fight: The Political Socialization of Youth in Fascist Italy, 1922–45* (Chapel Hill: U of North Carolina P, 1985).

70 For discussion of women during Fascism, see Piero Meldini's now classic anthology, *Sposa e madre esemplare: Ideologia e politica della donna e della famiglia*

durante il fascismo (Florence: Guaraldi, 1975); Pickering-Iazzi, ed., *Mothers of Invention*; and de Grazia, *How Fascism Ruled Women.*

71 See Roberta Gilchrist and Paul Meyvaert, 'The Medieval Monastic Claustrum,' *GESTA* 12 (1973), 53–60.

72 See Giorgio Muratore, 'Gli anni della Ricostruzione,' *Controspazio* (Nov. 1974), 6–25.

2: Barracks and Borders, Prisons and Masculinity

1 Dino Buzzati, 'I sette piani,' in *180 racconti* (Milan: Mondadori, 1982), 22. All references will be to this edition. 'I sette piani' appeared first in *La Lettura*, no. 3, and was later included in the collection *I sette messaggeri*, published in 1942. See Giovanna Iolì, *Dino Buzzati* (Milan: Mursia Editori, 1988), 63n109, for the story's complete publication history.

2 We can compare this to Foucault's thoughts in *Discipline and Punish* when he writes that 'the law inflicting penalties, some of which are more serious than others, cannot allow the individual condemned to light penalties to be imprisoned in the same place as the criminal condemned to more serious penalties ...' (Michel Foucault, *Discipline and Punish: The Birth of the Prison*, tr. Alan Sheridan [New York: Vintage, 1979], 233–4).

3 Windows are present throughout Buzzati's work, as Walter Geerts points out. See Walter Geerts, 'La forma, spazio, visione,' in *Dino Buzzati*, ed. Alvise Fontanella (Florence: Olschki, 1982), 157–67.

4 See Nancy Hartsock, 'Foucault on Power: A Theory for Women?' in *Feminism/ Postmodernism*, ed. Linda Nicholson (New York: Routledge, 1990), 157–75.

5 Iolì also believes that 'La nostra ora,' published in the 25 December 1936 issue of *Il convegno*, is a source for *Il deserto dei Tartari.*

6 Luigi Baldacci, 'Buzzati trascina all'inferno l'architetto Dorigo,' *Epoca*, 5 May 1963, 127.

7 See also Yves Panafieu, 'Un uomo delle frontiere,' *Cahiers Buzzati* 2 (1978), 76.

8 I refer to De Felice's multi-volume biography of Mussolini, *Mussolini il Duce*, especially volume 1, *Gli anni del consenso*, and volume 2, *Lo stato totalitario* (Turin: Einaudi, 1974 and 1981 respectively). Cf. Victoria de Grazia, *The Culture of Consent: The Organization of Mass Leisure in Fascist Italy* (New York and Cambridge: Cambridge UP, 1981). For a critique of De Felice's influence on Italian historiography, see Emilio Gentile, 'Renzo de Felice: A Tribute,' *Journal of Contemporary History* 32 (1997), 139–51; and Borden Painter, 'Renzo de Felice and the Historiography of Italian Fascism,' *American Historical Review* 95 (April 1990), 391–405. The complacency of Buzzati's characters recalls the 'indifference' of the characters in Morvavia's 1929 novel, *Gli indifferenti.*

Published almost a decade apart, Buzzati's and Moravia's novels sketch the quiescence that would have been essential to establishing the sort of 'consensus' De Felice described.

9 Panafieu identifies the same alienation and estrangement from the 'normal' world in the short story 'In quel momento preciso': 'Nous ne nous rejoindrons jamais. Nous sommes des îles solitaires, semées dans l'océan, et qu'un immense espace sépare. Baisers, promesses, larmes sont des sortes de petits ponts; de ridicules brindilles que nous tendons en direction de la rive pour franchir les abîmes.' See Panafieu, 'Un uomo delle frontiere,' 81.

10 Indro Montanelli, quoted in Mario Mignone, *Anormalità e angoscia nella narrativa di Dino Buzzati* (Ravenna: Longo, 1981), 104.

11 In an interview in the *Corriere della sera* on 21 March 1965, Buzzati 'confesses' to having felt victimized by critics who found his work derivative of Kafka's. As Fausto Gianfranceschi observes, despite an obviously shared thematics, Buzzati 'ha ideato uno dei suoi racconti più "kafkaniani," "L'inaugurazione della strada," prima che i libri dell'autore boemo fossero pubblicati in Italia.' See Fausto Gianfranceschi, *Dino Buzzati* (Turin: Borla, 1967), 136. For analyses of the general similarities between Kafka and Buzzati, see Joseph Strelka, 'Kafkaesque Elements in Kafka's Novels and in Contemporary Narrative Prose,' *Comparative Literature Studies* 21 (1984), 434–44; and Léon Riegel, 'Waiting for the War to Break Out: Jünger, Buzzati, and Gracq,' in *Literature and War,* ed. David Bevan (Amsterdam: Rodopi Press, 1989), 97–108. See also Indro Montanelli in *Il mistero di Dino Buzzati,* ed. Romano Battaglia (Milan: Ruscioni, 1980).

12 See Alberico Sala, 'Introduzione,' in *Il deserto dei Tartari,* by Dino Buzzati (Milan: Mondadori, 1983); Stefano Jacomuzzi, '1939: L'armata del Nord: Davanti al deserto dei Tartari (per una rilettura del romanzo di Dino Buzzati),' in *La cultura italiana negli anni 1930–45* (Naples: Edizioni scientifiche italiane, 1984), 113–28.

13 Quoted in Antonia Veronese Arslan, *Invito alla lettura di Dino Buzzati* (Milan: Mursia, 1974), 40.

14 See Dennis Mack Smith, *Mussolini's Roman Empire* (New York: Viking Press, 1976); Alberto Sbacchi, *Ethiopia under Mussolini: Fascism and the Colonial Experience* (London: Zed Books, 1985); and the succinct opening pages of Marcello Carlino's *Come leggere 'Il deserto dei Tartari' di Dino Buzzati* (Milan: Mursia, 1976).

15 Andrew Ross, 'Cowboys, Cadillacs, and Cosmonauts: Families, Film Genres, and Technocultures,' in *Engendering Men: The Question of Male Feminist Criticism,* ed. Joseph Boone and Michael Cadden (New York: Routledge, 1990), 87–101.

16 Homi Bhabha, 'Postcolonial Authority and Postcolonial Guilt,' in *Cultural Studies*, ed. Lawrence Grossberg, Cary Nelson, and Paula Treichler (London and New York: Routledge, 1992), 56.

17 Primo Levi, *La chiave a stella* (Turin: Einaudi, 1978).

18 See R. Shields, *Places on the Margin* (London: Routledge, 1991), esp. 264–78.

19 Edgar Morin, quoted in Geoffrey Bennington, 'Postal Politics and the Institution of the Nation,' in *Nation and Narration*, ed. Homi K. Bhabha (New York: Routledge, 1990), 121–37. Cf. Klaus Theweleit, *Male Fantasies, Volume I: Women, Floods, Bodies, History*, tr. Stephen Conway (Minneapolis: U of Minnesota P, 1986), esp. 300–5.

20 See Claudio Toscani, *Guida alla lettura di Buzzati* (Milan: Mondadori, 1987), 60.

21 Alberico Sala, 'Introduzione,' in *Il deserto dei Tartari* (Milan: Mondadori, 1960). For the correspondence to Buzzati's life, see Mignone, *Anormalità e angoscia*, 107n9.

22 I will discuss fashion and embodiment more fully in the pages that follow. On the expanding topic concerning the relation between architecture and fashion as discursive apparatuses, see the essays collected in *Architecture: In Fashion*, ed. Deborah Fausch, Paulette Singley, Rodolphe El-Khoury, and Zvi Efrat (New York: Princeton Architectural Press, 1994). See also Jacques Derrida, *The Truth in Painting*, tr. Geoff Bennington and Ian McLeod (Chicago: U of Chicago P, 1987), esp. 52–3, where Kant's tandem interest in clothing and columns is discussed; Gilles Deleuze and Félix Guattari, *Thousand Plateaus: Capitalism and Schizophrenia*, tr. Brian Massumi (Minneapolis: U of Minnesota P, 1987), esp. 476; and Eugenia Paulicelli, 'Le narrative della moda: Egemonia, genere, identità,' *Annali d'Italianistica* 16 (1998), 315–37.

23 I am in agreement with Barbara Spackman, who cautions against collapsing the categories of masculinity and virility. At the same time, glossing Fascist Teresa Labriola, Spackman writes that '"virility" can never be cleansed entirely of its relation to "masculinity."' See her *Fascist Virilities: Rhetoric, Ideology and Social Fantasy in Italy* (Minneapolis: U of Minnesota P, 1996), 43. Also on the discourse of virility in the military during the *ventennio*, see Bruno Wanrooij, *La storia del pudore: La questione sessuale in Italia* (Venice: Marsilio, 1990; and Tracy Koon, *Believe, Obey, Fight: The Political Socialization of Youth in Fascist Italy, 1922–45* (Chapel Hill: U of North Carolina P, 1985).

24 For a consonant reading of the importance of borders in the constitution of 'virility' in the work of the futurist F.T. Marinetti, see Spackman, *Fascist Virilities*, 7–16.

25 Critics stand divided over the possibility of political allegory in this novel. See Giorgio Barberi-Squarotti, 'Il romanzo fantastico degli anni 1930–1940:

Buzzati, Morovich, Terracini, Delfini,' in *La cultura italiana negli anni 1930–45* (Naples: Edizioni scientifiche, 1984), 17–49; Pietro Pancrazi, *Corriere della sera*, 2 August 1940; Giuseppe Carlo Marino, *L'autarchia della cultura: Intellettuali e fascismo negli anni trenta* (Rome: Riuniti, 1983), 100–2; and Yves Panafieu, 'Aspetti storici, morali, e politici del discorso dell'impotenza,' in Fontanella, ed., *Dino Buzzati*, 23–47.

26 Edgar Morin, quoted in Bennington, 'Postal Politics'; and the editors' introduction to *Nationalisms and Sexualities*, ed. Andrew Parker, Mary Russo, Doris Sommers, and Patricia Yeager (New York: Routledge, 1992), 1–18. Cf. Theweleit, *Male Fantasies*; and Benedict Anderson, *Imagined Communities: Reflections on the Origin and Spread of Nationalism* (London: Verson, 1983).

27 See Piero Meldini, *Sposa e madre esemplare: Ideologia e politica della donna e della famiglia durante il fascismo* (Florence: Guaraldi, 1975); *Mothers of Invention: Women, Italian Fascism, and Culture*, ed. Robin Pickering-Iazzi (Minneapolis: U of Minnesota P, 1995); Victoria de Grazia, *How Fascism Ruled Women: Italy 1922–43* (Berkeley: University of California P, 1992); Robin Pickering-Iazzi, *The Politics of the Visible: Writing Women, Culture, and Fascism* (Minneapolis: U of Minnesota P, 1997); and Spackman, *Fascist Virilities*.

28 Juliana Schiesari, 'In Praise of Virtuous Women? For a Genealogy of Gender Morals in Renaissance Italy,' *Annali d'Italianistica* 7 (1989), quoted in Spackman, *Fascist Virilities*, 46–7.

29 See Spackman, *Fascist Virilities*; and Chiara Saraceno, 'Redefining Maternity and Paternity: Gender, Pronatalism and Social Policies in Fascist Italy,' in *Maternity and Gender Policies: Women and the Rise of the European Welfare States, 1880s-1950s*, ed. Gisela Bock and Pat Thane (New York: Routledge, 1991), 196–212.

30 See *Piccole italiane: Un raggiro durato vent'anni*, ed. Maria Rosa Cutrufelli et al. (Milan: Anabasi, 1994), 67–9.

31 See Luisa Passerini's 'Donne operaie e aborto,' *Italia contemporanea* 151/152 (1983), 83–109, in which she provides an overview of resistance to the Regime's laws proscribing celibacy and abortion.

32 de Grazia, *How Fascism Ruled Women*, 69.

33 Quoted in de Grazia, *How Fascism Ruled Women*, 70.

34 As Vercellotti later recounted, 'One time at a meeting, at the Bianchi Club in Piazza Statuto, they wanted me to go home and make children – you'll excuse the language – for me to go home and mount my wife. But who [would do such a thing]? We're already poor, dammit! Well, I just can't stomach it' (quoted in Passerini, 'Donne operaie e aborto,' 85).

35 Giorgio Gattei, quoted in de Grazia, *How Fascism Ruled Women*.

36 Spackman, *Fascist Virilities*, 3. See also Philip V. Cannistraro, *La fabbrica di con-*

senso: Fascismo e mass media (Bari: Laterza, 1975); and Giuliano Manacorda, *Letteratura e cultura del periodo fascista* (Milan: Principato, 1974).

37 Karen Pinkus, *Bodily Regimes: Italian Advertising under Fascism* (Minneapolis: U of Minnesota P, 1995), 17. For Mussolini's instructions to the press, see Cannistraro, *La fabbrica di consenso,* esp. 67–98; and Spackman, *Fascist Virilities,* 2–3.

38 Spackman, *Fascist Virilities,* 155.

39 For a succinct précis of the problem, see Antonio Sema, 'La cultura dell'esercito,' in *Cultura e società negli anni del fascismo,* ed. Luigi Dadda and Mario Invernicci (Milan: Cordani, 1987). See also J.T.T. Sweet, *Iron Arm: The Mechanization of Mussolini's Army, 1920–40* (Westport, CT: Greenwood Press, 1980); Giorgio Rochat, 'La politica militare dell'Italia fascista,' *Storia d'Italia,* vol. 2 (Turin: Einaudi, 1973), 1883–91; and 'L'esercito e il fascismo,' in *Fascismo e società italiana,* ed. Guido Quazza (Turin: Einaudi, 1973), 89–123. On the training of officers during Fascism, see Agostino Gemelli, O.F.M., *Il nostro soldato: Saggi di psicologia militare* (Milan: Treves, 1917); and Ettore Grasselli, who, in *Corso di cultura militare* (Milan: Giuffrè, 1937), demonstrates Gemelli's currency in the interwar period.

40 See Pickering-Iazzi, *Politics of the Visible,* esp. 89–120.

41 Sema, 'La cultura dell'esercito,' 101.

42 Benito Mussolini, 'Il morale' (29/7/1917), in *Opera omnia,* ed. Duilio and Edoardo Susmel (Florence: La Fenice, 1951), 5:82–4.

43 Bruno Wanrooij, 'The Rise and Fall of Italian Fascism as Generational Revolt,' *Journal of Contemporary History* 22 (1987), 401–18.

44 See Koon, *Believe, Obey, Fight: The Political Socialization of Youth in Fascist Italy, 1922–45.* Edward Tannenbaum and Bruno Wanrooij disagree over exactly what happened to Italian youth during Fascism: it appears either they were made into sympathizers or just the opposite, that is, were made into resisters, precisely because of their supposed youthful susceptibility. Cf. Edward Tannenbaum, 'Fascist Socialization and Conformity,' in his *The Fascist Experience: Italian Society and Culture, 1922–45* (New York: Basic Books, 1975) 117–49. See also Bruno Wanrooij, '"Il Bo" 1935–1944. Italian Students between Fascism and Anti-Fascism,' *Risorgimento,* 1/2 (1982), 79–86; 'Youth Generation Conflict, and Political Struggle in Twentieth-century Italy,' *The European Legacy* 4:1 (1999), 72–88; and Luca La Rovere, 'Fascist Groups in Italian Universities: An Organisation at the Service of the Totalitarian State,' *Journal of Contemporary History* 34 (1999), 457–75.

45 There is no study of the Italian military and masculinity equivalent to Theweleit's research on the Freikorps. Possible source materials include Virgilio Ilari and Antonio Sema, *Marte in Orbace: Guerra, esercito e milizia nella con-*

cezione fascista della nazione (Ancona: Nuove Ricerche, 1988); Oreste Bovio, *L'ufficio storico dell'esercito: Un secolo di storiografia militare* (Rome: USSME, 1987); Giorgio Rochat, *L'esercito italiano da Vittorio Veneto a Mussolini 1919–25* (Bari: Laterza, 1967); and Gen. Mario Montanari, *L'esercito italiano alla vigilia della Seconda Guerra Mondiale* (Rome: USSME, 1982).

46 Raymond Firth, *Symbols, Public and Private* (Ithaca, NY: Cornell UP, 1973), 342. See also Eric Hobsbawm, *The Invention of Tradition* (New York: Cambridge UP, 1983). Cf. Ferdinand de Saussure, who compared military signals to linguistic signification: 'Language,' Saussure wrote toward the beginning of the twentieth century, 'is a system of signs expressing ideas and as such is comparable to writing, the deaf and dumb alphabet, symbolic rites, forms of courtesy, military signals, etc ... But [language] is the most important of these systems' (quoted in Tadeusz Kowzan, 'The Sign in the Theater: An Introduction to the Semiology of the Art of the Spectacle,' tr. Simon Pleasance, *Diogène* 61 [1968], 53).

47 Firth, *Symbols*, 339, 341.

48 The following laws – *regio decreti* or R.D. – were enacted during this period: 3 December 1934, 9 August 1935, nos. 2042 and 2043 on 14 December 1935, 16 April 1936, 1 October 1936, 7 June 1938, 25 September 1938, 21 October 1938, 7 December 1939, 22 January 1942, 30 March 1943, 12 August 1943. See Oreste Bovio, *Le bandiere dell'esercito* (Rome: USSME, 1981).

49 Bovio, 119.

50 Dino Buzzati, *Il deserto dei Tartari* (Milan: Mondadori, 1979), 22. All references are to this edition and hereafter appear parenthetically in the text.

51 As Marie-Hélène Caspar notices, it marks the beginning to the crucial first four-year period Drogo stays at the fort, which is concluded by his descent during his first furlough into the town, where his destiny at Bastiani is decided. After the description of the first approach, 'le lecteur n'a plus rien à s'apprendre. Il sait déjà presque tout.' The first sighting of the flag functions in analogous fashion to Drogo's initial four years at the fort: from the signal of the limp flag, the reader 'already knows' everything she needs to know. See her *Fantastique et mythe dans l'oeuvre de Buzzati* (La Garenne-Colombes: Editions Erasme, n.d.), 158.

52 I am thinking of the famous verse from Torquato Tasso's *Gerusalemme liberata*, 'Ed ecco ormai, l'ora fatale è giunta.'

53 Again, comparison between Moravia's *Gli indifferenti* and *Il deserto* is appropriate. Michele's failure to 'shoot' Leo at the novel's climax is comparable to the flaccidity and impotence I am describing. For a more contemporary coupling of impotence and a shrinking motif, see Paul Wells, 'The Invisible Man: Shrinking Masculinity in the 1950s Science Fiction B-Movie,' in *You*

Tarzan: Masculinity, Movies, and Men, ed. Pat Kirkham and Janet Thurmin (New York: St Martin's Press, 1993), 181–99.

54 Quoted in Ilari and Sema, *Marte in Orbace,* 61.

55 Ilari and Sema, 61.

56 Romano Luperini, *Il Novecento,* 2 vols (Turin: Loescher, 1981), 406–7. I discussed this in greater detail in the preceding chapter.

57 Yves Panafieu, 'Aspetti storici, morali e politici del discorso dell'impotenza,' in *Dino Buzzati,* ed. Alvise Fontanella (Florence: Olschki, 1982), 31.

58 Sigmund Freud, 'The Uncanny,' in *Freud: Standard Edition,* vol. 17, ed. James Strachey (London: Hogarth, 1957), 245.

59 Cf. Theweleit, *Male Fantasies, Volume II,* 201.

60 See Gillian Rose, *Feminism and Geography: The Limits of Geographical Knowledge* (Minneapolis: U of Minnesota P, 1993), 86–112. As Françoise Roussery-Harpe observes, the triangle is 'Lieu de mystère et d'interdit, lieu du désir et de la peur, *c'est bien une symbolique de la femme que Buzzati développe autour du désert*' (emphasis added; quoted in Caspar, *Fantastique et mythe,* 158).

61 On prefascist geographical irredentism, see P. Revelli, 'Una questione di geografia politica: l'Adriatico e il dominio del Mediterraneo orientale,' *Rivista geografica italiana* (1913), 111–12, anthologized in Costantino Caldo, *Il territorio come dominio: La geografia italiana durante il fascismo* (Naples: Loffredo, 1982).

62 Romance languages offer a similar collapse within the gendered system of language used to describe the symbol of the nation – namely, the flag. In Italian and Spanish, the flag is gendered feminine (la bandiera, la bandera), and the concept of the Patria gendered feminine in all three major languages (la Patria, la Madre Patria [Sp.], and la Patrie). While in current parlance the flag in French is masculine (le drapeau), significantly 'se bander' was seventeenth-century slang for male masturbation. For the relationship between impotence and the nation in revolutionary France, see Lynn Hunt 'Pornography and the French Revolution,' in *The Invention of Pornography,* ed. Lynn Hunt (New York: Zone Books, 1993), 301–40; and Lynn Hunt, 'The Many Bodies of Marie Antoinette: Political Pornography and the Problem of the Feminine in the French Revolution,' in *Eroticism and the Body Politic,* ed. Lynn Hunt (Baltimore: Johns Hopkins UP, 1991) 108–30.

63 See Klaus Theweleit, *Male Fantasies, Volume II: Psychoanalyzing the White Terror,* tr. Erica Carter and Chris Turner (Minneapolis: U of Minnesota P, 1989), esp. 223; as well as Hal Foster, 'Armor Fou,' *October* 56 (Spring 1991), 65–97. See also Mark Seltzer, *Serial Killers: Death and Life in American Wound Culture* (New York and London: Routledge, 1998), 50–1. Moretto's 'faccia dura' also recalls the hardened surface of what Jeffrey Schnapp calls the 'metallized'

body under Fascism. For his distinction between the 'mechanic' body (Bolshevik) and its 'metallized' counterpart (Fascist), see his *Staging Fascism: 18BL and the Theater of the Masses for the Masses* (Stanford: Standord UP, 1996), 109–11.

64 See Andrea Viotti, *Uniformi e distintivi dell'esercito italiano nella seconda guerra mondiale 1940–45* (Rome: USSME, 1988). For comments on the 'fashion system' deploying and/or exploding plastic visions of sexual difference in service to the nation, see Beverly Allen, 'The Novel, the Body, and Giorgio Armani,' and Eugenia Paulicelli, 'Fashion as a Text: Talking about Femininity and Feminism,' in Parker et al., eds, *Feminine Feminists: Cultural Practices in Italy*, ed. Giovanna Miceli-Jeffries (Minneapolis: Minnesota UP, 1995), 153–70 and 171–89, respectively. For a shrewd discussion of the role of consumer fashion and economic nationalism, see Norman Holland, 'Fashioning Cuba,' in Parker et al., eds, *Nationalisms and Sexualities*, 147–56. I follow Louis Althusser's discussion of ideological apparatuses and interpellation. See Althusser, 'Ideology and Ideological State Apparatuses: Notes toward an Investigation,' in *Lenin and Philosophy and Other Essays*, trans. B. Brewster (New York: Monthly Review, 1971), esp. 164, 175.

65 On fascist spectacle, see Schnapp, *Staging Fascism*.

66 Viotti, *Uniformi e distintivi dell'esercito italiano*, 11.

67 See Mary McLeod, 'Undressing Architecture: Fashion, Gender, and Modernity,' in Fausch et al., eds, *Architecture: In Fashion*, 39.

68 See Gilles Deleuze, *The Fold: Leibniz and the Baroque*, foreword and tr. Tom Conley (Minneapolis: U of Minnesota P, 1993), esp. 121.

69 Richard Dellamora, *Masculine Desire: The Sexual Politics of Victorian Aestheticism* (U of North Carolina P, 1990), 210. Cf. Schnapp's distinction between the 'dictator and the dandy' in *Staging Fascism*, 97–112.

70 On male masochism, see Kaja Silverman, *Male Subjectivity at the Margins* (New York: Routledge, 1992). See also Maurizia Boscagli's excellent *Eye on the Flesh: Fashions of Masculinity in the Early Twentieth Century* (Boulder, CO: Westview P, 1996), esp. 7–11, where she outlines the opposed possibilities for male masochism as (1) potentially radical (per Silverman) and (2) only a suspension of the sexual order of things within patriarchy. On masochism as the temporary 'solution' to patriarchy, see Paul Smith, *Clint Eastwood: A Cultural Production* (Minneapolis: U of Minnesota P, 1995).

71 See Paulette Singley and Deborah Fausch, 'Introduction,' in Fausch et al., eds, *Architecture: In Fashion*, 29n1. See also Deborah Fausch, '"Towards an Architecture of Our Times": Scaffold and Drapery in the Architecture of Venturi, Scott Brown and Associates,' in *Architecture: In Fashion*, 344–61. And the architectural presence does not stop here. Although this homophone

does not work in Italian one could point out the relationship – in Buzzati's text also thematic – between 'freeze' and 'frieze.'

72 The term 'sartorial gaze' is Joan Copjec's. See her 'The Sartorial Superego,' *October* 50 (Fall 1989), 56–95.

73 See Kachig Tölölyan, 'The Nation-State and Its Others,' *Diaspora* 1:1 (Spring 1991).

74 See George Mosse, *Nationalism and Sexuality: Middle-Class Morality and Sexual Norms in Modern Europe* (Madison: U of Wisconsin P, 1985); Eve Kosofsky Sedgwick, 'Nationalisms and Sexualities in the Age of Wilde,' in Parker et al., eds, *Nationalisms and Sexualities*, 235–45; Anderson, *Imagined Communities*.

75 Anderson, *Imagined Communities*, 5.

76 Neil Hertz, *The End of the Line: Essays on Psychoanalysis and the Sublime* (New York: Columbia UP, 1985), esp. 161–93.

77 Lamberto Mercuri, *L'Epurazione in Italia, 1943–48* (Cuneo: L'Arciere, 1988), esp. 9–20. See also Hans Woller, *I conti con il fascismo: L'epurazione in Italia 1943–48* (Bologna: Il Mulino, 1997); as well as *Transitional Justice: How Emerging Democracies Reckon with Former Regimes*, vol. 2, ed. Neil Kritz (Washington, DC: United States Institute of Peace P, 1995).

78 Paul Ginsborg, *A History of Contemporary Italy: Society and Politics 1943–88* (London: Penguin, 1990), 148.

79 Giuseppe Di Palma, 'Italy: Is There a Legacy and Is It Fascist?' in Kritz, ed., *Transitional Justice*, 162.

80 Roy Palmer Domenico, *Italian Fascists on Trial, 1943–48* (Chapel Hill: U of North Carolina P, 1991), 14.

81 See Domenico, 15–17.

3: Penitents and Penitentiaries: Interstices, Resistance, Freedom

1 Curzio Malaparte, *Kaputt* (Florence: Vallechi Editori, 1960), 619. All references are to this edition and hereafter appear parenthetically in the text.

2 We could contrast this soldier's cultural ignorance with the character of Bergmann, the Nazi commandant in Roberto Rossellini's *Rome: Open City* (1946). From a windowless room in Nazi headquarters in Via Tasso, Bergmann surveilles Rome by way of maps and photographs, and in this way successfully rounds up Resistance activists. For a reading of Bergmann's relationship to Rome, see Millicent Marcus, *Italian Film in the Light of Neorealism* (Princeton: Princeton UP, 1993), esp. 46–8.

3 On the relation between the Church and State, see Giovanni Miccoli, 'La chiesa e il fascismo,' in *Fascismo e società italiana*, ed. Guido Quazza. (Turin: Einaudi, 1973), 185–208; see also S.W. Halperin, *The Separation of the Church*

and State in Italian Thought from Cavour to Mussolini (Chicago: U of Chicago P, 1937); D.A. Binchy, *Church and State in Fascist Italy* (Oxford: Oxford UP, 1941); A. de Marsanich, *Lo stato nel ventennio fascista (1922–43): Principi e istituti* (Rome: Aniene Editori, 1958); A.C. Jemolo, *Church and State in Italy 1850–1950*, tr. David Morre (Oxford: Basil Blackwell, 1960); and Renato Moro, 'La modernizzazione cattolica tra fascismo e postfascismo come problema storiografico,' *Storia contemporanea* 19:4 (Aug. 1988), 625–716.

4 See 'Cenni storici,' undated and unpaginated source provided by the Amministrazione peniteniziaria. The Mantellate, mantled nuns, refers to Via delle Mantellate, one of the streets bounding the prison, which I discuss below. Alcide De Gasperi, also detained in Regina Coeli during Fascism, wrote in his letters of the disconnection between what was once a pious place and the prison into which it had been transformed: 'Queen of Heaven [Regina Coeli], rejoice, Hallelujah, though Regina Coeli, at present is a synonym for bitterness' (Charles Klopp, *Sentences: The Memoirs and Letters of Italian Political Prisoners from Bevenuto Cellini to Aldo Moro* [Toronto: U of Toronto P, 1999], 135).

5 See C.L. Morichini, *Degli istituti di carità per la sorveglianza e l'educazione dei poveri e dei prigionieri in Roma* (Rome, 1870); and Luigi Daga, 'Sistemi penitenziari,' in *Enciclopedia del diritto* (Milan: Giuffrè, 1992). Articles 21 and 22 of the Atti di soppressione (laws of suppression) (n. 3036 of 7 July 1866) called for 'il trasferimento in proprietà a province e comuni degli edifici conventuali meno famosi e meno legati ad una tradizione culturale.' See *L'archivio della direzione generale delle antichità e belle arti* (1860–90), ed. Matteo Musacchio (Rome: Ufficio centrale per i beni archivistici, 1994), 399.

6 See Klopp, *Sentences*, 125, and 220n50.

7 Klopp, 145.

8 Silvio Pellico, *Le mie prigioni* (Bari: Edizioni Paoline, 1970), 62. See Klopp's reading of Pellico's later detainment in the Spielberg in *Sentences*, 38–45. Later in the nineteenth century, Sigismondo Castromediano would make a similar observation: '"It's a curious twist of fate how in all these localities where once there were monks, their places have been taken by criminals"' (quoted in Klopp, 5).

9 By postmodern geography, I mean the re-examination of the 'interpretive significance of space in the historically privileged confines of contemporary critical thought.' See Edward Soja, *Postmodern Geographies: The Reassertion of Space in Critical Social Theory* (London and New York: Verso, 1989), 11, but esp. 10–42. Fellini makes visible this jumble of Rome in *La Dolce Vita* (1959), especially in the establishing sequences that, from aerial position, sweep across Rome's various realities, mixing Imperial, Christian, and con-

temporary Rome together. See Marguerite Waller's fine reading of this in her 'Whose Dolce Vita Is It, Anyway?' *Quaderni d'Italianistica* 11:1 (1990), 127–35.

10 Giancarlo Rocca, *Donne religiose: Contributo a una storia della condizione femminile in Italia nei secoli XIX–XX* (*Claretianum* 32 [1992]), 265.

11 R. Hostie, 'Emancipazione della donna e istituti religiosi,' *Dizionario degli Istituti di Perfezione* 3 (1976), 1126.

12 For reference to the gothicized carceral, see Katherine Gill, 'Open Monasteries for Women in Late Medieval and Early Modern Italy: Two Roman Examples,' in *The Crannied Wall: Women, Religion, and the Arts in Early Modern Europe*, ed. Craig Monson (Ann Arbor: U of Michigan P, 1992), 15–47.

13 See Elissa Gelfand, 'Imprisoned Women: Toward a Socio-Literary Feminist Analysis,' *Yale French Studies* 62 (1981), 85–203, and her *Imagination in Confinement: Women's Writings from French Prisons* (Ithaca and London: Cornell UP, 1983). See also chapter 1, where I discuss this in greater detail.

14 *Vita e processo di Suor Virginia Maria de Leyva, Monaca di Monza*, ed. Umberto Colombo (Milan: Garzanti, 1985), 676. For Manzoni's relation to Ripamonti, see *I promessi sposi*, ed. Angelo Marchese (Milan: Mondadori, 1985), 175n5.

15 See Henri Lefebvre, *The Production of Space*, tr. Donald Nicholson-Smith (Oxford: Blackwell, 1991), esp. 286.

16 See Diane Ghirardo, 'Virtually Visible,' *Thresholds* 19 (1999), 41–7; and Paul Meyvaert, 'The Medieval Monastic Claustrum,' *GESTA* 12 (1973), 53–60.

17 Cf. Iris Marion Young, 'Throwing like a Girl: A Phenomenology of Feminine Body Comportment, Motility, and Spatiality,' in *The Thinking Muse: Feminism and Modern French Philosophy*, ed. Jeffner Allen and Iris Marion Young (Bloomington: Indiana UP, 1979), 51–70.

18 See Lucy Sargisson, *Contemporary Feminist Utopianism* (New York and London: Routledge, 1996), esp. 63–97; Vincent Geoghegan, *Utopianism and Marxism* (London: Methuen, 1987); Francis Bartkowski, *Feminist Utopias* (Lincoln: U of Nebraska P, 1989); and *Utopias*, ed. Peter Alexander and Roger Gill (London: Duckworth, 1984).

19 For a history of forced vocation, see Romano Canosa, *Il Velo e il Cappuccio: Monacazioni forzate e sessualità nei conventi femminili in Italia tra Quattrocento e Settecento* (Rome: Sapere 2000, 1991).

20 For Piovène's work as a censor during the Regime, see Barbara Zaczek, 'Guido Piovène's *Lettere di una novizia*: Misreading a Nun,' in *The Flight of Ulysses: Studies in Memory of Emmanuel Hatzantonis* (Chapel Hill: Annali d'Italianistica, 1997), 298n18; and Giovanni Falaschi,' Interventi redazionali negli anni trenta,' *Belfagor* 40 (1985), 497–528. In the preface to his 1962 novel *La coda di paglia*, Piovène issued a blanket 'apology' for his collaboration with

the Regime. See Guido Sommavilla, 'Ierologia di Guido Piovène,' *Letture* 31 (1976), 7n4.

21 See Giorgio Pullini, 'Piovène romanziere,' in *Guido Piovène*, ed. Stefano Rosso-Mazzinghi (Vicenza: Neri Pozza Editore, 1980), 29–45; Enzo Bettizia, 'L'attività giornalistica di Piovène,' in *Guido Piovène*, 46–52; Giorgio Barberi Squarotti, 'I primi romanzi di Piovène,' in *Guido Piovène*, 53–70; Gino Nogara, 'La terra di Piovène,' in *Guido Piovène*, 105–14; and Piero Bigongiari, 'La mezza verità come momento dinamico della narrativa di Piovène,' in *Guido Piovène*, 164–72. See also G. Catalano, *Piovène* (Florence: Il Castoldo, 1967), 67–83.

22 Guido Piovène, *Lettere di una novizia*, 14th ed. (Milan: Bompiani, 1963), 14. All references will be to this edition and hereafter appear parenthetically in the text.

23 Rita's wandering offers an excellent and contrary example to Emanuela's 'errance' in Alba de Céspedes's novel *Nessuno torna indietro*, which I examine in detail below. For an excellent reading of Emanuela's charting of exterior, urban geography, see Robin Pickering-Iazzi, *Politics of the Visible: Writing Women, Culture, and Fascism* (Minneapolis: U of Minnesota P, 1997), 164–88. See also Panivong Norindr, '"Errances" and Memories in Marguerite Duras's Colonial Cities,' *differences* 5:3 (1993), 52–79.

24 Emilio Cecchi observes that Piovène's Po landscape is painted in the customary 'whispy' grace of a watercolourist. See Rosso-Mazzinghi, ed., *Guido Piovène*, 105.

25 This is not the last time that fog will be used to depict moral ambiguity, especially as regards Fascism. Fog in Piovène's novel anticipates a cinematic example of the equivalency between fog, haze, and Fascism. While not exactly the Po countryside that Piovène accurately portrays, the fog Fellini photographs in *Amarcord* (1976) bears some similarities. See James Hay, *Popular Film Culture in Fascist Italy* (Bloomington: U of Indiana P, 1987), xi–xvii.

26 For more on windows in Piovène and a comparison with Moravia, see Andrea Afribo, 'La finestra e altro: Guido Piovène,' in *Guido Piovène tra idoli e ragione: Atti del convegno di studi Vicenza, 24–26 novembre 1994*, ed. Stefano Strazzabosco (Venice: Marsilio, 1996), 297–310.

27 Louis Marin, *Utopics: The Semiological Play of Textual Spaces*, tr. Robert Vollrath (Atantic Highlands, NJ: Humanities International P, 1984), xxiv.

28 See Gabriella Zarri, 'De monialibus (secoli XVI-XVII-XVIII),' *Rivista di storia e letteratura religiosa* 33:3 (1997), 643–69; Canosa, *Il Velo e il Cappuccio*; Colombo, ed., *Vita e processo di Suor Virginia Maria de Leyva, Monaca di Monza*.

29 See, for example, Jules Kirschner, *Pursuing Honor While Avoiding Sin* (Milan: Giuffrè, 1978); Jules Kirschner and Anthony Molho, 'The Dowry Fund and

the Marriage Market in Early Quattrocento Florence,' *Journal of Modern History 50* (1978), 403–38; Christiane Klapisch-Zuber and David Herlihy, *Tuscans and Their Families* (New Haven: Yale UP, 1985); and Christiane Klapisch-Zuber, *Women, Family, and Ritual in Renaissance Italy,* tr. Lydia Cochrane (Chicago: U of Chicago P, 1985).

30 Quoted in Gabriella Zarri, 'Monasteri femminili e città,' in *La chiesa e il potere politico dal medioevo all'età contemporanea*, vol. 9 of *Storia d'Italia*, ed. G. Chittolini and G. Miccoli (Turin: Einaudi, 1986), 365; see also n19 on the same page.

31 The novel was thought so attune to the rhythms of this genre that it was optioned for a film and de Céspedes herself was invited to collaborate on the screenplay. For the history of the novel's transition to the screen, see Jacqueline Reich, 'Fear of Filming: Alba de Céspedes and the 1943 Film Adaptation of *Nessuno torna indietro,*' in *Writing beyond Fascism: Cultural Resistance in the Life and Works of Alba de Céspedes,* ed. Carole C. Gallucci and Ellen Nerenberg (Cranbury, NJ: Fairleigh-Dickinson UP, 2000), 132–54.

32 See Jacqueline Reich's 'Reading, Writing, and Rebellion: Collectivity, Specularity, and Sexuality in the Italian Schoolgirl Comedy, 1934–43,' in *Mothers of Invention: Women, Italian Fascism, and Culture,* ed. Robin Pickering-Iazzi (Minneapolis: U of Minnesota P, 1995), 220–51. The popularity of the Hungarian model, which Reich usefully situates, would not preclude the popularity of a single film from German cinema like *Mädchen in Uniforme,* which, as Rich says, had gained international acclaim. See B. Ruby Rich 'From Repressive Tolerance to Erotic Liberation: *Maedchen in Uniform,*' *Re-vision: Essays in Film Criticism* (AFI), 3 (1984), 100–30.

33 Maria Borgese, 'Letteratura femminile,' *Nuova antologia,* 16 July 1939, 232–5.

34 On the history and fortune of the alternative ending – which was never seen in Germany – see Rich, 128n9. Rich tells us also (101) that Sagan's film was based on Christa Winsloe's play *Gestern und Heute* (Yesterday and Today), which, following the 'tremendous initial popularity both within Germany and internationally,' appeared as the novel *The Child Manuela*. The film is the only version in which Manuela does not die. See Richard Dyer, *Studies on Lesbian and Gay Film* (New York: Routledge, 1990), 30.

35 The Catholic Church, as witnessed by the *Casta Connubi,* upheld its time-honoured tradition of exhorting believers to procreate. See Carole Gallucci, 'There's No Turning Back: Challenging the New Woman's Future,' in Pickering-Iazzi, ed., *Mothers of Invention,* 200–19. See also Annarita Buttafuoco, 'Motherhood as a Political Strategy: The Role of the Italian Women's Movement in the Creation of the Cassa Nazionale di Maternità,' in *Maternity and Gender Policies: Women and the Rise of the European Welfare States, 1880s–*

1950s, ed. Gisela Bock and Pat Thane (New York: Routledge, 1991), 178–95; and Chiara Saraceno, 'Redefining Maternity and Paternity: Gender, Pronatalism and Social Policies in Fascist Italy,' in *Maternity and Gender,* 196–212.

36 See Assunta Parsani and Neria de Giovanni, *Femminile al confronto* (Rome: Lacaita, 1984); Ellen Nerenberg, '"Donna proprio ... proprio donna": The Social Construction of Femininity in Alba de Céspedes's *Nessuno torna indietro*,' *Romance Languages Annual* 3 (1991), 267–73; Gallucci, 'There's No Turning Back; Pickering-Iazzi, *Politics of the Visible*; and Sandra Carletti, 'Internalizing the Gaze,' in Gallucci and Nerenberg, eds, *Writing beyond Fascism*.

37 Although Silvia, the protagonist Parsani and de Giovanni identify, is an important spokeswoman, Emanuela is the protagonist in the classical sense: she promotes and orchestrates action and story in the novel.

38 The final portrait of Silvia, writing to her friends at Il Grimaldi from her new boarding-school room in Littoria, suggests neither of Parsani's and de Giovanni's categories of 'success' or 'failure.' Rather, it illustrates Silvia's lack of spatial and social development.

39 See *Wall Tappings: An Anthology of Writing by Women Prisoners,* ed. Judith Scheffler (Boston: Northeastern UP, 1986), 21.

40 Alba de Céspedes, *Nessuno torna indietro* (Milan: Mondadori, 1938), 12. All references will be to this edition and hereafter appear parenthetically in the text.

41 See Laura Maraini, *Quelle dell'idea* (Bari: De Donato, 1982), and Cesira Fiori, *Una donna nelle carceri fasciste* (Rome: Riuniti Editori, 1965).

42 See Michela De Giorgio, *Le italiane dall'Unità a oggi: Modelli culturali e comportamenti sociali* (Rome-Bari: Laterza, 1992), and Victoria de Grazia, *How Fascism Ruled Women, Italy 1922–43* (Berkeley: U of California P, 1992), esp. 154–7.

43 See Pickering-Iazzi, *Politics of the Visible,* 171–2; and Carletti, 'Internalizing the Gaze.'

44 The book ran through thirteen editions before it was censored in 1942. See Michele Giocondi, *Lettori in camicia nera: Narrativa di successo nell'Italia fascista* (Messina and Florence: G. D'Anna, 1978), 16–23.

45 Virginia Woolf, *A Room of One's Own* (New York: Harcourt, Brace, Jovanovich, 1957), 4.

46 The bodies Pinkus examines in 'The Body Disappears' are not specifically gendered. See her *Bodily Regimes: Italian Advertising under Fascism* (Minneapolis: U of Minnesota P, 1995), 195–243.

47 In addition to feature films, shorts on the subject of religious women were also produced in this period: Piero Costa's 1949 *Santa Cecilia, regina delle*

armonie, Arrigo Cinotti's 1949 *Chiara d'Assisi,* and Dante Moccheggiani's 1950 documentary, *La fanciulla di Corinaldo.* On the importance of this cinematic genre, see Giovanna Grignaffini, 'Sante e suore sullo schermo,' in *Donna e fede: Santità e vita religiosa in Italia,* ed. Lucetta Scaraffia and Gabriella Zarri (Rome-Bari: Laterza, 1994), 517–30

48 For holy anorexia, see Caroline Walker Bynum, *Holy Feast and Holy Fast* (Berkeley: U of California P, 1987); Rudolph Bell, *Holy Anorexia* (Chicago: U of Chicago P, 1985); and Linda Carroll, 'Holy Anorexia Revisited,' *Psychohistory Review* 26:2 (1998), 115–36.

49 Cf. Susan Bordo, 'Anorexia nervosa: Psychopathology as the Crystallization of Culture,' in *Feminism and Foucault: Reflections on Resistance,* ed. Irene Diamond and Lee Quinby (Boston: Northeastern UP, 1988).

50 De Céspedes's representation of Silvia's homeliness and femininity aligns *Nessuno torna indietro* with other 1930s discussions of the spectacular aspects of femininity. Joan Rivière, for example, published her influential essay 'Womanliness as a Masquerade' in the *International Journal of Psychoanalysis* in 1929. See also Judith Butler's fine reading of Rivière in *Gender Trouble: Feminism and the Subversion of Identity* (New York: Routledge, 1990), 50–4.

51 See Piero Meldini, *Sposa e madre esemplare: Ideologia e politica della donna e della famiglia durante il fascismo* (Florence: Guaraldi, 1975); Emiliana Noether, 'Italian Women under Fascism: A Reevaluation,' *Italian Quarterly* 32 (90) (Fall 1982), 69–80; Lesley Caldwell, 'Reproducers of the Nation: Women and the Family in Fascist Policy,' in *Rethinking Italian Fascism: Capitalism, Populism, and Culture,* ed. David Forgacs (London: Lawrence and Wishart, 1986); de Grazia, *How Fascism Ruled Women;* Saraceno, 'Redefining Maternity'; Buttafuoco, 'Motherhood as a Political Strategy'; and Pickering-Iazzi, ed., *Mothers of Invention.*

52 See Gill, 'Open Monasteries.' For the role of these women in nineteenth- and twentieth-century convent practices in Italy, see Lucetta Scaraffia, '"Il cristianesimo l'ha fatta libera, collocandola nella famiglia accanto all'uomo" (dal 1850 alla *Mulieris dignitatem*),' in Scaraffia and Zarri, eds, *Donna e fede,* 441–93; and Rocca, *Donne religiose.*

53 Sally Gearhart 'Future Visions: Today's Politics: Feminist Utopias in Review,' in *Women in Search of Utopia: Mavericks and Mythmakers,* ed. Ruby Rohrlick and Baruch Elaine Hoffman (New York: Schocken Books, 1984), 296. See also Sargisson, *Contemporary Feminist Utopianism,* esp. 63–97.

54 Cf. Carletti, 'Internalizing the Gaze.'

55 Lefebvre, *The Production of Space,* 209–10.

56 Cf. chapter 1, where I discuss Macciocchi's analysis and its role in studies of

women's involvement in Italian Fascism. On the organization of women
within the PNF, see de Grazia, *How Fascism Ruled Women*, 234–71.

57 For Church dicta concerning twentieth-century convent practice, see Rocca,
Donne religiose, esp. 239–71.

58 See Laura Gellott and Michael Phayer, 'Dissenting Voices: Catholic Women
in Opposition to Fascism,' *Journal of Contemporary History* 22 (1987), 91–114.

59 Jo Ann Kay McNamara, *Sisters in Arms: Catholic Nuns through Two Millennia*
(Cambridge: Harvard UP, 1996), 271.

60 The formulation 'imagination in confinement' is Elissa Gelfand's. See her
Imagination in Confinement: Women's Writings from French Prisons.

61 Enza Biagini, *Anna Banti* (Milan: Mursia, 1978), 43n1.

62 On this subject, see also Daria Valentini, 'Anna and Her Sisters: The Idyll of
the Convent in Anna Banti,' *Forum Italicum* 30:2 (Fall 1996), 332–50.

63 Anna Banti, 'Lavinia fuggita,' in *Il coraggio delle donne* (Milan: La Tartaruga,
1983). All references will be to this edition and hereafter appear parenthetically in the text.

64 Biagini, *Anna Banti*, 79.

65 See also Ioan Davies, *Writers in Prison* (Oxford: Basil Blackwell, 1990).

66 Pellico, *Le mei prigioni*, 77. See also *Kaputt* (185–7), where Malaparte discusses the liberation of the spirit during his stay in Regina Coeli.

67 Banti addresses a more complex system of patrons and women artists in the
seventeenth century in *Artemisia*. As she will in the short story, Banti conjoins
writing (her original manuscript lost in the 1944 bombing of Florence
opposed to the revisions she later quilts together from memory) and time
(author and imagined protagonist consoling each other's losses across the
centuries). Further, the classical names (Artemisia, Lavinia) similarly layer
time in mythic fashion.

68 Elsa Morante, 'Via dell'Angelo,' in *Lo sciallo andaluso* (Turin: Einaudi, 1963),
61. All references will be to this edition and hereafter appear parenthetically
in the text.

4: Love for Sale; or, That's *Amore*: Brothels, Prison, Revision

1 For the lability of the sign of prostitution, see, for example, Laurie Teal, 'The
Hollow Women: Modernism, the Prostitute, and Commodity Aesthetics,' *differences: A Journal of Feminist Cultural Studies* 7:3 (1995), 80–108, for an analysis
of the prostitute in French and German modernism; Michael Rothberg, 'The
Prostitution of Paris: Late Capital of the Twentieth Century,' *Found Object* 1:1
(1992), 2–22, for an analysis of the prostitute as the figure for urbanizing
Paris; Elizabeth Helsinger 'Consumer Power and the Utopia of Desire: Chris-

tina Rossetti's "Goblin Market,"' *ELH* 58 (1991), 903–33; and Joseph Lenz, 'Base Trade: Theater as Prostitution,' *ELH* 60 (1993), 833–55, for an analysis of the juxtaposition of theatres and brothels in Shakespeare's London. See also Lynne Sharon Chancer, 'Prostitution, Feminist Theory, and Ambivalence: Notes from the Sociological Underground,' *Social Text* 37 (Winter 1993), 143–71; and Jann Matlock, *Scenes of Seduction: Prostitution, Hysteria, and Reading Difference in Nineteenth-Century France* (New York: Columbia UP, 1994).

2 Tripolina and Salomé, in Millicent Marcus's view, enact the two opposing terms of the film's title, 'Love' and 'Anarchy,' a tension Wertmüller stages in their bathroom brawl the morning of the planned assassination. See Millicent Marcus, *Italian Film in the Light of Neorealism* (Princeton: Princeton UP, 1993), 320.

3 Peter Bondanella writes that the brothel in the film serves as 'metaphor for all of Italy: Both the fascist government and the bordello are organized around authoritarian principles.' Like Wertmüller's prostitutes, the boarders in Alba de Céspedes's novel *Nessuno torna indietro* – a focus in the preceding chapter – hail from all over the Peninsula. See *Italian Cinema from Neorealism to the Present* (New York: Continuum, 1990), 357–8.

4 Carlo Lucarelli's recent novel *Via delle Oche* (Palermo: Sellerio, 1996) documents some of these practices and draws attention to the brief periods (often thirty days) that prostitutes were billeted at the various official *case chiuse* before being circulated to a different town. I will have the opportunity to describe this and other practices concerning the *case chiuse* below.

5 See Katherine Gill, 'Open Monasteries for Women in Late and Early Modern Italy: Two Roman Examples,' in *The Crannied Wall: Women, Religion, and the Arts in Early Modern Europe*, ed. Craig Monson (Ann Arbor: U of Michigan P, 1992), 15; and Graciela Daichman, *Wayward Nuns in Medieval Literature* (Syracuse: Syracuse UP, 1986).

6 *Lettere dalle case chiuse*, ed. Lina Merlin and Carla Barberis (Milan-Rome: Edizioni Avanti!, 1955), 112.

7 See Homa Fardjadi and Moshen Mostafavi, *Delayed Space* (New York: Princeton Architectural P, 1999).

8 A similar 'pogrom,' in fact, took place in Rome soon after Mussolini's ouster, and is best illustrated by the arrest of actress Stefania Rossi and her daughter Bibi at the Pensione Trinità dei Monti. As Roy Palmer Domenico notes, the 'interest in love and prostitution particularly reveals the general inability to identify Fascists ... [L]overs and mistresses ... embodied a kind of corruption that many associated with fascism.' See Palmer Domenico, *Italian Fascists on Trial, 1943–48* (Chapel Hill: U of North Carolina P, 1991), 50.

9 See Antonio Palermo, 'Gli anni Trenta: Per una nuova periodizzazione della

storiografia letteraria,' in *La cultura italiana negli anni 1930–45* (Naples: Edizioni scientifiche italiane, 1984), 159–81; Claudia Koonz, *Mothers in the Fatherland: Women, the Family, and Nazi Politics* (New York: St Martin's Press, 1987); and *Gender, Patriarchy, and Fascism in the Third Reich*, ed. Elaine Martin (Detroit: Wayne State UP, 1993). Given the historical parameters and the 'real world' conditions prostitutes lived in/under in newly Republican Italy, Karen Newman's objection to the critique of prostitution, while taken under advisement, can be pre-empted. She writes: 'Reading women repeatedly as the object of male exchange constructs a victim's discourse that risks reinscribing the very sexual politics it seeks to expose and change.' See her 'Directing Traffic: Subjects, Objects, and the Politics of Exchange,' *differences: A Journal of Feminist Cultural Studies* 2 (1990), 47. For a critique of the 'reinscription' of such victim's status, see Audrey Ecstavasia, 'Fucking (with Theory) for Money: Toward an Introduction of Escort Prostitution,' in *Essays in Postmodern Culture*, ed. Eyal Amiran and John Unsworth (Oxford and New York: Oxford UP, 1993), 177–98.

10 On the problem of periodizing neorealist practice, see Romano Luperini, *Il Novecento*, 2 vols (Turin: Loescher, 1981) esp. 406–7; Pasquale Voza, 'Il problema del neorealismo negli anni Trenta: *Il Saggiatore, Il Cantiere*,' *Lavoro critico* 21–2 (1981), 65–105; Ruth Ben-Ghiat, 'The Politics of Realism: *Corrente di Vita Giovanile* and the Youth Culture of the 1930s,' *Stanford Italian Review* 8:1–2 (1990), 139–64; 'Neorealism in Italy 1930–1950: From Fascism to Resistance,' *Romance Languages Annual* 3 (1991), 155–9; *Fascist Modernities: Italy 1922–45* (Berkeley: U of California P forthcoming); and Bruno Falcetto, *Storia della narrativa neorealista* (Milan: Mursia, 1992). For the politics of neorealist aesthetics, see Lucia Re, *Calvino and the Age of Neorealism: Fables of Estrangement* (Stanford: Stanford UP, 1992), 15–30; and Robin Pickering-Iazzi, *Politics of the Visible: Writing Women, Culture, and Fascism* (Minneapolis: U of Minnesota P, 1997), esp. 124–88. For the poetic/poets' response to the neorealist agenda, see Keala Jewell, *The Poiesis of History: Experimenting with Genre in Postwar Italy* (Ithaca, NY: Cornell UP, 1992), esp. 1–22. My focus on the way Pratolini's novel disavows the liberatory politics believed present in the season of neorealism does not exclude readings of the novel that train on the author's oppositional practice outside of the relation of textual/sexual politics. For example, Silvia Ross has recently explored Pratolini's use of Florentine annual festivals, so numerous in the novel, as a means of staging a Bahktinian reading of Pratolini's 'resistance' to Fascism (Silvia Ross, 'Resistance and the Carnivalesque: Florentine Festivals in Pratolini's *Cronache di poveri amanti*,' unpublished paper presented at the American Association of Italian Studies, February 1997, Winston-Salem, North Carolina).

11 Although received knowledge of neorealism placed Pratolini in its vanguard, recent scholarship has called into question the political engagement of his art. As Re observes, 'Giuseppe Alicata uses [the term *neorealismo*] in his 1941 review of Pavese's novel [*Paesi tuoi*], and Eugenio Montale also employs it in his review of Vasco Pratolini's 1942 "slice-of-life" novel *Via de' Magazzini*. In both of these works, however, a sense of political commitment and a passionate adherence to the social issues of the present are either negligible or absent altogether' (Re, *Calvino and the Age of Neorealism*, 12). However, the lack of attention to then-contemporary social issues may be deliberate and may not impugn the author's political commitment in the way that Re believes.

12 Reported in *Gli alleati e la ricostruzione in Toscana*, ed. Roger Absalom (Florence: Olschki, 1988), 469, 472.

13 In their letters to Senator Merlin during parliamentary discussions of the proposed Merlin Law, prostitutes complained that they were unable to expunge their past in prostitution from their police records and, consequently, encountered serious difficulties relocating and finding work outside the sex trade; even though many wanted to leave the brothels, they chose to stay with the work and shelter that the *case chiuse* provided them. Cf. Merlin and Barberis, eds, *Lettere dalle case chiuse*, 94, 96, 109.

14 'Appendice documentaria,' in Merlin and Barberis, eds, *Lettere dalle case chiuse*, 163–203, esp. 163–72. See also Victoria de Grazia, *How Fascism Ruled Women: Italy 1922–45* (Berkeley: U of California P, 1992), esp. 44; Donato Francesco di Migliardo, 'Brevi considerazioni sulla legge 20 febbraio 1958,' *Archivio penale* 14 (1958), 462–5; and 'Il delitto di sfruttamento negli articoli 534 C.P. e negli artt. 3n8 e 4 della legge 20 febbraio 1958,' *Archivio penale* 15 (1959), 77–83; and Aldo Casalinuovo, 'Un nuovo capitolo nella storia del diritto italiano: Le norme penali della legge Merlin,' *Rivista penale* (1958), 553–72.

15 See Title X, Articles 545–55 in *Codice Penale e norme complementari*, 3rd ed., ed. Giovanni Conso (Milan: Giuffrè Editori, 1982), 200–2.

16 See 'Appendice documentaria' in Merlin and Barberis, eds, *Lettere dalla case chiuse*; and Mary Gibson, *Prostitution and the State in Italy, 1860–1915* (New Brunswick: Rutgers UP, 1986).

17 *La costituzione della repubblica italiana*, ed. Vincenzo Carullo (Bologna: Zuffi, 1950), 56. See also 56n3, in which prostitution is specifically included in this article. In fact, the criminalization of prostitution breaches Art. 2 (concerning inviolable human rights before the State), Art. 32 (concerning the right of the citizen to deny a prescribed medical treatment), and Art. 41 (concerning economic self-determination). See Tamar Pitch, 'La sessualità,

le norme, lo stato: Il dibattito sulla legge Merlin,' *memoria* 17:2 (1986), 24–41.

18 Gibson, *Prostitution and the State in Italy,* 224. Gibson observes that the advent of penicillin took the air out of the argument concerning public hygiene. She adds that women's suffrage, too, contributed to the ratification of the Merlin Law. However, I maintain that ten years (and these ten years, in particular) is no negligible amount of time in which to stage, time and again, the 'same' arguments recycled from a century earlier.

19 For more on the coeval constructions of nationalism and sexual identity, see George Mosse, *Nationalism and Sexuality: Middle-Class Morality and Sexual Norms in Modern Europe* (Madison: U of Wisconsin P, 1985); Klaus Theweleit, *Male Fantasies I: Women, Floods, Bodies, History* (Minneapolis: U of Minnesota P, 1987); Benedict Anderson, *Imagined Communities: Reflections on the Origin and Spread of Nationalism* (London: Verso, 1991); and *Nationalisms and Sexualities,* ed. Andrew Parker, Mary Russo, Doris Sommer, and Patricia Yeager (New York: Routledge, 1992).

20 See Pitch, 'La sessualità, le norme, lo stato'; and Lina Merlin's autobiography, *La mia vita,* ed. Elena Marinucci (Florence: Giunti Barbera, 1989).

21 Indeed, Pratolini's itemization bears remarkable resemblance to the details the prostitutes outline themselves in their letters to Senator Merlin. Cf. Merlin and Barberis, eds, *Lettere dalle case chiuse,* esp. 119–20 and 143–4.

22 Vasco Pratolini, *Cronache di poveri amanti,* in *Romanzi* (Milan: Mondadori, 1993), 737. All references will be to this edition and hereafter appear parenthetically in the text.

23 Cf. Alberto Asor Rosa, *Vasco Pratolini* (Rome: Edizioni Moderne, 1958), 130, where the critic blindly accepts Pratolini's seemingly egalitarian evaluation. I will say more directly of Asor Rosa's participation in Pratolini's assessment of prostitution, as well as of the evaluation of the author as a practitioner in the neorealist group.

24 Elio Vittorini's 1956 short novel, *Erica e i suoi fratelli* (which also lies within the time frame of ratification of the Merlin Law), documents the hypocrisy of working-class morality and offers an interesting comparison. The fourteen-year-old of the title, abandoned by her parents, becomes a prostitute in order to feed herself and her younger siblings; what results is general censure on the part of her neighbours, who, although barely subsisting themselves, have managed not to 'sink' to prostitution in order to survive.

25 The brothel appears as a refuge for the politically disparate in the literature of this, time as well as in cinema seeking to represent this era. Consider, for example, the brothel as social space in Vittorini's *Il garofano rosso* or Alberto Moravia's *La romana* (1947), which I will return to briefly below, or in films

like De Sica's *Ladri di bicicletta* (The Bicycle Thief; 1948) and Wertmüller's (re)vision in *Film d'amore e d'anarchia*.

26 For Lizzani's and Pratolini's responses to the film, see Lizzani's '"Cronache di poveri amanti": Il film,' in *Vasco Pratolini e il cinema*, ed. Andrea Vannini (Florence: Edizioni La Bottega del Cinema, 1987), 23–8; and, in the same volume, Pratolini's 'Testimonianza su "Cronache di poveri amanti,"' 29–30.

27 Ugo withdraws from the 'family' of Via del Corno, a manoeuvre Pratolini delineates literally in his removal from the Caressis' home. The hotel offers useful counterpoint to the home, and anticipates the next chapter concerning the space of home. As Mary Douglas says, 'The idea of the hotel is the perfect opposite of the home, not only because it uses market principles for its transactions, but because it allows its clients to buy privacy as a right of exclusion. This offends doubly the principle of the home whose rules and separations provide some limited privacy for each member.' See Mary Douglas, 'The Idea of a Home: A Kind of Space,' *Social Research* 58 (1991), 305.

28 Merlin and Barberis, eds, *Lettere dalle case chiuse*, 62.

29 This episode is based on an historical account of actual events in Florence in 1926. See Antoine Ottavi, 'La formation d'un romancier italien dans l'entre-deux-guerres: Vasco Pratolini,' in *Hommage à Louise Cohen: Langue et littérature italiennes (Annales de la faculté des lettres et sciences humaines de Nice* 42 [1982], 175–201).

30 This retreat performs an important function of signification and implies Pratolini's interest in the capacity of prose fiction to reproduce mimetically the real. In his review of Romano Bilenchi's 1935 novel *Il capofabbrica* for *Il Bargello*, Pratolini comments that 'The word is intended as "essentiality," without being the fruit of cerebral or forced virtuosity: Bilenchi's language gives back to the word its representational function by virtue of its Tuscan purity which stems from the best tradition' (quoted in Frank Rosengarten, *Vasco Pratolini: The Development of a Social Novelist* [Carbondale: Southern Illinois UP, 1965]). At the same time, Ben-Ghiat, in 'Neorealism in Italy, 1930–1950,' comments that it is just this kind of concern for 'Tuscan purity' that makes her call into question Pratolini's relationship to neorealist politics.

31 The original reads: '... Lentamente si avvicinavano, scorgendosi appena sotto la scorza delle diverse esperienze, che a poco a poco cadevano come la borraccina raschiata dalla pietra, ed apparivano le loro anime, che erano ugualmente *senza peccato*. Ed erano piante giovani, desiderose di affondare le radici in una terra sana. Diciamo: Amore' (869, emphasis added). This innocent state ('senza peccato') is virginal indeed, even more so since it directly concerns the transition from the sale and purchase of sex to sex given 'freely.'

32 Furthermore, the welter of detail required to distinguish between the many splinter factions that were constantly evolving under the Regime may have proved too cumbersome for Pratolini to manage in the narrative. Cf. Ben-Ghiat, 'The Politics of Realism.'

33 We may want to compare this kind of (suspect, fascist) voyeurism to that of Clerici in Bernardo Bertolucci's 1970 cinematic version of Moravia's *The Conformist*.

34 Karl Marx, 'The Economic and Philosophic Manuscripts of 1844,' in *The Marx-Engels Reader*, ed. Robert Tucker (New York: W.W. Norton, 1978), 103; emphases in original.

35 De Grazia, *How Facism Ruled Women*, 45.

36 Jeffrey Schnapp, in his *Staging Fascism: 18BL and the Theater of the Masses for the Masses* (Stanford: Stanford UP, 1996), offers a reading of the Fascist spectacle, '18BL ... teatro di masse per masse,' staged in Florence in April 1934. For advertising during Fascism, see Karen Pinkus, *Bodily Regimes: Italian Advertising under Fascism* (Minneapolis: U of Minnesota P, 1995). See also Marla Stone 'Staging Fascism: The Exhibition of the Fascist Revolution,' *Journal of Contemporary History* 28:2 1993, 215–43. See also Mabel Berezin *Making the Fascist Self: The Political Culture of Interwar Italy* (Ithaca: Cornell UP, 1997), for the primacy of the piazza during the Regime.

37 Dante, to use an early literary example, links spectacle, illusion, fraud, and prostitution together in the figure of Thais in *Inferno* 18.That this figure derives from Terence's play *Eunuco* serves also to bolster the performative (i.e., spectacular) aspects of this scene. In the *Inferno*, Thais endlessly repeats lines from the Roman play: 'Ho io grazie grandi apo te? / Anzi, maravigliose!' This constant iteration, which shows the *contrapasso* at work, meaningfully closes the canto. Thais's deceitful declaration implies the contamination of both speech and the content it tries to express, something rendered plastically by the image of her immersion in shit. Significantly, Dante and Virgil, at the beginning of the following canto, enter into the realm of the Simoniacs, those who have commercialized sacred things, creating a structural connection to prostitution in the *Comedy*. Thais is more than a spectacular figure from a spectacle (i.e., a play), for Dante, too, comments on the *vision* of the spectacle that her never-ending performance provides. The last verse of the canto states: 'E quinci sian le nostre *viste* sazie.' Pratolini makes a suprahistorical leap, linking Florence of the interwar and postwar period to the Florence of one of Dante's cohorts, Dino Compagni, a strategy that Re reminds us is redeployed in Pratolini's 'Cronache fiorentine XX secolo,' published in Vittorini's journal *Il Politecnico* in 1947. See Re, *Calvino and the Age of Neorealism*, 94–5.

38 In the system of the *case chiuse*, workers' earnings were eroded by petty corruption. Prostitution offered many angles of exploitation, some of which, while ethically suspect, were perfectly legal. These included, for example, office visits to physicians authorized to declare the prostitutes' state of health. These physicians often invented small medical excuses (lice or parasites, etc.) for which the sex workers would need to remove themselves from work for several days, endangering their next payment to either the physician or to the Madam.

Closer to home, the prostitutes were expected to pay the Madam varying sums in the form of 'tips' (*mance*) every two weeks. This sum, as detailed by the prostitute correspondents as well as an accountant who had worked for fifteen years in a well-known Milanese locale, significantly ate into the workers' earnings. For example, if the *signorine* were paid 100,000 lire per day, the tip was expected to be 15,000 lire at the end of two weeks. See Merlin and Barberis, eds, *Lettere dalle case chiuse*, esp. 124–5.

39 From beginning to end, the novel is not unlike Thornton Wilder's *Our Town*; it is a popular drama whose dramatic apparatus includes a narrator, direct address to the audience, stage directions and 'dialoghetti paralleli' (the unmediated speech between the lovers) like those in a Goldoni play. The novel itself brims with reference to performance: while Via del Corno is described as a stage, there are also references to the 'comedy' of life, theatrical characters (e.g., Stenterello), the 'chorus' of the *cornacchiai*, to street theatre like the annual *scampanata* or Carnival masques, and to song and dance. See Ruggero Jaccobi, 'Uno spettacolo a scena fissa e multipla,' in *Vasco Pratolini*, ed. Luciano Lusi (Taranto: Mandes Editore, 1988), 172–6.

40 Jaccobi, 'Uno spettacolo,' 172.

41 Re, *Calvino and the Age of Neorealism*, 96.

42 Elio Vittorini, *Il garofano rosso* (Milan: Mondadori, 1947), 221.

43 Cf. Pier Raimondo Baldini's work on the variants of the novel in his 'Varianti vittoriniane: *Il garofano rosso*,' *Canadian Journal of Italian Studies* 7:26–7 (1984), 1–15.

44 Written while Moravia was in Fondi in 1943, *La romana* does not, I would say, echo the public discourse of the Merlin Law in the way of *Cronache*. For the composition of the novel, see Thomas Peterson, *Alberto Moravia* (New York: Twayne, 1996), 41–50.

45 For the way his sexual 'perversion' subtends his political perversion, we may care to see Astarita as a precursor to Clerici, the protagonist of Moravia's 1951 novel *Il conformista* (The Conformist).

46 Cinematic representation of Fascists routinely depicts them as sexual deviants, especially, it appears, in the 1970s. Cf. Pontecorvo's *Kapò* (1959), Ber-

tolucci's *The Conformist* (1970) and *1900* (1975–6), Cavani's *Il portiere di notte* (The Night Porter; 1974), Pasolini's *Salò* (1975), and Wertmüller's *Pasqualino Settebellezze* (Seven Beauties; 1976).

47 Cf. Ann McClintock, 'Sex Workers and Sex,' *Social Text* 37 (Winter 1993), 1–10.

48 'Olympe' was in France one of the *noms-de-guerre* frequently assumed by upper-class prostitutes. Dumas *fils* gave the name 'Olympe' to the mercenary courtesan, modern rival of the sentimental Marguerite, in *La dame aux camélias*, and the name was used frequently in the popular literature and drama of the 1860s (such as Augier's *Le Mariage d'Olympe*). Another critic points to yet two earlier theatrical instances of Olympias: Félicien David's opera *Herculanum*, popular throughout the 1850s, and Zacherie Astruc's unpublished play 'Les dialogues des vierges folles et des vierges sages.' See Charles Bernheimer, *Figures of Ill Repute: Representing Prostitutes in Nineteenth-Century France* (Cambridge: Harvard UP, 1989); Sharon Flescher, 'More on a Name: Manet's *Olympia* and the Defiant Heroine in Mid-Nineteenth-Century France,' *Art Journal* 45 (1985), 27–35; Amy Millstone, 'French Feminist Theater and the Subject of Prostitution,' in *The Image of the Prostitute in Modern Literature*, ed. Pierre Horn and Mary Beth Pringle (New York: Frederick Ungar, 1984), 19–27; and Hollis Clayson, *Painted Love: Prostitution in French Art of the Impressionist Era* (New Haven: Yale UP, 1991).

49 Cesira Fiori, *Una donna nelle carceri fasciste* (Rome: Riuniti Editori, 1965), 82. See also Barbara Spackman, *Decadent Genealogies: The Rhetoric of Sickness from Baudelaire to D'Annunzio* (Ithaca and London: Cornell UP, 1988); and Nancy Harrowitz, *Anti-Semitism, Misogyny, and the Logic of Cultural Difference* (Lincoln: U of Nebraska P, 1995). In *La psicoanalisi nella cultura italiana* (Turin: Boringhieri, 1966), Michel David cites an article from *La stampa* in December 1965 that claimed Lombrosianism was alive and well ('redignified'). For Lombroso's importance to Fascist criminal anthropology, see G.G. Perrando, 'La medicina legale italiana nell'ultimo decennio,' *Archivio di antropologia criminale* 47 (1927), 562–89.

50 See Franco Pelella, 'Riabilitare Lombroso,' *Risorgimento* 41:3 (1989), 283–314; and Elena Bernart and Marello Tricarico, 'Per una rilettura dell'opera di C. Lombroso,' *Physis* 18:2 (1976), 179–84.

51 Elisa's 'diseased heart' nicely dovetails with the story of another prostitute in Pratolini's work, Bianca in *Le amiche* (1939), who, significantly, dies of heart disease.

52 Prostitution offers the quintessentially consensual act (saving, naturally, the way in which women may find coercive factors in dismal socio-economic conditions). Seen in this light, Pratolini's conflation of prositution and fascism paves the way for the notion of 'consent' that will characterize the postwar

critical evaluation of Fascism. The belief that the Italian public acquiesced to Fascism, consenting to and therefore permitting its advent, will find its chief spokesperson in Renzo de Felice, whose *Interpretazioni del fascismo* appeared first in 1969. The belief that consent is a prerequisite to Fascism seems to be alive and well, judging from the clamour surrounding Daniel Goldhagen's recent study of National Socialism, *Hitler's Willing Executioners: Ordinary Germans and the Holocaust* (New York: A.A. Knopf, 1996).

53 It is worth noting how Pratolini architecturally ensures the Signora's conflation with the Duce. Following her massive stroke (*emorragia cerebrale*), which the *cornacchiai* misinterpret as her desire to defenestrate herself, the Signora, greatly diminished, performs her own kind of pantomime for the street from her windowsill. 'Ella si spenzola dalla finestra, agita le mani per scacciare gli importuni, segna col dito i due orizzonti, abbraccia le case con un gesto, si batte il petto, *mugola* risentita come dire "Questo è tutto mio! Via! Sciò! Tutti!" (988, emphasis added). The satirical dumbshow completes itself when she is reduced to blowing bubbles for the (delighted) children in the street. Diane Ghirardo has commented on the architectural primacy of the balcony itself in the construction of the New Towns in the Agro Pontine, the triumph of Fascist rebuilding of the State that took place between 1928 and 1940. Discussing the central piazza of Littoria, she notes that the balcony and the tower, positioned above the square, provide a 'stage for the theatrical presentation of the Duce. The tower is emblematic of the Duce's figure standing above ... either in reality or symbolically through his representative. The gesture of the Fascist salute ... corresponds to the gestural funtion of the tower ... The tower ... becomes itself the locus of memory, power, and order, an ever-present, starkly compelling backdrop for the virtual presence of the Duce' (Diane Ghirardo, *Building New Communities: New Deal America and Fascist Italy* [Princeton: Princeton UP, 1989], 89).

54 Asor Rosa, *Vasco Pratolini*, 140.

55 Asor Rosa, 142.

56 Pickering-Iazzi, *Politics of the Visible*, 183–4.

57 Gibson, *Prostitution and the State in Italy*, 194; quoted in Pickering-Iazzi, *Politics of the Visible*.

58 The other two episodes of 'Una storia italiana' are *Lo scialo* (1960) and *Allegoria e derisione* (1966).

59 Fernand Braudel, *On History*, tr. Sarah Matthews (Chicago: U of Chicago, 1980), 2.

60 The aforementioned 'Cronache fiorentine xx secolo' and both *Cronaca familiare* and *Cronache* all appeared in 1947. Critics tend to see the analogy between Compagni and Pratolini more readily than the one between Prato-

lini and another early Florentine chronicler, Giovanni Villani, for the reason that Compagni (and Pratolini following his lead) concentrates on the political factionalism of Florence.

61 Pratolini, 'Cronache fiorentine xx secolo,' quoted in Asor Rosa, *Vasco Pratolini*, 136 (attribution of emphasis unknown).

62 Asor Rosa, 137 (attribution of emphasis unknown).

63 Asor Rosa, 143.

64 Asor Rosa, 144.

65 Gayle Rubin, 'The Traffic in Women: Notes on the "Political Economy" of Sex,' in *Toward an Anthropology of Women*, ed. Rayna Reiter (New York: Monthly Press, 1975), 172.

5: House Arrest

1 Simone Weil, *Cahiers I* (Paris: Plon, 1951), 53.

2 For an intelligent reading of homicide in Ginzburg and de Céspedes, see Sandra Carletti, '"Gli ho sparato negli occhi": Gender Conflict and Homicide in Alba de Céspedes's *Dalla parte di lei* and Natalia Ginzburg's *È stato così*,' in *Gendered Contexts*, ed. Julia Harrison et al. (New York: P. Lang, 1996), 153–64. Margherita Di Fazio identifies a thematic of homicidal women in fin-de-siècle Italian narrative; see her 'La donna omicida: Narrative italiana fra Ottocento e Novecento,' in *Diritto e rovescio: Studi sulle donne e il controllo sociale*, ed. Tamar Pitch (Naples: Edizioni scientifiche italiane, 1987), 237–56. See also Ruth Harris, *Murders and Madness: Medicine, Law, and Society in the Fin-de-siècle* (Oxford: Clarendon P, 1989). In both *Dalla parte di lei* as well as her interventions in *Mercurio*, the journal of art and politics that she edited, de Céspedes addresses the absence of women in the Italian judiciary. See Ellen Nerenberg, 'Resistance and Remorse: Alba de Céspedes's Withdrawal from the Public Sphere,' in *Writing beyond Fascism: Cultural Resistance in the Life and Works of Alba de Céspedes*, ed. Carole Gallucci and Ellen Nerenberg (Cranbury, NJ: Fairleigh-Dickinson UP, 2000). Significantly, women were not permitted to take a degree in law until 1919 and were not eligible for judgeships until 1962; early visionaries included, for example, Lidia Poët, Teresa Labriola, Romelia Troise, Elisa Comani in Ancona, Fausta Dogliotti in Genoa, and Bice Daneo in Milan. For more on women jurists, see Michaela De Giorgio, *Le italiane dall'Unità a oggi: Modelli culturali e comportamenti sociali* (Rome-Bari: Laterza, 1992), 479–84.

3 Biddy Martin and Chandra Mohanty, 'Feminist Politics: What's Home Got to Do with It?' in *Feminist Studies/Cultural Studies*, ed. Teresa de Lauretis (Bloomington: Indiana UP, 1986), 191–212.

4 Sigmund Freud, 'The Uncanny,' in *Freud, Standard Edition*, ed. James Strachey (London: Hogarth, 1957), 17:226.
5 For the no/place of home, see *Utopias*, ed. Peter Alexander and Roger Gill (London: Duckworth, 1984). With specific interest in the feminist aspect of the good/no place, see Lucy Sargisson, *Contemporary Feminist Utopianism* (New York and London: Routledge, 1996); Frances Bartkowski, *Feminist Utopias* (Lincoln: U of Nebraska P, 1989); Gillian Rose, *Feminism and Geography* (London and New York: Routledge, 1993), esp. 53–60; and Yi-Fu Tuan, *Space and Place: The Perspective of Experience* (Minneapolis: U of Minnesota P, 1987), esp. 136–41. In the growing bibliography concerning Utopia and its spatial variants, see Louis Marin, *Utopics* (Atlantic Highlands, NJ: Humanities International P, 1990), and 'Frontiers of Utopia: Past and Present,' *Critical Inquiry* 19:3 (1992), 397–420. See also Gianni Vattimo, *Transparent Society*, tr. David Webb (Baltimore: Johns Hopkins UP, 1992), esp. 62–75; Michel Foucault, 'Of Other Spaces,' *Diacritics* 16:1 (1986), 22–7; and Kevin Heatherington, *The Badlands of Modernity: Heterotopia and Social Ordering* (London and New York: Routledge, 1997).
6 Mary Douglas, 'The Idea of a Home: A Kind of Space,' *Social Research* 58 (1991), 289; see also Akiko Busch, *Geography of Home: Writings on Where We Live* (New York: Princeton Architectural P, 1999).
7 As I point out in chapter 1, this is the same logic by which Barbara Spackman impugns Marie Antonietta Macciocchi's study of the participation of Italian women in the Regime, *La donna 'nera': 'Consenso' femminile e fascismo* (Milan: Feltrinelli, 1976). See Barbara Spackman, *Fascist Virilities: Rhetoric, Ideology, and Social Fantasy in Italy* (Minneapolis: U of Minnesota P, 1996), 27.
8 Although Peter Hainsworth does not take the representation of women as a prime index, he arrives at a similar conclusion with regard to the subject's position vis-à-vis the Fascist State in Gadda's work. Gadda, he writes, 'oscillates between analysis of Fascism as an objective phenomenon and a mode of writing which is itself contaminated with at least some of the features he lays at Mussolini's doors.' However, Hainsworth also points out how dangerous it may have been for Gadda to claim his attraction to Mussolini and to Fascism. See Hainsworth, 'Fascism and Anti-fascism in Gadda,' in *Carlo Emilio Gadda: Contemporary Perspectives*, ed. Manuela Bertone and Robert Dombroski (Toronto: U of Toronto P, 1997), 229.
9 The lack of 'completion' in the *Pasticciaccio* is a well-established *topos* in Gadda criticism. See Arnaldo Ceccaroni, 'Per una lettura del Pasticciaccio,' *Lingua e stile* 5 (1975), 57–85; Walter Pedullà, 'La dialettica degli opposti come fondamento dell'incompiutezza,' in *Leggere Gadda: Antologia della critica gaddiana*, ed. Arnaldo Ceccaroni (Bologna: Zanichelli, 1978), 133–6;

Michel Butor, 'Gadda e la tragedia dell'incompiuto,' in Ceccaroni, ed., *Leggere Gadda*, 68–70; JoAnn Cannon, 'The Reader as Detective: Notes on Gadda's *Pasticciaccio*,' *Modern Language Studies* 10 (Fall 1980), 41–50; and Gerhard van der Linde, 'The Body in the Labyrinth: Detection, Rationality, and the Feminine in Gadda's *Pasticciaccio*,' *American Journal of Italian Studies* 21:57 (1998), 26–40.

10 Benito Mussolini, *Opera omnia*, ed. Edoardo and Duilio Susmel (Florence: La Fenice, 1951) 17:363–4. For reworkings of this theory later in the Regime, see Manlio Pompei, 'Demografia: Punto e daccapo,' *Critica fascista* 15:9 (1 March 1937), 135–6; 'Stato fascista e famiglia fascista' [anonymous author], *Critica fascista* 15:8 (15 Feb. 1937), 113–16; and Vittorio Zincone, 'Politica demografica,' *Critica fascista* 18:8 (15 Feb. 1940), 136. The newly designed homes in the Agro Pontine New Towns featured increased numbers of bedrooms to accommodate the predicted – and desired – growth in population. See Diane Ghirardo, *Building New Communities: New Deal America and Fascist Italy* (Princeton: Princeton UP, 1989).

11 Dolores Hayden, *The Power of Place* (Cambridge: MIT P, 1995), 22.

12 For boys and young men's organizations, see chapter 3 above; and Tracy Koon, *Believe, Obey, Fight: The Political Socialization of Youth in Fascist Italy, 1922–45* (Chapel Hill, NC: U of North Carolina P, 1985). For the organization of adults into afterwork programs, see Victoria de Grazia, *The Culture of Consent: The Organization of Mass Leisure in Fascist Italy* (New York and Cambridge: Cambridge UP, 1981). For the ONMI, see Victoria de Grazia, *How Fascism Ruled Women: Italy, 1922–45* (Berkeley: U of California P, 1992).

13 Dennis Doordan, *Building Modern Italy: Italian Architecture, 1914–1936* (New York: Princeton Architectural P, 1988), 137. For the ways in which the spatial relations in the New Towns of the Agro Pontine displayed political and social strategies of the PNF, see Ghirardo, *Building New Communities*, 62 ff. See also L. Ferrario and D. Pastore, *Giuseppe Terragni: La casa del fascio* (Rome: Istituto Mides, 1982); Thomas Schumacher, *Surface and Symbol: Giuseppe Terragni and the Architecture of Italian Rationalism* (Princeton: Princeton UP, 1991); and *Giuseppe Terragni*, ed. Bruno Zevi (Bologna: Zanichelli, 1980), esp. 78–83.

14 See *Il razionalismo e l'architettura in Italia durante il fascismo*, ed. Silvia Danesi and Luciano Panetta (Venice: Edizioni del Biennale, 1976), esp. 7–52. Not all *case del fascio* exemplified such architectural trends in the way of Terragni; many were instated in retrofitted *palazzi* or in newer buildings designed along the lines of a more traditional architectural style. I thank Joseph Siry for this observation.

15 Spackman, *Fascist Virilities*, 52.

16 See Giulio Ernesti, *La costruzione dell'utopia: Architetti e urbanisti nell'Italia fascista* (Rome: Edizioni lavoro, 1988).

17 See Doordan, *Building Modern Italy*, 137–41.

18 See Marla Stone, *The Patron State: Culture and Politics in Fascist Italy* (Princeton: Princeton UP, 1998), 148.

19 See Lidia Sciama, 'The Problem of Privacy in Mediterranean Anthropology,' in *Women and Space*, ed. Shirley Ardener (New York: St Martin's, 1981), 89–111; and Douglas, 'The Idea of a Home.'

20 See Millicent Marcus, *Italian Film in the Light of Neorealism* (Princeton: Princeton UP, 1992), 33–53.

21 See Marguerite Waller, 'Back to the Future: Dante and the Languages of Post-War Italian Film,' in *Dante in the Movies and on Television*, ed. Amilcare Iannucci (Toronto: U of Toronto P, forthcoming).

22 Cf. Federico Bellini, *Mario Ridolfi* (Bari-Rome: Laterza, 1993), esp. 51–79.

23 Ernesto Nathan Rogers, 'The House of Man,' *Domus* (1946), quoted in Vittorio Gregotti, *New Directions in Italian Architecture*, tr. Giuseppina Salvadori (New York: George Braziller, 1968), 38.

24 Quoted in Gregotti, *New Directions in Italian Architecture*, 38. Cf. Carlo Aymonino, 'Storia e cronaca del Quartiere Tiburtino,' *Casabella continuità* [*Domus*] 215 (1957), 20.

25 See Giorgio Muratore, 'Gli anni della Ricostruzione,' *Controspazio* (Nov. 1974), 6–25. In an interview, Zevi described the political commitment of the APAO membership: 'L'APAO nacque come formazione politica, il nostro era un impegno in primo luogo politico ... Per il resto noi appartenevamo a diversi partiti, sempre della sinistra, sempre del rinnovamento' (quoted in Bellini, *Mario Ridolfi*, 159n6). On the political composition of the APAO, see also Manfredo Tafuri, *Ludovico Quaroni e lo sviluppo dell'architettura moderna in Italia* (Milan: Garzanti, 1964), 79ff.

26 Paul Ginsborg, *A History of Contemporary Italy: Society and Politics 1943–88* (London: Penguin, 1990), 246–7.

27 See Ginsborg, *A History of Contemporary Italy*; Marcello Fabbri, *L'urbanistica italiana dal dopoguerra a oggi* (Bari: De Donato, 1983); 'Provvedimenti urgenti per la ricostruzione,' *Rassegna del primo convegno nazionale per la ricostruzione edilizia* 3 (1945); *La situazione della casa in Italia*, ed. Nicola Sinopoli (Milan: Franco Angeli, 1976); Giorgio Ruffolo, *Riforme e controriforme* (Bari-Rome: Laterza, 1975); *Inchiesta sulla miseria in Italia*, ed. Paolo Braghin (Turin: Einaudi, 1978); Marianella Pirzio Biroli Sclavi, 'L'inchiesta sulla miseria in Italia,' *Memoria* 6 (1982), 96–100; Franco Crespi and Franco Martinelli, 'La dinamica delle relazioni sociali nel contesto urbano,' *Rivista di sociologia* 6:16 (1968), 5–50; Ludovico Quaroni, 'Politica del quar-

tiere,' in *La città fisica,* ed. Antonio Terranova (Bari-Rome: Laterza, 1981), 105–23.

28 This comparison may be extended to include Ridolfi's designs for the new prison in Cosenza as well, built, like the Nuoro prison, during 1953–5.

29 See chapter 3 for a full discussion of the history of penal architecture in Italy. See also Renzo Dubbini, *Architettura delle prigioni: I luoghi e il tempo della punizione (1700–1880)* (Milan: Franco Angeli, 1986).

30 Cinema offers an example of the proximity to and role of the prison in residential Naples in a film like Vittorio De Sica's 1964 *Ieri, Oggi, e domani* (Yesterday, Today, and Tomorrow) with Sophia Loren and Marcello Mastroianni.

31 See Massimo Pavarini, 'La città e il suo rovescio: Note in tema di carcere e metropoli,' *La nuova città* 1 (April 1983), 12–29; and his 'La periferia penitenziaria,' in *Un fossile chiamato carcere: Scritti sul carcere,* ed. Corrado Marcetti and Nicola Solimano (Florence: Angelo Pontecorboli, 1993), 14–24. The relocation to the urban periphery of carceral space only increased in importance, especially in the 1970s, when Italy began constructing maximum security prisons. Three pairs of comparisons make this point clear: In Rome, Regina Coeli and Rebibbia; the Murate complex (now the faculty of architecture at the university, a fact not without some irony) and Sollicciano in Florence; and, in Milan, San Vittore and Opera.

32 See Giorgio Muratore, 'Le nuove carceri di Nuoro,' *Controspazio* 3 (1974), 44–9; Federico Bellini and Valerio Palmieri, *Mario Ridolfi: Guida all'architettura* (Verona: Arsenale Editrice, 1997), esp. 45–53.

33 See Peter Rowe, *Modernity and Housing* (Cambridge: MIT P, 1993).

34 For a history of the *concorsi,* or competitions, see Carlo Aymonino, 'Storia e cronaca del Quartiere Tiburtino,' *Casabella continuità* 215 (1957), 19–23.

35 Manfredo Tafuri, *History of Italian Architecture, 1944–85,* tr. Jessica Levine (Cambridge: MIT P, 1989), 17. See also Carlo Chiarini and Marcello Girelli, 'Dal Tiburtino a Matera,' *Domus* 231 (1959), 25–6; and Giancarlo De Carlo, 'Architetture italiane,' *Casabella continuità* 199 (1957), 19–33.

36 Tafuri, *History of Italian Architecture,* 17.

37 Gimsborg, *A History of Contemporary Italy,* 244; see also Laura Balbo, *Stato di famiglia* (Milan: Garzanti, 1976), esp. 184–5.

38 Ginsborg, *A History of Contemporary Italy,* 215. We remember the finale of Mario Monicelli's 1958 film *I soliti ignoti* (Big Deal on Madonna Street), when Tiberio (Marcello Mastroianni) derides Cappanelle (Carlo Pisacane) for his infatuation with the novelty of the 'icebox' in the kitchen of the apartment they have just failed to burgle.

39 See Annalisa Avon, '"La casa all'italiana": Modernismo, ragione, e tradizione nell'organizzazione dello spazio domestico dal 1927 al 1930,' in *La*

costruzione dell'utopia: Architetti e urbanisti nell'Italia fascista, ed. Guilio Ernesti (Rome: Edizioni lavoro, 1988), 47–66; Marjan Boot, Ineke van Hamersveld, and Juliette Roding, *La casalinga riflessiva: La cucina razionale come mito domestico negli anni '20 e '30* (Rome: Multigrafica, 1983); and de Grazia, *How Fascism Ruled Women*, 101–2. See also Dolores Hayden, *The Grand Domestic Revolution: A History of Feminist Designs for American Homes, Neighborhoods, and Cities* (Cambridge: MIT P, 1981); and Barbara Ehrenreich and Deirdre English. 'The Manufacture of Housework,' *Socialist Revolution* 26 (1975), 5–40.

40 I discuss the split between the 1947 writing of the novel and its historical setting in the preceding chapter.

41 Alberto Moravia, *La romana* (Milan: Bompiani, 1980), 305. All references are to this edition and hereafter appear parenthetically in the text.

42 Loris Rambelli, *Storia del 'giallo' italiano* (Milan: Garzanti, 1979), 12.

43 Quoted in Stefano Tani, *The Doomed Detective: The Contribution of the Detective Novel to Postmodern Italian and American Fiction* (Carbondale: Southern Illinois UP, 1984), 21 (emphasis added). We might consider other 'containers' featured in detective stories in the vein Benjamin describes. On this front, we could consider Romualdo Natoli's *La camera sigillata* (Milan: Sonzogno, 1938); Pietro Mormino's *Mezzanotte al castello* (Milan: Sonzogno, 1938); or the 'astuccio cinese' [Chinese pocketbook] in Umberto Foccaccia's 'giallo' of the same name (*L'astuccio cinese* [Milan: Sonzogno, 1940]). For the development of Gothic space in Italian cinema of the latter half of the 1950s, see Stefano della Casa, *The Stepbrothers of Neorealism*, catalog for the 27th Rotterdam International Film Festival (Feb 1998).

44 Quoted in Rambelli, *Storia del 'giallo' italiano*, 115. See also Ernest Mandel, *Delitti per diletto: Storia del romanzo poliziesco* (Milan: Intern Giallo, 1990).

45 Rambelli, 115. See also Angela Felice, 'Il "giallo" a scuola: I ragazzi,' *Problemi* 79 (May–Aug. 1987), 192–209.

46 Rambelli, 37.

47 See Sigmund Freud, 'The Uncanny,' in *Freud, Standard Edition*, ed. James Strachey (London: Hogarth, 1957), 17:219–52.

48 'The Detective and the Boundary: Some Notes on the Postmodern Literary Imagination,' *Boundary 2* 1(Fall 1972), 159. See also Claus Reinert, 'Beschreibung des *Unheimlichen*,' in *Das Unheimliche und die Detektivliteratur* (Bonn: Bouvier Verlag Herbert Grundmann, 1973), 16–26.

49 Jürgen Thorwald outlines the developments in these laboratory methods in his *Crime and Science*, tr. Richard and Clara Winston (New York: Harcourt, Brace & World, 1967).

50 For the Girardi case, see Thorwald 38–45; for the Canella case, see Leonardo

Sciascia, *Il teatro della memoria* (Turin: Einaudi, 1981). See also Karen Pinkus, '"Black" and "Jew": Race and the Resistance to Psychoanalysis in Italy,' *Annali d'Italianistica* 16 (1998), esp. 151–4.

51 Rambelli attests to the success of detective novels in translation in the Italian market of the '20s.

52 See Thomas Sebeok and Jean Umiker-Sebeok, '"You Know My Method": A Juxtaposition of Charles S. Peirce and Sherlock Holmes,' in *The Sign of Three: Dupin, Holmes, Peirce*, ed. Umberto Eco and Thomas Sebeok (Bloomington: Indiana UP, 1983), 11–54, esp. 39ff. See also Irving Copi, *Introduction to Logic* (New York: Macmillan, 1961), 433–45.

53 Carlo Emilio Gadda, *Quer pasticciaccio brutto de via Merulana* [1957] (Milan: Garzanti, 1983), 73–5. All references are to this edition and hereafter appear parenthetically in the text.

54 See Joan McConnell, *A Vocabulary Analysis of Gadda's 'Pasticciaccio'* (University, MS: Romance Monographs, 1973).

55 Freud, 'The Uncanny,' 228.

56 In an exhaustive reading of the semantic and philosophical significance of the word 'pasticcio' as it appears throughout Gadda's corpus, Gian Carlo Roscioni observes that in *Quer pasticciaccio*, 'pasticcio' intends 'l'aspetto concreto, oggettivo fisico del crimine.' See *La disarmonia prestabilita* (Turin: Einaudi, 1969), esp. 82–100.

57 '*Heimlich*; adj. and adv. vernaculus, occultus' (Freud, 'The Uncanny,' 225). Also: '*Heimlich*, as used of knowledge – mystic, allegorical: A *heimlich* meaning mysticus, divinus, occultus, figuratus' ('The Uncanny,' 226).

58 The Christian Democrats warned against the Communist excesses of 'free love' should they take the April election. See Ginsborg, *A History of Contemporary Italy*, 117; *C'era una volta la DC*, ed. Luca Romano and Paolo Scabello (Rome, 1975); and Antonio Gambino, *Storia del dopoguerra dalla Liberazione al potere DC* (Rome- Bari: Laterza, 1975).

59 For such schemata, see, among others, Emiliana Noether, 'Italian Women under Fascism: A Reevaluation,' *Italian Quarterly*, 32 (1982), 69–80; *When Biology Becomes Destiny: Women in Weimar and Nazi Germany*, ed. R. Bridenthal, A. Grossmann, and M. Kaplan (New York: Monthly Review, 1984); Elisabetta Mondello, *La nuova italiana: La donna nella stampa e nella cultura del ventennio* (Rome: Riuniti, 1987); de Grazia, *How Fascism Ruled Women*; Mariolina Graziosi, 'Gender Struggle and the Social Manipulation of Gender Identity in the Interwar Years,' in Pickering-Iazzi, ed., *Mothers of Invention*, 26–51; Lucia Re, 'The Fascist Theories of "Woman" and the Construction of Gender,' in Pickering-Iazzi, ed., *Mothers of Invention*, 76–99. On the homoerotic aspect of the gynaeceum see Elaine Marks, 'Lesbian Intertextuality,' in *Homosexualities*

and French Literature, ed. Elaine Marks and George Stambolian (Ithaca, NY: Cornell UP, 1979), 357–8.

60 I share Manuela Bertone's view of the nearly compulsive repetition of matricide in Gadda's oeuvre. Given the so noticeable missing maternity for Liliana, one wonders if this murder isn't a sort of matricide manqué. See Manuela Bertone, 'Murderous Desires: Gaddian Matricides from *Novella seconda* to *La cognizione del dolore*,' in Bertone and Dombroski, eds, *Carlo Emilio Gadda*, 112.

61 In chapter 2 I discussed the relation between Drogo's enthralled paralysis as he stood before the 'vaginalized' desert and the uncanny. Don Ciccio, too, recalls that neurotic man who, Freud writes, 'feel[s] there is something uncanny about the female genital organs. This *Unheimlich* place, however, is the entrance to the former Heim [home] of all human beings, to the place where each of us lived once upon a time and in the beginning. There is a joke saying that "Love is home-sickness"; and whenever a man dreams of a place or a country and says to himself, while he is dreaming: "this place is familiar to me, I've been here before," we may interpret the place as being his mother's genitals or her body ... the prefix "un" is the token of repression' (Freud, 'The Uncanny,' 245). With reference to *La cognizione del dolore*, Manuela Bertone believes that Gadda 'represents, perhaps unintentionally, Freud's aetiology of neurosis' (Bertone, 'Murderous Desires,' 129n5).

62 I am referring to Julia Kristeva's classic 1982 study *The Powers of Horror: An Essay on Abjection*, tr. Leon Roudiez (New York: Columbia UP, 1982), and the process of abjection she outlines 'wherein the subject repels and seeks escape from the horrific mother.' Freeland's objections to the near constant deployment of the abject as a heuristic in cinema studies are reasonable: All births are not monstrous and all fears are not associated to the primal mother. The alternation between love for the mother and fear of becoming engulfed by the mother and all of her soil (and specifically menstrual blood) strikes me as particularly salient in Gadda's treatment of motherhood in *Quer pasticciaccio*. See Cynthia Freeland, 'Feminist Frameworks for Horror Films,' in *Post-Theory: Reconstructing Film Studies*, ed. David Bordwell and Noël Carroll (Madison: U of Wisconsin P, 1996), esp. 195–203.

63 See also van der Linde, 'The Body in the Labyrinth.'

64 See Laura Kipnis, '(Male) Desire vs. (Female) Disgust: Reading *Hustler*,' in *Cultural Studies*, ed. Lawrence Grossman, Cary Nelson, and Paula Treichler (New York: Routledge, 1992), 373–91. The position of Liliana's body, specifically the skirt thrown back over the head, is reminiscent of another woman, namely Claretta Petacci, whose death scene – popularized through its repetition in the press – also featured the up-ended skirt of an inert female body.

65 Margherita Sarfatti, 'Italia d'oggi,' *Augustea* 23 (1933), 655, anthologized in *Sposa e madre esemplare*, ed. Piero Meldini (Florence and Rimini: Guaraldi Editori, 1975), 228–30. Sarfatti's concern for the 'cell' of the family hardly disappears following the ouster of the Regime. However, rather than Fascists espousing such pro-family rhetoric, it is Communists who deploy such language. In 1946, Leonilde Lotti opines in the pages of *Rinascita*, the official organ of the PCI (Communist Party) that the family 'si presenta ora più che mai come nucleo primordiale ... per il rinnovamento materiale e morale della vita italiana.' See *Rinascita* (Rome: Riuniti, 1976), 224. I thank Anna Maria Torriglia for pointing out this to me.

66 Carlo Emilio Gadda, *Eros e Priapo* (Milan: Grazanti, 1967), 73. See also Spackman's exceptional analysis in *Fascist Virilities*, 1–7 and 24–6.

67 See Spackman, *Fascist Virilities*, Karen Pinkus, *Bodily Regimes: Italian Advertising under Fascism* (Minneapolis: U of Minnesota P, 1995); Robin Pickering-Iazzi, *Politics of the Visible* (Minneapolis: U of Minnesota P, 1997); and Marie Antonietta Macciocchi, *La donna 'nera': 'Consenso' femminile e fascismo* (Milan: Feltrinelli, 1976), esp. 29–105.

68 See de Grazia, *How Fascism Ruled Women*, 18–20; and Christopher Seton-Watson, *Italy from Liberalism to Fascism, 1870–1925* (London: Methuen, 1967).

69 Carlo Emilio Gadda, 'Quer pasticciaccio,' *Letteratura* 28 (1947), 74–5.

70 Robert Dombroski, *Introduzione allo studio di Gadda* (Florence: Vallechi Editore, 1967), 113–14. See also Gian Paolo Biasin, *I sapori della modernità: Cibo e romanzo* (Bologna: Il Mulino, 1991), 134 and 139n32. For other important legal trials of women in the period, including the Montesi scandal, see Michaela De Giorgio, *Le italiane dall'Unità a oggi: Modelli culturali e comportamenti sociali* (Rome-Bari: Laterza, 1992), esp. 479ff.; and A. Garofalo, *L'italiana in Italia* (Bari, Laterza, 1956).

71 Gadda, 'Quer pasticciaccio,' *Letteratura* 29 (1947), 54.

72 The female body often showcases physical deformity in Gadda's oeuvre. See Margaret Baker, 'The Women Characters of Carlo Emilio Gadda,' in *Visions and Revisions*, ed. Mirna Cicioni and Nicole Prunster (Oxford: Berg Publishers, 1993), 53–5.

73 In her germinal study of witchcraft in Western Europe, M.A. Murray writes that 'every contemporary writer who gives a general view of religion, observes the witches' power over human fertility' (M.A. Murray, *The Witch Cult in Western Euope* [Oxford: Clarendon P, 1962], 173). Carlo Ginzburg endorsed Murray's claims about the relation between witchcraft and fertility rites. In the preface to the English edition of *I benandanti* (The Night Battles, in Italian in 1966 and English in 1983), he confirms at least her cardinal point. See *The Night Battles*, tr. John and Anne Tedeschi (Baltimore: Johns

Hopkins UP, 1983), xiii.

74 Quoted in Murray, *The Witch Cult,* 24.

75 Nina Auerbach, *Communities of Women: An Idea in Fiction* (Cambridge: Harvard UP, 1978).

76 Cf. Julia Kristeva, 'Women's Time,' in *The Kristeva Reader,* ed. Toril Moi (New York: Columbia UP, 1986), 187–213.

77 *Relazione ministeriale al Re per l'approvazione del testo definitivo del Codice penale,* 19 October 1930, quoted in Denise Detragiach, 'Un aspect de la politique démographique de l'Italie fasciste: La répression de l'avortement,' *Mélanges Moyen Age – Temps Modernes* 92:2 (1980), 693–735. See also Fortunato Montuoro, 'La gravidanza nel concetto di malattia,' *Archivio di antropologia criminale* 55 (1935), 211–14; and Luigi Torchiana and Bruno Guaraldi, 'Gravidanza extra-uterina e procurato aborto,' *Archivio di Antropologia Criminale* 51 (1931), 626–34. Such prohibitions notwithstanding, Italian women did administer and receive abortions during the *ventennio,* as Luisa Passerini has documented. See her 'Donne operaie e aborto,' *Italia contemporanea* 151–2 (1983), 83–109.

78 See Guido Lucchini, 'Gadda's Freud,' in Bertone and Dombroski, eds, *Carlo Emilio Gadda,* 177–94. See also Robert Dombroski, *L'esistenza ubbidiente: Letterati italiani sotto il fascismo* (Naples: Guida Editori, 1984), esp. 91–114.

79 Indeed, Lucchini shows that Gadda's critique of Freud is framed by the culture of positivism. See Lucchini, 'Gadda's Freud,' 182.

80 See Michel David, *La psicoanalisi nella cultura italiana* (Turin: P. Boringhieri, 1966); see also A. Viziano, 'Ancora valide le idee di Lombroso,' *La Stampa,* 7 Dec. 1965, n.p.; G.G. Perrando, 'La medicina legale italiana nell'ultimo decennio,' *Archivio di antropologia criminale* 47 (1927) 562–89; Lorenzo Ellero, 'Il coraggio scientifico di Cesare Lombroso,' *Archivio di antropologia criminale* 49 (1929), 629–35; Elena Bernart and Marello Tricarico, 'Per una rilettura dell'opera di C. Lombroso,' *Physis* 18:2 (1976), 179–84; Daniel Pick, 'The Faces of Anarchy: Lombroso and the Politics of Criminal Science in Post-Unification Italy,' *History Workshop* 21 (Spring 1986), 60–86; Renzo Villa, *Il deviante e si suoi segni: Lombroso e la nascita dell'antropologia criminale* (Milan: Franco Angeli, 1985); Ludmilla Jordanova, *Sexual Visions: Images of Gender in Science and Medicine between the Eighteenth and Twentieth Centuries* (Madison: U of Wisconsin P, 1985); and Franco Pelella, 'Riabilitare Lombroso,' *Risorgimento* 41:3 (1989), 283–314. See also Pinkus, '"Black" and "Jew,"' 149n7.

81 See Guido Neppi Modona, 'Carcere e società civile,' *Storia d'Italia: I documenti,* V, Pt. 2 (Turin: Einaudi, 1977), 1903–98.

82 Stephen Jay Gould, *The Mismeasure of Man* (New York: W.W. Norton, 1981), 108.

83 In *Pedagogical Anthropology* (English edition, 1913). Montessori simply inverts Lombroso's paradigm in order to demonstrate women's intellectual superiority to men. See Gould, 107.

84 De Grazia, *How Fascism Ruled Women*, 48–9.

85 Ibid.

86 Cesare Lombroso and G. Ferrero, *La donna delinquente, la prostituta e la donna normale* (Milan-Turin-Rome: Bocca Editori, 1915), 223–34.

87 Cf. Dombroski, *Introduzione*, esp. 141.

88 Is the Countess's jewelbox the miniature representation of the breach of the *interieur* that Benjamin identifies? Is the 'piega nera' formed by the girl's eyebrows at novel's end a reference back to that other 'fold,' the 'solcatura del sesso' [furrow of sex] Ingravallo remembers while viewing Liliana's cadaver?

89 Dacia Maraini, *E tu chi eri?* (Milan: Bompiani Editori, 1973), 19.

90 Michael Keith and Steve Pile, 'Conclusion: Towards New Radical Geographies,' in *Place and the Politics of Identity*, ed. Michael Keith and Steve Pile (New York and London: Routledge, 1993), 220–6.

91 See, among others, Elizabeth Grosz, *Space, Time, and Perversion* (London and New York: Routledge, 1995); Edward Soja, *Postmodern Geographies: The Reassertion of Space in Critical Social Theory* (London and New York: Verso, 1989); Henri Lefevbre, *The Production of Space*, tr. Donald Nicholson-Smith (Oxford: Blackwell, 1991); Louis Marin, *Utopics: The Semiological Play of Textual Places* [1984], tr. Robert Vollrath (Atlantic Highlands, NJ: Humanities International P, 1990); Tuan, *Space and Place*; Michel de Certeau, *The Practice of Everyday Life*, tr. Stevan Rendall (Berkeley: U of California P, 1988); Gaston Bachelard, *The Poetics of Space*, tr. Maria Jolas (Boston: Beacon P, 1958); Riccardo Gúllon, 'On Space and Time in the Novel,' *Critical Inquiry* 2 (1975), 11–28; and Joseph Frank, 'Spatial Form: An Answer to Critics,' *Critical Inquiry* 4 (1977), 126–34.

92 The subject of women's involvement in the Resistance is enjoying much-deserved attention in recent criticism. See, for example, Miriam Mafai, *Pane nero: Donne e vita quotidiana nella Seconda guerra mondiale* (Milan: Mondadori: 1987); Jane Slaughter, *Women and the Italian Resistance* (Denver, CO: Arden P, 1997); and Marina Addis Saba, *Partigiane: Tutte le donne della resistenza* (Milan: Mursia, 1998).

Bibliography

Abelson, Elaine. *When Ladies Go A-thieving: Middle-Class Shoplifters in the Victorian Department Store.* New York: Oxford UP, 1989.

Abramowitz, Isidore. *The Great Prisoners: The First Anthology of Literature Written in Prison.* New York: Dutton, 1946.

Absalom, Roger, ed. *Gli alleati e la ricostruzione in Toscana.* Florence: Olschki, 1988.

Accrocca, Elio Filippo. *Ritratti su misura.* Venezia: Sodalizio del libro, 1960.

Addis Saba, Marina. *Partigiane: Tutte le donne della resistenza.* Milan: Mursia, 1998.

– ed. *La corporazione delle donne.* Florence: Vallechi, 1988.

Afribo, Andrea. 'La finestra e altro: Guido Piovène.' In *Guido Piovène tra idoli e ragione: Atti del convegno di studi Vicenza, 24–26 novembre 1994.* Ed. Stefano Strazzabosco. Venice: Marsilio, 1996. 297–310.

Agrest, Diana. 'Toward a Theory of Production of Sense in the Built Environment.' In *On Streets.* Ed. Stanford Anderson. Cambridge: MIT P, 1978. 213–21.

Alexander, Peter, and Roger Gill, eds. *Utopias.* London: Duckworth, 1984.

Allen, Beverly. 'Terrorism Tales: Gender and the Fictions of Italian National Identity.' *Italica* 69:2 (1992), 161–76.

– 'The Novel, the Body, and Giorgio Armani.' In *Feminine Feminists: Cultural Practices in Italy.* Ed. Giovanna Miceli-Jeffries. Minneapolis: Minnesota UP, 1995. 153–70.

Althusser, Louis. *Lenin and Philosophy and Other Essays.* Tr. B. Brewster. New York: Monthly Review, 1971.

Anderson, Benedict. *Imagined Communities: Reflections on the Origin and Spread of Nationalism.* London: Verso, 1991.

Anonymous. 'Il delitto di sfruttamento negli articoli 534 C.P. e negli artt. 3 n. 8 e 4 della legge 20 febbraio 1958.' *Archivio penale* 15 (1959), 77–83.

Anonymous. 'Stato fascista e famiglia fascista.' *Critica fascista* 15:8 (15 Feb. 1937), 113–16.

'Argo.' 'Punti fermi sull'educazione femminile.' *Critica fascista* 18:21 (1 Sept. 1940), 357–59.

Arslan, Antonia Veronese. *Invito alla lettura di Dino Buzzati.* Milan: Mursia, 1974.

Asor Rosa, Alberto. *Vasco Pratolini.* Rome: Edizioni Moderne, 1958.

Aspesi, Natalia. *Il lusso e l'autarchia: Storia dell'eleganza italiana 1930–44.* Milan: Rizzoli, 1982.

Auerbach, Nina. *Communities of Women: An Idea in Fiction.* Cambridge: Harvard UP, 1978.

Avon, Annalisa. '"La casa all'italiana": Modernismo, ragione, e tradizione nell'organizzazione dello spazio domestico dal 1927 al 1930.' In *La costruzione dell'utopia: Architetti e urbanisti nell'Italia fascista.* Ed. Guilio Ernesti. Rome: Edizioni lavoro, 1988. 47–66.

Aymonino, Carlo. 'Storia e cronaca del Quartiere Tiburtino.' *Casabella continuità* 215 (1957), 19–23.

Bachelard, Gaston. *The Poetics of Space.* Tr. Maria Jolas. Boston: Beacon, 1958.

Baker, Margaret. 'The Women Characters of Carlo Emilio Gadda.' In *Visions and Revisions.* Ed. Mirna Cicioni and Nicole Prunster. Oxford: Berg Publishers, 1993. 53–69.

Bakhtin, Mikhail. *The Dialogic Imagination: Four Essays.* Tr. Caryl Emerson and Michael Holquist. Austin: U of Texas P, 1981. 84–258.

Balbo, Laura. *Stato di famiglia.* Milan: Garzanti, 1976.

Baldacci, Luigi. 'Buzzati trascina all'inferno l'architetto Dorigo.' *Epoca,* 5 May 1963, 127.

Banti, Anna. *Artemisia.* Milan: Mondadori, 1953.

– *La monaca di Sciangai e altri racconti.* Milan: Mondadori, 1957.

– *Il coraggio delle donne.* Milan: La Tartaruga, 1983.

– *Artemisia.* Tr. Shirley D'Ardia Caracciolo. Lincoln: U of Nebraska P, 1988.

Barberi-Squarotti, Giorgio. 'Il romanzo fantastico degli anni 1930–1940: Buzzati, Morovich, Terracini, Delfini.' In *La cultura italiana negli anni 1930–45.* Naples: Edizioni scientifiche, 1984. 17–49.

Bartkowski, Frances. 'Epistemic Drift in Foucault.' In *Feminism and Foucault: Reflections on Resistance.* Ed. Irene Diamond and Lee Quinby. Boston: Northeastern UP, 1988. 43–58.

– *Feminist Utopias.* Lincoln: U of Nebraska P, 1989.

Bartky, Sandra Lee. 'Foucault, Femininity, and the Modernization of Patriarchal Power.' In *Writing on the Body: Female Embodiment and Feminist Theory.* Ed. Katie Conboy, Nadia Medina, and Sarah Stanbury. New York: Columbia UP, 1997. 129–54.

Beccaria, Cesare. *Dei delitti e delle pene.* Ed. Franco Venturi. Turin: Einaudi, 1965.
- *On Crimes and Punishments, and Other Writings.* Tr. Richard Davies et al. Ed. Richard Bellamy. New York: Cambridge UP, 1995.
Bell, David, and Gill Valentine, eds. *Mapping Desire: Geographies of Sexualities.* London and New York: Routledge, 1995.
Bell, Rudolph. *Holy Anorexia.* Chicago: U of Chicago P, 1985.
Bellini, Federico. *Mario Ridolfi.* Bari-Rome: Laterza, 1993.
Bellomo, Manlio. *La condizione giuridica della donna in Italia.* Turin: ERI, 1970.
Ben-Ghiat, Ruth. 'The Politics of Realism: *Corrente di Vita Giovanile* and the Youth Culture of the 1930s.' *Stanford Italian Review* 8:1–2 (1990), 139–64.
- 'Neorealism in Italy 1930–1950: From Fascism to Resistance.' *Romance Languages Annual* 3 (1991), 155–9.
- *Fascist Modernities: Italy 1922–45.* Berkeley: U of California P, forthcoming.
Bender, John. *Imagining the Penitentiary: Fiction and the Architecture of the Mind in 18th-Century England.* Chicago: U of Chicago P, 1987.
Bennington, Geoffrey. 'Postal Politics and the Institution of the Nation.' In *Nation and Narration.* Ed. Homi K. Bhabha. New York: Routledge, 1990. 121–37.
Berezin, Mabel. *Making the Fascist Self: The Political Culture of Interwar Italy.* Ithaca: Cornell UP, 1997.
Bernart, Elena, and Marello Tricarico. 'Per una rilettura dell'opera di C. Lombroso.' *Physis* 18:2 (1976), 179–84.
Bernheimer, Charles. *Figures of Ill Repute: Representing Prostitutes in 19th-Century France.* Cambridge: Harvard UP, 1989.
Bertoldi, Silvio. *Soldati a Salò: L'ultimo esercito di Mussolini.* Milan: Rizzoli, 1995.
Bertone, Manuela. 'Murderous Desires: Gaddian Matricides from *Novella seconda* to *La cognizione del dolore.*' In *Carlo Emilio Gadda: Contemporary Perspectives.* Ed. Manuela Bertone and Robert Dombroski. Toronto: U of Toronto P, 1997. 111–31.
Bertone, Manuela, and Robert Dombroski, eds. *Carlo Emilio Gadda: Contemporary Perspectives.* Toronto: U of Toronto P, 1997.
Betti, Ugo. *Crime on Goat Island.* Tr. Henry Reed. San Francisco: Chandler Publishers, 1961.
- *Teatro completo.* Ed. Silvio D'Amico and Achille Fiocco. Bologna: Cappelli, 1971.
Bhabha, Homi. 'Postcolonial Authority and Postcolonial Guilt.' In *Cultural Studies.* Ed. Lawrence Grossberg, Cary Nelson, and Paula Treichler. London and New York: Routledge, 1992. 56–66.
Biasin, Gian Paolo. *I sapori della modernità: Cibo e romanzo.* Bologna: Il Mulino, 1991.

Blelloch, Paola. 'Anna Banti da *Il coraggio delle donne* a *Le donne muoiono.*' *Nemla Italian Studies* 11–12 (1987–8), 97–103.

Bloomer, Jennifer. *Architecture and the Text: The (S)crypts of Joyce and Piranesi.* New Haven: Yale UP, 1993.

Bock, Gisela, and Giuliana Nobili, eds. *Il corpo delle donne.* Bologna: Transeuropa, 1988.

Bondanella, Peter. *Italian Cinema from Neorealism to the Present.* New York: Continuum, 1990.

Boot, Marjan, Ineke van Hamersveld, and Juliette Roding. *La casalinga riflessiva: La cucina razionale come mito domestico negli anni '20 e '30.* Rome: Multigrafica, 1983.

Bordo, Susan. 'Anorexia nervosa: Psychopathology as the Crystallization of Culture.' In *Feminism and Foucault: Reflections on Resistance.* Ed. Irene Diamond and Lee Quinby. Boston: Northeastern UP, 1988.

– 'Feminism, Foucault and the Politics of the Body.' In *Up against Foucault: Explorations of Some Tensions between Foucault and Feminism.* Ed. Caroline Ramazanoglu. London: Routledge, 1993. 179–202.

Borgese, Maria. 'Letteratura femminile.' *Nuova antologia CDIV* (16 July 1939), 232–5.

Boscagli, Maurizia. 'The Power of Style: Fashion and Self-Fashioning in Irene Brin's Journalistic Writing.' In *Mothers of Invention: Woman, Italian Fascism, and Culture.* Ed. Robin Pickering-Iazzi. Minneapolis: U of Minnesota P, 1995. 121–36.

– *Eye on the Flesh: Fashions of Masculinity in the Early Twentieth Century.* Boulder, CO: Westview P, 1996.

Bourdieu, Pierre *Outline of a Theory of Practice.* Tr. Richard Nice. Cambridge: Cambridge UP, 1977.

Bovio, Oreste. *Le bandiere dell'esercito.* Rome: USSME, 1981.

– *L'ufficio storico dell'esercito: Un secolo di storiografia militare.* Rome: USSME, 1987.

Boxer, Sarah. 'So That's Why Walls Conceal Heating Vents,' *New York Times,* 5 June 2000, B7, 9.

Braghin, Paolo, ed. *Inchiesta sulla miseria in Italia.* Turin: Einaudi, 1978.

Braudel, Fernand. *On History.* Tr. Sarah Matthews. Chicago: U of Chicago P, 1980.

Braun, Emily. *Mario Sironi and Italian Modernism: Art and Politics under Fascism.* Cambridge: Cambridge UP, 2000.

Briamonte, Nino. '"Un caso clinico" e "L'adaptation" di Albert Camus.' In *Dino Buzzati: La lingua, le lingue.* Ed. Nella Giannetto. Milan: Mondadori, 1994. 115–34.

Brombert, Victor. *The Romantic Prison.* Princeton: Princeton UP, 1978.

Burghartz, Susanna. 'The Equation of Women and Witches: A Case Study of Witchcraft Trials in Lucerne and Lausanne in the Fifteenth and Sixteenth Centuries.' In *The German Underworld: Deviants and Outcasts in German History.* Ed. Richard Evans. London: Routledge, 1988. 57–74.

Busch, Akiko. *Geography of Home: Writings on Where We Live.* New York: Princeton Architectural P, 1999.

Butler, Judith. 'Variations on Gender: Beauvoir, Wittig, and Foucault.' *Praxis International* 5 (1985/86), 505–16.

– *Gender Trouble: Feminism and the Subversion of Identity.* New York and London: Routledge, 1990.

Butor, Michel. 'The Space of the Novel.' In *Inventory.* Ed. Richard Howard. New York: Simon and Schuster, 1968. 31–8.

– 'Gadda e la tragedia dell'incompiuto.' In *Leggere Gadda: Antologia della critica gaddiana.* Ed. Arnaldo Ceccaroni. Bologna: Zanichelli, 1978. 68–70.

Buttafuoco, Annarita. *Le Mariuccine: Storia di un'istituzione laica l'Asilo Mariuccia.* Milan: Franco Angeli, 1988.

– 'Motherhood as a Political Strategy: The Role of the Italian Women's Movement in the Creation of the Cassa Nazionale di Maternità.' In *Maternity and Gender Policies: Women and the Rise of the European Welfare States, 1880s-1950s.* Ed. Gisela Bock and Pat Thane. New York: Routledge, 1991. 178–95.

Buzzati, Dino. *Il deserto dei Tartari.* Milan: Mondadori: 1979.

– *The Tartar Steppe.* Tr. Stuart Hood. Boston: Godine P, 1995.

Bynum, Caroline Walker. *Holy Feast and Holy Fast.* Berkeley: U of California P, 1987.

– *Fragmentation and Redemption: Essays on Gender and the Human Body in Medieval Religion.* New York: Zone Books, 1991.

Cain, Maureen. 'Foucault, Feminism and Feeling: What Foucault Can and Cannot Contribute to Feminist Epistemology.' In *Up against Foucault: Explorations of Some Tensions between Foucault and Feminism.* Ed. Caroline Ramazanoglu. London: Routledge, 1993. 73–96.

Calamandrei, Piero. 'La costituzione inattuata.' *L'Attualità* 9 (May 1956) [74 pp.; published as a separate supplement].

Caldo, Costantino. *Il territorio come dominio: La geografia italiana durante il fascismo.* Naples: Loffredo, 1982.

Caldwell, Lesley. 'Reproducers of the Nation: Women and the Family in Fascist Policy.' In *Rethinking Italian Fascism: Capitalism, Populism, and Culture.* Ed. David Forgacs. London: Lawrence and Wishart, 1986. 110–41.

Calvino, Italo. 'Multiplicity.' In *Six Memoes for the Next Millenium.* Cambridge: Harvard UP, 1988. 105–24.

Cammarota, Paolo. 'Osservazioni sulle nuove norme in materia di meretricio.'
Rivista penale (1959), 359–62 [no volume given].

Canella, Guido, and Aldo Rossi. 'Architetti italiani: Mario Ridolfi.' *Comunità* 41
(1966), 50–5.

Cannistraro, Philip V. *La fabbrica di consenso: Fascismo e mass media.* Bari: Laterza,
1975.

Cannistraro, Philip V., and Brian Sullivan. *Il Duce's Other Woman.* New York:
William Morrow, 1993.

Cannon, JoAnn. 'The Reader as Detective: Notes on Gadda's Pasticciaccio.' In
Modern Language Studies 10 (Fall 1980), 41–50.

– *Postmodern Italian Fiction: The Crisis of Reason in Calvino, Eco, Sciascia, Malerba.*
London: Associated UP, 1989.

Canosa, Romano. *Il Velo e il Cappuccio: Monacazioni forzate e sessualità nei conventi
femminili in Italia tra Quattrocento e Settecento.* Rome: Sapere 2000, 1991.

Caplan, Jane, ed. *Written on the Body: The Tattoo in European and American History.*
Princeton: Princeton UP, 2000.

Carletti, Sandra. '"Gli ho sparato negli occhi": Gender Conflict and Homicide in
Alba de Cèspedes's *Dalla parte di lei* and Natalia Ginzburg's *È stato così.*' In *Gen-
dered Contexts.* Ed. Laura Benedetti, Julia Hairston, and Silvia Ross. New York:
P. Lang, 1996. 153–64.

– 'Internalizing the Gaze.' In *Writing beyond Fascism: Cultural Resistance in the Life
and Works of Alba de Cèspedes.* Ed. Carole C. Gallucci and Ellen Nerenberg.
Cranbury, NJ: Fairleigh-Dickinson UP, 2000. 110–31.

Carlino, Marcello. *Come leggere 'Il deserto dei Tartari' di Dino Buzzati.* Milan: Mursia,
1976.

Carnochan, W.B. 'The Literature of Confinement.' In *The Oxford History of
Prison.* Oxford and New York: Oxford UP, 1995. 427–55.

Carroll, Linda. 'Holy Anorexia Revisited.' *Psychohistory Review* 26:2 (1998),
115–36.

Casalinuovo, Aldo. 'Un nuovo capitolo nella storia del diritto italiano: Le norme
penali della legge Merlin.' *Rivista penale* (1958), 553–72 [no volume given].

Caspar, Marie-Hélène. 'L'organizzazione spaziale nei romanzi di Dino Buzzati.'
In *Dino Buzzati.* Ed. Alvise Fontanella. Florence: Olshki, 1982. 121–38.

– *L'Africa di Buzzati. Libia: 1933. Etiopia: 1939–40.* Paris: Centre de Recherches
Italiennes, 1997.

– *Fantastique et mythe dans l'oeuvre de Buzzati.* La Garenne-Colombes, France: Editions Erasme, n.d.

Cavallero, Daniela. 'Liliana e Zamira: Due riflessi dell'altro. *Quer pasticciaccio
brutto de via Merulana* visto attraverso le donne.' *Romance Languages Annual* 7
(1998), 218–21.

Ceccaroni, Arnaldo. 'Per una lettura del Pasticciaccio.' *Lingua e stile* 5 (1975), 57–85.

– ed. *Leggere Gadda: Antologia della critica gaddiana.* Bologna: Zanichelli, 1978.

Chancer, Lynne Sharon. 'Prostitution, Feminist Theory, and Ambivalence: Notes from the Sociological Underground.' *Social Text* 37 (Winter 1993), 143–71.

Chesney-Lind, Meda. *The Female Offender: Girls, Women, and Crime.* Thousand Oaks: Sage Publications, 1995.

Chiarini, Carlo, and Marcello Girelli. 'Dal Tiburtino a Matera.' *Domus* 231 (1959), 25–6.

Cicioni, Mirna, and Nicole Prunster, eds. *Visions and Re-visions: Women in Italian Culture.* Providence and Oxford: Berg Publishers, 1993.

Ciucci, Giorgio. *Gli architetti e il fascismo.* Turin: Einaudi, 1989.

Cixous, Hélène. 'We Who Are Free, Are We Free?' In *Freedom and Interpretation: The Oxford Amnesty Lectures, 1992.* Ed. Barbara Johnson. New York: Basic Books (HarperCollins), 1993. 17–44.

Clayson, Hollis. *Painted Love: Prostitution in French Art of the Impressionist Era.* New Haven: Yale UP, 1991.

Cohn, Norman. *Europe's Inner Demons: An Enquiry Inspired by the Great Witch Hunt.* Sussex: Sussex UP, 1975.

Colamina, Beatriz, ed. *Sexuality and Space.* Princeton: Princeton Architectural Papers, 1992.

Colombo, Umberto, ed. *Vita e processo di Suor Virginia Maria de Leyva, Monaca di Monza.* Milan: Garzani, 1985.

Conso, Giovanni, ed. *Codice Penale e norme complementari.* 3rd ed. Milan: Giuffrè Editori, 1982.

Contini, Gianfranco. 'Introduzione,' *La cognizione del dolore.* Turin: Einaudi, 1963.

Copi, Irving. *Introduction to Logic.* New York: Macmillan, 1961.

Copjec, Joan. 'The Sartorial Superego.' *October* 50 (Fall 1989), 56–95.

Cotrell, Jane. *Alberto Moravia.* New York: Frederick Ungar, 1974.

Crespi, Franco, and Franco Martinelli. 'La dinamica delle relazioni sociali nel contesto urbano.' *Rivista di sociologia* 6:16 (1968), 5–50.

Crotti, Ilaria. *Buzzati.* Florence: Il Castoldo, 1977.

Cutrufelli, Maria Rosa, ed. *Piccole italiane: Un raggiro durato vent'anni.* Milan: Anabasi, 1994.

Daga, Luigi. 'Ospedali psichiatrici giudiziari, sistema penale e sistema penitenziario.' *Rassegna penitenziaria e criminologica* 7:1–3 (Jan.–Dec. 1985), 1–52.

– 'Sistemi penitenziari.' In *Enciclopedia del diritto.* Milan: Giuffrè, 1992.

Danesi, Silvia, and Luciano Patetta, eds. *Il razionalismo e l'architettura in Italia durante il fascismo.* Venice: Edizioni del Biennale, 1976.

David, Michel. *La psicoanalisi nella cultura italiana.* Turin: Boringhieri,1966.

Davies, Ioan. *Writers in Prison.* Oxford: Blackwell, 1990.

Davis, John A. *Conflict and Control: Law and Order in Nineteenth-Century Italy.* Atlantic Highlands, NJ: Humanities International P, 1988.

D'Azeglio, Massimo. *I miei ricordi.* 2 vols. Milan: Mursia, 1966.

– *Things I Remember.* Tr. E.R. Vincent. Oxford UP, 1966.

De Carlo, Giancarlo. 'Architetture italiane.' *Casabella continuità* 199 (1957), 19–33.

de Certeau, Michel. *The Practice of Everyday Life.* Tr. Steven Rendall. Berkeley: U of California P, 1988.

de Céspedes, Alba. *Nessuno torna indietro.* Milan: Mondadori, 1938.

– *There's No Turning Back.* Tr. Jan Noble. London: Jarrold, 1941.

– *Dalla parte di lei.* Milan: Mondadori, 1948.

– *The Best of Husbands (Dalla parte di lei).* Tr. Frances Frenaye. New York: Macmillan, 1952.

De Felice, Renzo. *Mussolini il Duce. I. Gli anni del consenso.* Turin: Einaudi, 1974.

– *Interpretations of Fascism.* Tr. Brenda Huff. Cambridge: Harvard UP, 1977.

– *Mussolini il Duce.* II. *Lo Stato totalitario.* Turin: Einaudi, 1981.

– *Storia degli ebrei sotto il fascismo.* Turin: Einaudi, 1988.

De Gennaro, Domenico. 'Prostituzione e lotta contro lo sfruttamento della prostituzione altrui.' *Archivio penale* 14 (1958), 216–29.

De Giorgio, Michela. *Le italiane dall'Unità a oggi: Modelli culturali e comportamenti sociali.* Rome-Bari: Laterza, 1992.

De Grand, Alexander. 'Fascism in Italian History.' *Italian Americana* 14:2 (1996), 159–62.

de Grazia, Victoria. *The Culture of Consent: The Organization of Mass Leisure in Fascist Italy.* New York and Cambridge: Cambridge UP, 1981.

– *How Fascism Ruled Women: Italy 1922–45.* Berkeley: U of California P, 1992.

de Lauretis, Teresa. 'Narrative Discourse in Calvino: Praxis or Poiesis.' *PMLA* 90 (1975), 414–25.

– *Technologies of Gender: Essays on Theory, Film, and Fiction.* Bloomington: Indiana UP, 1987.

De Luna, Giovanni. *Storia del Partito d'Azione.* Milan: Feltrinelli, 1982.

– *Donne in oggetto: L'antifascismo nella società italiana 1922–39.* Turin: Bollati Boringhieri, 1995.

De Nicola, Francesco. *Introduzione a Vittorini.* Bari: Laterza, 1993.

De Robertis, G. *Scrittori del Novecento.* Florence: 1940.

Del Re, Alisa. 'Politiche demografiche e controllo in Francia, Italia, e Germania negli anni '30.' In *Stato e rapporti sociali di sesso.* Ed. A. Del Re. Milan: Franco Angeli, 1989.

– ed. *Stato e rapporti sociali di sesso*. Milan: Franco Angeli Libri, 1989.

Deleuze, Gilles. *Cinema I: The Movement-Image*. Minneapolis: U of Minnesota P, 1986.

– *Dialogues*. New York: Columbia UP, 1987.

– *The Fold: Leibniz and the Baroque*. Foreword and tr. Tom Conley. Minneapolis: U of Minnesota P, 1993.

Deleuze, Gilles, and Félix Guattari. 'City/State.' In *Zone* 1/2 (1986).

Dellamora, Richard. *Masculine Desire: The Sexual Politics of Victorian Aestheticism*. Chapel Hill: U of North Carolina P, 1990.

Derrida, Jacques. 'The Purveyor of Truth.' Tr. Willis Domingo. *Yale French Studies* 52 (1975), 31–113.

Detragiach, Denise. 'Un aspect de la politique démographique de l'Italie fasciste: La repressione de l'avortement.' *Mélanges Moyen Age – Temps Modernes* 92:2 (1980), 693–735.

Di Cori, Paola. 'Rosso e bianco: La devozione al Sacro Cuore di Gesù nel primo dopoguerra.' *Memoria* 5 (1982), 82–107.

di Migliardo, Donato Francesco. 'Brevi considerazioni sulla legge 20 febbraio 1958.' *Archivio penale* 14 (1958), 462–5.

Diamond, Irene, and Lee Quinby, eds. *Feminism and Foucault: Reflections on Resistance*. Boston: Northeastern UP, 1988.

Diderot, Denis. *La religieuse*. Ed. R. Mauzi. Paris: Colin, 1961.

– *The Nun*. Tr. Leonard Tancock. Harmondsworth: Penguin, 1974.

Dombroski, Robert. *Introduzione allo studio di Gadda*. Florence: Vallechi Editore, 1967.

– *L'esistenza ubbidiente: Letterati italiani sotto il fascismo*. Naples: Guida Editori, 1984.

Domenico, Roy Palmer, *Italian Fascists on Trial, 1943–48*. Chapel Hill: U of North Carolina P, 1991.

Doordan, Dennis. *Building Modern Italy: Italian Architecture 1914–1936*. New York: Princeton Architectural P, 1988.

Doria, Anna Rossi. *Diventare cittadine: Il voto alle donne in Italia nel 1945*. Florence: Giunti, 1996.

Douglas, Mary. 'The Idea of a Home: A Kind of Space.' *Social Research* 58 (1991), 287–307.

Dubbini, Renzo. 'Carcere e architettura in Italia nel XIX secolo: Tecnologia punitiva e strategie spaziali.' In *Le macchine imperfette: Architettura, programma, istituzioni, nel XIX secolo*. Ed. P. Morachiello and G. Teyssot. Rome: Officina, 1980.

– *Architettura delle prigioni: I luoghi e il tempo della punizione (1700–1880)*. Milan: Franco Angeli, 1986.

Duncan, Martha. *Romantic Outlaws, Beloved Prisons: The Unconscious Meanings of Crime and Punishment*. New York: New York UP, 1996.

Dunnage, Jonathan, ed. *After the War: Violence, Justice, Continuity and Renewal in Italian Society.* Leicester: Troubador, 1999.

During, Simon. *Foucault and Literature: Towards a Genealogy of Writing.* New York and London: Routledge, 1992.

Dyer, Richard. *Studies on Lesbian and Gay Film.* New York: Routledge, 1990.

Ecstavasia, Audrey. 'Fucking (with Theory) for Money: Toward an Introduction of Escort Prostitution.' *Essays in Postmodern Culture.* Ed. Eyal Amiran and John Unsworth. Oxford and New York: Oxford UP, 1993. 177–98.

Ehrenreich, Barbara, and Deirdre English. 'The Manufacture of Housework.' *Socialist Revolution* 26 (1975), 5–40.

Eisenstein, Sergei. 'Piranesi, or the Fluidity of Forms.' Tr. Roberta Reeder. *Oppositions* 11 (1978), 83–110.

Ellero, Lorenzo. 'Il coraggio scientifico di Cesare Lombroso.' *Archivio di Antropologia Criminale* 49 (1929), 629–35.

Enciclopedia del diritto. Dir. Costantino Mortafi and Francesco Santoro-Pasarelli. Florence: Giuffrè Editore, 1980.

Ernesti, Giulio. *La costruzione dell'utopia: Architetti e urbanisti nell'Italia fascista.* Rome: Edizioni lavoro, 1988.

Etlin, Richard. *Modernism in Italian Architecture 1890–1940.* Cambridge: MIT P, 1991.

Fabbri, Marcello. *L'urbanistica italiana dal dopoguerra a oggi.* Bari: De Donato, 1983.

Falcetto, Bruno. *Storia della narrativa neorealista.* Milan: Mursia, 1992.

Fardjadi, Homa, and Moshen Mostafavi. *Delayed Space.* New York: Princeton Architectural P, 1999.

Fausch, Deborah. '"Towards an Architecture of our Times": Scaffold and Drapery in the Architecture of Venturi, Scott Brown and Associates.' In *Architecture: In Fashion.* Ed. Deborah Fausch, Paulette Singley, Rodolphe El-Khoury, and Zvi Efrat. New York: Princeton Architectural P, 1994. 344–61

Fausch, Deborah, Paulette Singley, Rodolphe El-Khoury, and Zvi Efrat, eds. *Architecture: In Fashion.* New York: Princeton Architectural Press, 1994.

Felice, Angela. 'Il "giallo" a scuola: I ragazzi.' *Problemi* 79 (May–Aug. 1987), 192–209.

Ferrario, L., and D. Pastore, *Giuseppe Terragni: La casa del fascio.* Rome: Istituto Mides, 1982.

Fiori, Cesira. *Una donna nelle carceri fasciste.* Rome: Riuniti Editori, 1965.

Firth, Raymond. *Symbols, Public and Private.* Ithaca, NY: Cornell UP, 1973.

Flescher, Sharon. 'More on a Name: Manet's *Olympia* and the Defiant Heroine in Mid-Nineteenth-Century France.' *Art Journal* 45 (1985), 27–35.

Fontanella, Alvise, ed. *Dino Buzzati.* Florence: Olshki, 1982.

Forgacs, David, ed. *Rethinking Italian Fascism; Capitalism, Populism, and Culture.* London: Lawrence and Wishart, 1986.

Forti, Marco, ed. *Gianna Manzini tra letteratura e vita.* Milan: Fondazione Arnaldo e Alberto Mondadori, 1985.

Foster, Hal. 'Armor Fou.' *October* 56 (Spring 1991), 65–97.

Foucault, Michel. *The Birth of the Clinic: An Archaeology of Medical Perception.* Tr. Alan Sheridan. New York: Vintage, 1975.

– *Discipline and Punish: The Birth of the Prison.* Tr. Alan Sheridan. New York: Vintage, 1977.

– 'The Eye of Power.' In *Power/Knowledge.* Ed. Colin Gordon. New York: Pantheon Books, 1980. 146–65.

– *The History of Sexuality I: An Introduction.* Tr. Robert Hurley. New York: Vintage, 1980.

– 'Space, Knowledge, and Power.' In *The Foucault Reader.* Ed. Paul Rabinow. New York: Pantheon, 1984. 239–56

– 'Of Other Spaces.' *Diacritics* 16:1 (1986), 22–7.

– *The History of Sexuality III: The Care of the Self.* Tr. Robert Hurley. New York: Vintage, 1988.

– *The Order of Things: An Archaeology of the Human Sciences.* New York: Vintage, 1994.

Franco Crespi, and Franco Martinelli, 'La dinamica delle relazioni sociali nel contesto urbano.' *Rivista di sociologia* 6:16 (1968), 5–50.

Frank, Joseph. 'Spatial Form: An Answer to Critics.' *Critical Inquiry* 4 (1977), 126–34.

Frasson, Alberto. 'Piovène e l'ambiguità del suo tempo.' *L'Osservatore politico letterario* 20:12 (1974), 31–40.

Freeland, Cynthia. 'Feminist Frameworks for Horror Films.' In *Post-Theory: Reconstructing Film Studies.* Ed. David Bordwell and Noël Carroll. Madison: U of Wisconsin P, 1996. 195–218.

Freud, Sigmund. 'The Uncanny.' In *Freud, Standard Edition.* Ed. James Strachey. London: Hogarth, 1957. 17:219–52.

Friedland, Roger, and Deirdre Boden. 'NowHere: An Introduction to Space, Time, and Modernity.' In *NowHere: Space, Time, and Modernity.* Ed. Roger Friedland and Deirdre Boden. Berkeley: U of California P, 1994. 1–60.

Gadda, Carlo Emilio. *That Awful Mess on Via Merulana.* Tr. William Weaver. New York: George Braziller, 1965.

– *Eros e Priapo.* Milan: Grazanti, 1967.

– *Quer pasticciaccio brutto de via Merulana.* Milan: Garzanti, 1983.

Gallerano, Nicola. *La resistenza fra storia e memoria.* Milan: Mursia, forthcoming.

Gallucci, Carole. '*There's No Turning Back: Challenging the New Woman's Future.*' In

Mothers of Invention: Woman, Italian Fascism, and Culture. Ed. Robin Pickering-Iazzi. Minneapolis: U of Minnesota P, 1995. 200–19.

Gambino, Antonio. *Storia del dopoguerra: Dalla Liberazione al potere DC.* Rome-Bari: Laterza, 1975.

Garofalo, A. *L'italiana in Italia.* Bari, Laterza, 1956.

Gearhart, Sally. 'Future Visions: Today's Politics: Feminist Utopias in Review.' In *Women in Search of Utopia: Mavericks and Mythmakers.* Ed. Ruby Rohrlick and Baruch Elaine Hoffman. New York: Schocken Books, 1984.

Geerts, Walter. 'La forma, spazio, visione.' In *Dino Buzzati.* Ed. Alvise Fontanella. Florence: Olschki, 1982. 157–67.

Gelfand, Elissa. 'Imprisoned Women: Toward a Socio-Literary Feminist Analysis.' *Yale French Studies* 62 (1981), 185–203.

– *Imagination in Confinement: Women's Writings from French Prisons.* Ithaca and London: Cornell UP, 1983.

Gellott, Laura, and Michael Phayer. 'Dissenting Voices: Catholic Women in Opposition to Fascism.' *Journal of Contemporary History* 22 (1987), 91–114.

Gemelli, Agostino, O.F.M. *Il nostro soldato: Saggi di psicologia militare.* Milan: Treves, 1917.

Gentile, Emilio. 'Alcune considerazioni sull'ideologia fascista.' *Storia contemporanea* 5:1 (Jan. 1974), 115–25.

– 'Renzo de Felice: A Tribute.' Tr. Anne Heaton-Ward. *Journal of Contemporary History* 32:2 (1997), 139–51.

Geoghegan, Vincent. *Utopianism and Marxism.* London: Methuen, 1987.

Ghirardo, Diane. *Building New Communities: New Deal America and Fascist Italy.* Princeton, NJ: Princeton UP, 1989.

– 'Virtually Visible.' *Thresholds* 19 (1999), 41–7.

Gianfranceschi, Fausto. *Dino Buzzati.* Turin: Borla, 1967.

Gibson, Mary. *Prostitution and the State in Italy, 1860–1915.* New Brunswick: Rutgers UP, 1986.

Gilchrist, Roberta. *Gender and Material Culture: The Archaeology of Religious Women.* London and New York: Routledge, 1994.

Gill, Katherine. 'Open Monasteries for Women in Late and Early Modern Italy: Two Roman Examples.' In *The Crannied Wall: Women, Religion, and the Arts in Early Modern Europe.* Ed. Craig Monson. Ann Arbor: U of Michigan P, 1992. 15–47.

Ginatempo, Nella. *La casa in Italia: Abitazioni e crisi del capitale.* Milan: Gabriele Mazzotta Editore, 1975.

Ginsborg, Paul. *A History of Contemporary Italy: Society and Politics 1943–88.* London: Penguin, 1990.

- 'Resistenza e riforma in Francia e Italia, 1943–48.' *Ventesimo secolo*, 2:5–6 (1992), 297–319.

Ginzburg, Carlo. *I benandanti: Stregoneria e culti agrari tra Cinquecento e Seicento.* Turin: Einaudi, 1966.

- *Night Battles.* Tr. John and Anne Tedeschi. Baltimore: Johns Hopkins UP, 1983.

- *Storia notturna.* Turin: Einaudi, 1989.

Ginzburg, Natalia. *È stato così.* Turin: Einaudi, 1974.

- *'The Road to the City' and 'The Dry Heart.'* Tr. Frances Frenaye. Manchester: Carcanet P, 1989.

Giocondi, Michele. *Lettori in camicia nera: Narrativa di successo nell'Italia fascista.* Messina and Florence: G. D'Anna, 1978.

Giovagnoli, Agostino. *Le premesse della Ricostruzione.* Milan: Nuovo Istituto editoriale, 1982.

Goldhagen, Daniel. *Hitler's Willing Executioners: Ordinary Germans and the Holocaust.* New York: A.A. Knopf, 1996.

Golsan, Richard. *Fascism's Return: Scandal, Revision, and Ideology since 1980.* Lincoln: U of Nebraska P, 1998.

Gould, Stephen Jay. *The Mismeasure of Man.* New York: W.W. Norton, 1981.

Gramsci, Antonio. *Lettere dal carcere.* Ed. Sergio Caprioglio and Elsa Fubini. Turin: Einaudi, 1975.

- *Quaderni del carcere.* 4 vols. Ed. Valentino Gerratana.

- *Letters from Prison.* 2 vols. Tr. R. Rosenthal. New York: Columbia UP, 1984.

- *Prison Notebooks.* Tr. J. Buttigieg and A. Callari. Ed. J. Buttigieg. New York: Columbia UP, 1992.

Grasselli, Ettore. *Corso di cultura militare.* Milan: Giuffrè, 1937.

Grignaffini, Giovanna. 'Sante e suore sullo schermo.' In *Donna e fede: Santità e vita religiosa in Italia.* Ed. Lucetta Scaraffia and Gabriella Zarri. Rome-Bari: Laterza, 1994. 517–30.

Grosz, Elizabeth. *Space, Time, and Perversion.* London and New York: Routledge, 1995.

Guagnini, Elvio. 'Alcuni esemplari recenti di giallo italiano dentro e fuori.' *Problemi* 86 (Sept.–Dec. 1989), 257–88.

Guasco, Maurizio. 'La vita religiosa nell'Italia repubblicana.' *Italia contemporanea* 181 (Dec. 1990), 651–72.

Guglielmi, Guido. *La prosa italiana del Novecento: Umorismo, metafisica, grottesca.* Turin: Einaudi, 1986.

Guilleragues, Gabriel. *Lettres portugaises.* Ed. Frédéric Rougeot. Geneva: Droz, 1972.

- *The Portuguese Letters.* Tr. Donald Ericson. New York: Bennett-Edwards, 1986.

Gúllon, Riccardo. 'On Space and Time in the Novel.' *Critical Inquiry* 2 (1975), 11–28.

Hainsworth, Peter. 'Fascism and Anti-Fascism in Gadda.' In *Carlo Emilio Gadda: Contemporary Perspectives*. Ed. Manuela Bertone and Robert Dombroski. Toronto: U of Toronto P, 1997. 221–41.

Harris, Ruth. *Murders and Madness: Medicine, Law, and Society in the Fin-de-siècle*. Oxford: Clarendon P, 1989.

Harrowitz, Nancy. 'Matilde Serao's *La mano tagliata*: Figuring the Material in Mystery.' *Stanford Italian Review* 7 (1987), 191–204.

– *Anti-Semitism, Misogyny, and the Logic of Cultural Difference*. Lincoln: U of Nebraska P, 1995.

Harrowitz, Nancy, and Barbara Hyams, eds. *Jews and Gender: Responses to Otto Weininger.* Philadelphia: Temple UP, 1995.

Hartsock, Nancy. 'Foucault on Power: A Theory for Women?' In *Feminism/Postmodernism*. Ed. Linda Nicholson. New York: Routledge, 1990. 157–75.

Haycraft, Howard, ed. *The Art of the Mystery Story*. New York: Simon and Schuster, 1946.

Hayden, Dolores. *The Grand Domestic Revolution: A History of Feminist Designs for American Homes, Neighborhoods, and Cities*. Cambridge: MIT P, 1981.

– *The Power of Place*. Cambridge: MIT P, 1995.

Heatherington, Kevin. *The Badlands of Modernity: Heterotopia and Social Ordering*. London and New York: Routledge, 1997.

Heilbrun, Carolyn, and Judith Resnick. 'Convergences: Law, Literature, and Feminism.' *Yale Law Review* 99 (1989–90), 1913–56.

Hekman, Susan, ed. *Feminist Interpretations of Michel Foucault*. University Park: Pennsylvania State UP, 1996.

Helsinger, Elizabeth. 'Consumer Power and the Utopia of Desire: Christina Rossetti's "Goblin Market,"' *ELH* 58 (1991), 903–33.

Hertz, Neil. 'Freud and the Sandman.' In *Textual Strategies: Perspectives in Post-Structuralist Criticism*. Ed. Josué Harari. Ithaca, NY: Cornell UP, 1979. 296–321.

– *The End of the Line: Essays on Psychoanalysis and the Sublime*. New York: Columbia UP, 1985.

Hewitt, Andrew. 'Fascist Modernism, Futurism, and "Post-Modernity,"' In *Fascism, Aesthetics, and Culture*. Ed. Richard Golsan. Hanover, NH: University P of New England, 1992. 38–55.

Hobsbawm, Eric. *The Invention of Tradition*. New York: Cambridge UP, 1983.

Holland, Norman. 'Fashioning Cuba.' In *Nationalisms and Sexualities*. Ed.

Andrew Parker, Mary Russo, Doris Sommer, and Patricia Yeager. New York: Routledge, 1992.

Hostie, R. 'Emancipazione della donna e istituti religiosi.' In *Dizionario degli Istituti di Perfezione* 3 [1976], 1124–7.

Hughes, H. Stuart. *Prisoners of Hope: The Silver Age of Italian Jews, 1924–74.* Cambridge: Harvard UP, 1983.

Hunt, Lynn. 'The Many Bodies of Marie Antoinette: Political Pornography and the Problem of the Feminine in the French Revolution.' In *Eroticism and the Body Politic.* Ed. Lynn Hunt. Baltimore: Johns Hopkins UP, 1991. 108–30.

– 'Pornography and the French Revolution.' In *The Invention of Pornography.* Ed. Lynn Hunt. New York: Zone Books, 1993. 301–40.

Ilari, Virgilio, and Antonio Sema. *Marte in Orbace: Guerra, esercito e milizia nella concezione fascista della nazione.* Ancona: Nuove Ricerche, 1988.

Iolì, Giovanna. *Dino Buzzati.* Milan: Mursia Editori, 1988.

Irigaray, Luce. *Elemental Passions.* Tr. Joanne Collie and Judith Still. New York and London: Routledge, 1992.

Jaccobi, Ruggero. 'Uno spettacolo a scena fissa e multipla.' In *Vasco Pratolini.* Ed. Luciano Lusi. Taranto: Mandes Editore, 1988. 172–6.

Jacomuzzi, Stefano. 'I primi racconti di Buzzati.' In *Dino Buzzati.* Ed. A. Fontanella. Florence: Olschki, 1982.

– '1939: L'armata del Nord: Davanti al deserto dei Tartari (per una rilettura del romanzo di Dino Buzzati).' In *La cultura italiana negli anni 1930–45.* Naples: Edizioni scientifiche italiane, 1984. 113–28.

Jameson, Frederic. *The Political Unconscious: Narrative as a Socially Symbolic Act.* Ithaca and London: Cornell UP, 1981.

Jesi, Furio. *La cultura di destra.* Milan: Garzanti, 1979.

Jewell, Keala. *The Poiesis of History: Experimenting with Genre in Postwar Italy.* Ithaca, NY: Cornell UP, 1992.

– 'Sexual Commerce and Culture: Pier Paolo Pasolini's Caracalla Poems.' *Italica* 75(2) (1998), 192–209.

Johnson, Barbara. 'The Frame of Reference: Poe, Lacan, Derrida.' *Yale French Studies* 55/56 (1977), 457–505.

Jordanova, Ludmilla. *Sexual Visions: Images of Gender in Science and Medicine between the Eighteenth and Twentieth Centuries.* Madison: U of Wisconsin P, 1985.

Joyce, James. *Ulysses.* New York: Vintage, 1961.

Kamuf, Peggy. 'Replacing Feminist Criticism.' In *Conflicts in Feminism.* Ed. Marianne Hirsch and Evelyn Fox Keller. New York: Routledge, 1990. 105–11.

Kaplan, Alice Yeager. *Reproductions of Banality: Fascism, Literature, and French Intellectual Life.* Minneapolis: U of Minnesota P, 1986.

Keith, Michael, and Steve Pile. 'Conclusion: Towards New Radical Geographies.' In *Place and the Politics of Identity.* Ed. Michael Keith and Steve Pile. New York and London: Routledge, 1993. 220–6.

Kestner, Joseph. *The Spatiality of the Novel.* Detroit: Wayne State UP, 1978.

Khan, Victoria. 'Rhetoric and the Law.' *diacritics* 19:2 (Summer 1989), 21–34.

Kipnis, Laura. '(Male) Desire vs. (Female) Disgust: Reading *Hustler.*' In *Cultural Studies.* Ed. Lawrence Grossman, Cary Nelson, and Paula Treichler. New York: Routledge, 1992. 373–91.

Klopp, Charles. *Sentences: The Memoirs and Letters of Italian Political Prisoners from Bevenuto Cellini to Aldo Moro.* Toronto: U of Toronto P, 1999.

Koon, Tracy. *Believe, Obey, Fight: The Political Socialization of Youth in Fascist Italy, 1922–45.* Chapel Hill: U of North Carolina P, 1985.

Koonz, Claudia. *Mothers in the Fatherland: Women, the Family, and Nazi Politics.* New York: St Martin's P, 1987.

Kowzan, Tadeusz. 'The Sign in the Theater: An Introduction to the Semiology of the Art of the Spectacle.' Tr. Simon Pleasance. *Diogène* 61 (1968), 52–80.

Kristeva, Julia. *The Powers of Horror: An Essay on Abjection.* Tr. Leon Roudiez. New York: Columbia University P, 1982.

– 'Women's Time.' In *The Kristeva Reader.* Ed. Toril Moi. New York: Columbia UP, 1986. 187–213.

Kritz, Neil, ed. *Transitional Justice: How Emerging Democracies Reckon with Former Regimes.* 3 vols. Washington, DC: United States Institute of Peace P, 1995.

Kurzweil, Edith. 'Michel Foucault's History of Sexuality as Interpreted by Feminists and Marxists.' *Social Research* 53:4 (1986), 647–66.

La coscienza contemporanea tra 'pubblico' e 'privato': Atti del XLIX corso di aggiornamento culturale dell'Università Cattolica 9–14 settembre 1979. Milan: Pubblicazioni dell'Università Cattolica del Sacro Cuore, 1979.

La costituzione della repubblica italiana. Ed. Vincenzo Carullo. Bologna: Zuffi, 1950.

La Rovere, Luca. 'Fascist Groups in Italian Universities: An Organisation at the Service of the Totalitarian State.' *Journal of Contemporary History* 34 (1999), 457–75.

Lacan, Jacques. 'The Seminar on "The Purloined Letter,"' Tr. Jeffrey Mehlman. *Yale French Studies* 48 (1973), 38–72.

Laclau, Ernesto. *Politics and Ideology in Marxist Theory.* London: Verso, 1977.

Laforgia, Patrizia Guida. 'Dimensione narrativa e psicologia femminile in Anna Banti.' *Il Veltro.* 40:1–2 (Jan.–April 1996), 138–42.

Le Corbusier. 'L'Espace indicible.' *Art* (Jan. 1946), 6–10.

Lefebvre, Henri. *The Production of Space*. Tr. Donald Nicholson-Smith. Oxford: Blackwell, 1991.

Lenz, Joseph. 'Base Trade: Theater as Prostitution.' *ELH* 60 (1993), 833–55.

Levi, Fabio. 'Italian Society and Jews after the Second World War: Between Silence and Reparation.' In *After the War: Violence, Justice, Continuity and Renewal in Italian Society*. Ed. Jonathan Dunnage. Leicester: Troubador, 1999. 21–31.

Levi, Primo. *Moments of Reprieve*. Tr. Ruth Felman. New York: Summit Books, 1986.

– *Survival in Auschwitz*. Tr. Stuart Woolf. New York: Summit Books, 1986.

– *I sommersi e i salvati*. Turin: Einaudi, 1987.

– *The Drowned and the Saved*. Tr. Raymond Rosenthal. New York: Summit Books, 1988.

– *Racconti*. Turin: Einaudi, 1989.

– *Se questo è un uomo*. Turin: Einaudi, 1989.

– *La ricerca delle radici*. Turin: Einaudi, 1997.

Libera, Adalberto. 'Il quartiere Tusculano a Roma.' *Comunità* 31 (1955), 46–9.

Lindsey, Shelley Stamp. 'Horror, Femininity, and Carrie's Monstrous Puberty.' In *The Dread of Difference: Gender and the Horror Film*. Ed. Barry Keith Grant. Austin: U of Texas P, 1996. 279–95.

Linz, Juan. *The Breakdown of Democratic Regimes: Crisis, Breakdown, and Reequilibration*. Baltimore: Johns Hopkins UP, 1978.

Lizzani, Carlo. '"Cronache di poveri amanti": Il film.' In *Vasco Pratolini e il cinema*. Ed. Andrea Vannini. Florence: Edizioni La Bottega del Cinema, 1987. 23–8.

Lombroso, Cesare, and G. Ferrero. *La donna delinquente, la prostituta e la donna normale*. Milan-Turin-Rome: Bocca Editori, 1915.

– *The Female Offender*. New York: Philosophical Library, 1958.

Lucarelli, Carlo. *Via delle Oche*. Palermo: Sellerio, 1996.

Lucchini, Guido. 'Gadda's Freud.' In *Carlo Emilio Gadda*. Ed. Manuela Bertone and Robert Dombroski. Toronto: U of Toronto P, 1997. 177–94.

Luperini, Romano. *Il Novecento*. 2 vols. Turin: Loescher, 1981.

Luti, Giorgio. *Cronache letterarie tra le due guerre 1920/40*. Bari: Laterza, 1966.

Macaggi, Domenico. 'Vita apnoica extra-uterina ed infanticidio di fronte all'art. 577 del Testo definitivo del Progetto Rocco.' *Archivio di Antropologia Criminale* 50 (1930), 1536–47.

MacCannell, Dean, and Juliet Flower MacCannell. 'Violence, Power and Pleasure: A Revisionist Reading of Foucault from the Victim Perspective.' In *Up against Foucault: Explorations of Some Tensions between Foucault and Feminism*. Ed. Caroline Ramazanoglu. London: Routledge, 1993. 203–38.

Macciocchi, Marie Antonietta. *La donna 'nera': 'Consenso' femminile e fascismo.* Milan: Feltrinelli, 1976.

Mack Smith, Dennis. *Mussolini's Roman Empire.* New York: Viking, 1976.

Maier, Charles S. 'I fondamenti politici del dopoguerra.' In *Storia d'Europa. I. L'Europa di oggi.* Turin: Einaudi. 311–72.

Malaparte, Curzio. *Kaputt.* Florence: Vallechi Editori, 1960.

– *Kaputt.* Tr. Cesare Foligno. Marlboro: Marlboro P, 1982.

Manacorda, Giuliano. *Letteratura e cultura del periodo fascista.* Milan: Principato, 1974.

Mandel, Ernest. *Delitti per diletto: Storia del romanzo poliziesco.* Milan: Intern Giallo, 1990.

Mann, Coramae Richey. *Female Crime and Delinquency.* Birmingham: U of Alabama P, 1984.

Manzini, Gianna. *Tempo innamorato.* Milan: Mondadori, 1928.

Manzoni, Alessandro. *The Betrothed.* Tr. Bruce Penman. London: Penguin, 1972.

– *I promessi sposi.* Ed. Angelo Marchese. Milan: Mondadori, 1985.

Maradei, Manlio. 'Ancora nel rimpianto di Guido Piovène: "Come si fabbrica un'anima."' *L'Approdo letterario* 73 (1976), 117–24.

Maraini, Dacia. *E tu chi eri?* Milan: Bompiani Editori, 1973.

Marcetti, Corrado, and Nico Solimano, eds. *Carcere di tante carceri.* Florence: Angelo Pontecorboli, n.d.

Marcus, Sharon. *Apartment Stories: City and Home in Nineteenth-Century Paris and London.* Berkeley: U of California P, 1999.

Marin, Louis. *Utopics: The Semiological Play of Textual Places.* Tr. Robert Vollrath. Atlantic Highlands, NJ: Humanities International P, 1990.

– 'Frontiers of Utopia: Past and Present.' *Critical Inquiry* 19:3 (1992), 397–420.

Marino, Giuseppe Carlo. *L'autarchia della cultura: Intellettuali e fascismo negli anni trenta.* Rome: Riuniti, 1983.

Marks, Elaine. 'Lesbian Intertextuality.' In *Homosexualities and French Literature.* Ed. Elaine Marks and George Stambolian. Ithaca, NY: Cornell UP, 1979. 357–8.

Markus, Thomas. *Buildings and Power: Freedom and Control in the Origin of Modern Building Types.* London and New York: Routledge, 1993.

Martin, Biddy, and Chandra Mohanty, 'Feminist Politics: What's Home Got to Do with It?' In *Feminist Studies/Cultural Studies.* Ed. Teresa de Lauretis. Bloomington: Indiana UP, 1986. 191–212.

Martin, Elaine, ed. *Gender, Patriarchy, and Fascism in the Third Reich.* Detroit: Wayne State UP, 1993.

Massini, Luigi Carlo. 'La pericolosità criminosa nella nuova legislazione, il problema tecnico e dei tecnici.' *Archivio di Antropologia Criminale* 50 (1930), 1571–8.

Matlock, Jann. *Scenes of Seduction: Prostitution, Hysteria, and Reading Difference in Nineteenth-Century France*. New York: Columbia UP, 1994.

McClintock, Ann. 'Sex Workers and Sex.' *Social Text* 37 (Winter 1993), 1–10.

McConnell, Joan. *A Vocabulary Analysis of Gadda's Pasticciaccio*. University, MS: Romance Monographs, 1973.

McLeod, Mary. 'Undressing Architecture: Fashion, Gender, and Modernity.' In *Architecture: In Fashion*. Ed. Deborah Fausch, Paulette Singley, Rodolphe El-Khoury, and Zvi Efrat. New York: Princeton Architectural P, 1994. 39–123.

McNamara, Jo Ann Kay. *Sisters in Arms: Catholic Nuns through Two Millennia*. Cambridge: Harvard UP, 1996.

Meldini, Piero. *Sposa e madre esemplare. Ideologia e politica della donna e della famiglia durante il fascismo*. Florence: Guaraldi, 1975.

– ed. *Sposa e madre esemplare: Ideologia e politica della donna e della famiglia durante il fascismo*. Florence: Guaraldi, 1975.

Melis, Guido. *Storia dell'Amministrazione italiana 1861–1993*. Bologna: Il Mulino, 1993.

Mercuri, Lamberto. *L'Epurazione in Italia, 1943–48*. Cuneo: L'Arciere, 1988.

Merlin, Lina. *La mia vita*. Ed. Elena Marinucci. Florence: Giunti Barbera, 1989.

Merlin, Lina, and Carla Barberis, eds. *Lettere dalle case chiuse*. Rome and Milan: Edizioni Avanti! 1955.

Meyvaert, Paul. 'The Medieval Monastic Claustrum,' *GESTA* 12 (1973), 53–9.

Miccoli, Giovanni. 'La chiesa e il fascismo.' In *Fascismo e società italiana*. Ed. Guido Quazza. Turin: Einaudi, 1973. 185–208.

Michaelis, Meir. *Mussolini and the Jews: German-Italian Relations and the Jewish Question in Italy, 1922–45*. Oxford: Clarendon P, 1978.

Mignone, Mario. *Anormalità e angoscia nella narrativa di Dino Buzzati*. Ravenna: Longo, 1981.

Miller, D.A. *The Novel and the Police*. Berkeley: U of California P, 1988.

Millstone, Amy. 'French Feminist Theater and the Subject of Prostitution.' In *The Image of the Prostitute in Modern Literature*. Ed. Pierre Horn and Mary Beth Pringle. New York: Frederick Ungar, 1984. 19–27.

Modleski, Tania. *The Women Who Knew Too Much: Hitchcock and Feminist Theory*. New York: Methuen, 1988.

Mondello, Elisabetta. *La nuova italiana: La donna nella stampa e nella cultura del ventennio*. Rome: Riuniti, 1987.

Monson, Craig, ed. *The Crannied Wall: Women, Religion, and the Arts in Early Modern Europe*. Ann Arbor: U of Michigan P, 1992.

Montanari, Gen. Mario. *L'esercito italiano alla vigilia della Seconda Guerra Mondiale.* Rome: USSME, 1982.

Montanelli, Indro. *Il mistero di Dino Buzzati.* Ed. Romano Battaglia. Milan: Ruscioni, 1980.

Montuoro, Fortunato. 'La gravidanza nel concetto di malattia.' *Archivio di Antropologia Criminale* 55 (1935), 211–14.

Moore, Henrietta. *Space, Text, and Gender: An Anthropological Study of the Marakwet of Kenya.* Cambridge: Cambridge UP, 1986.

Morandi, Mario. 'Uomini e donne.' *Critica fascista* 16: 23 (1 Oct. 1938), 359–60.

Morante, Elsa. *Il gioco segreto.* Milan: Garzanti, 1942.

Moravia, Alberto. 'Perchè ho scritto *La Romana.*' *Fiera letteraria*, 13 March 1947.

– *The Woman of Rome.* Tr. Lydia Holland. New York: Farrar, Strauss, and Young, 1950.

– *The Conformist.* Tr. Angus Davidson. New York: Farrar, Strauss, and Young, 1951.

– *Il conformista.* Milan: Bompiani, 1966.

– *La romana.* Milan: Bompiani, 1980.

More, Thomas. *Utopia.* New York and London: W.W. Norton, 1975.

Morichini, C.L. *Degli istituti di carità per la sorveglianza e l'educazione dei poveri e dei prigionieri in Roma.* Rome, 1870.

Morin, Edgar. *La Méthode Vol. I: Nature de la nature.* Paris: Editions du Seuil, 1977.

Moro, Renato. 'La modernizazzione cattolica tra fascismo e postfascismo come problema storiografico.' *Storia contemporanea* 19:4 (Aug. 1988), 625–716.

Morris, Meaghan. 'The Pirate's Fiancée: Feminists and Philosophers, or Maybe Tonight It'll Happen.' In *Michel Foucault: Power, Truth, Strategy.* Ed. Meaghan Morris and Paul Patton. Sydney: Feral Publications, 1979. 148–68.

Mosse, George. *Nationalism and Sexuality: Middle-Class Morality and Sexual Norms in Modern Europe.* Madison: U of Wisconsin P, 1985.

Muratore, Giorgio. 'Gli anni della Ricostruzione.' *Controspazio* 3 (1974), 6–25.

– 'Le nuove carceri di Nuoro.' *Controspazio* 3 (1974), 44–9.

Murray, M.A. *The Witch Cult in Western Europe.* Oxford: Clarendon P, 1962.

Mussolini, Benito. *Opera omnia.* Ed. Edoardo and Duilio Susmel. 44. vols. Florence: La Fenice, 1951.

Neppi Modona, Guido. 'La magistratura e il fascismo.' In *Fascismo e società italiana.* Ed. Guido Quazza. Turin: Einaudi, 1973. 125–81.

– 'Carcere e società civile.' *Storia d'Italia: I documenti.* V, Pt. 2. Turin: Einaudi, 1977. 1903–98.

Nerenberg, Ellen. '"Donna proprio ... proprio donna": The Social Construction of Femininity in Alba de Céspedes's *Nessuno torna indietro.*' *Romance Languages Annual* 3 (1991), 267–73.

- 'Resistance and Remorse: Alba de Céspedes's Withdrawal from the Public Sphere.' In *Writing beyond Fascism: Cultural Resistance in the Life and Works of Alba de Céspedes.* Ed. Carole Gallucci and Ellen Nerenberg. Cranbury, NJ: Fairleigh-Dickinson UP, 2000. 223–46.

Newman, Karen. 'Directing Traffic: Subjects, Objects, and the Politics of Exchange.' *differences: A Journal of Feminist Cultural Studies* 2 (1990), 47.

Noether, Emiliana. 'Italian Women under Fascism: A Reevaluation.' *Italian Quarterly* 32:90 (Fall 1982), 69–80.

Norindr, Panivong. '"Errances" and Memories in Marguerite Duras's Colonial Cities.' *differences* 5:3 (1993), 52–79.

Oliva, Giovanni. 'Luoghi di pena-Luoghi di svago: La villeggiatura ad Alghero fra Ottocento e Novecento.' *Il Risorgimento* 2 (1993), 177–94.

Orsi, Gianfranco, and Lia Volpati. 'Il "giallo" Mondadori dal 1929 al 1941.' *Problemi* 73 (May–Aug. 1985), 152–7.

Ottavi, Antoine. 'La formation d'un romancier italien dans l'entre-deux-guerres: Vasco Pratolini.' *Annales de la faculté des lettres et sciences humaines de Nice* 42 *[Hommage à Louise Cohen: Langue et littérature italiennes]* (1982), 175–201.

Paci, Renzo, ed. *Scritti storici in memoria di Enzo Piscitelli.* Padua: Antenore, 1982.

Painter, Borden. 'Renzo de Felice and the Historiography of Italian Fascism.' *American Historical Review* 95:2 (April 1990), 391–405.

Palmer Domenico, Roy. *Italian Fascists on Trial, 1943–48.* Chapel Hill: U of North Carolina P, 1991.

Palermo, Antonio. 'Gli anni Trenta: Per una nuova periodizzazione della storiografia letteraria.' In *La cultura italiana negli anni 1930–45.* Naples: Edizioni scientifiche italiane, 1984. 159–81.

Palmieri, Valerio. *Mario Ridolfi: Guida all'architettura.* Verona: Arsenale, 1997.

Panafieu, Yves. 'Un homme des frontières.' *Cahiers Buzzati* 2 (1978), 69–83.

- 'Un uomo delle frontiere.' *Cahiers Buzzati* 2 (1978), 67–8.

- 'Aspetti storici, morali, e politici del discorso dell'impotenza.' In *Dino Buzzati.* Ed. Alvise Fontanella. Florence: Oischki, 1982. 23–47.

Pancrazi, Pietro. *Corriere della Sera*, 2 August 1940, n.p.

Parker, Andrew, Mary Russo, Doris Sommer, and Patricia Yeager, eds. *Nationalisms and Sexualities.* New York: Routledge, 1992.

Passeleqc, Georges, and Bernard Suchecky. *The Hidden Encyclical of Pius XI.* New York: Harcourt Brace, 1997.

Passerini, Luisa. 'Donne operaie e aborto.' *Italia contemporanea* 151–2 (1983), 83–109.

Paulicelli, Eugenia. 'Fashion as a Text: Talking about Femininity and Feminism.'

In *Feminine Feminists: Cultural Practices in Italy.* Ed. Giovanna Miceli-Jeffries. Minneapolis: Minnesota UP, 1995. 171–89.

– 'Le narrative della moda, egemonia, genere, identità.' *Annali d'Italianistica* 16 (1998), 315–37.

Pavarini, Massimo. 'La città e il suo rovescio: Note in tema di carcere e metropoli.' *La nuova città* 1 (April 1983), 12–29.

– 'La periferia penitenziaria.' In *Un fossile chiamato carcere: Scritti sul carcere.* Ed. Corrado Marcetti and Nicola Solimano. Florence: Angelo Pontecorboli, 1993. 14–24.

Pavone, Claudio. *Una guerra civile: Saggio storico sulla moralità nella Resistenza.* Turin: Bollati Boringhieri, 1991.

– *Alle origini della Repubblica: Scritti sul fascismo, antifascismo, e continuità dello Stato.* Turin: Bollati Boringhieri, 1995.

– 'Caratteri ed eredità della "zona grigia,"' *Passato e presente* 43 (1998), 5–12.

Pedullà, Walter. 'La dialettica degli opposti come fondamento dell'incompiutezza.' In *Leggere Gadda: Antologia della critica gaddiana.* Ed. Arnaldo Ceccaroni. Bologna: Zanichelli, 1978. 133–6.

Pelella, Franco. 'Riabilitare Lombroso.' *Risorgimento* 41:3 (1989), 283–314.

Pellegrini, Alessandro. 'La verità di Piovene.' *L'Osservatore politico letterario* 22:7 (1976), 47–67.

Pellico, Silvio. *Le mie prigioni.* Bari: Edizioni Paoline, 1970.

– *My Prisons.* Tr. I.G. Capaldi. Westport, CT: Greenwood P, 1978.

Perrando, G.G. 'La medicina legale italiana nell'ultimo decennio.' *Archivio di antropologia criminale* 47 (1927), 562–89.

Peterson, Thomas. 'The "Feminine" Writing of Anna Banti: *Un grido lacerante.*' *Nemla Italian Studies,* 11/12 (1987–8), 87–96.

– *Alberto Moravia.* New York: Twayne Publishers, 1996.

Petronio, Giuseppe. 'La letteratura poliziesca oggi.' *Problemi* 86 (Sept.–Dec. 1989), 208–32.

Pick, Daniel. 'The Faces of Anarchy: Lombroso and the Politics of Criminal Science in Post-Unification Italy.' *History Workshop* 21 (Spring 1986), 60–86.

Pickering-Iazzi, Robin. *Politics of the Visible: Writing Women, Culture, and Fascism.* Minneapolis: U of Minnesota P, 1997.

– ed. *Mothers of Invention: Women, Italian Fascism, and Culture.* Minneapolis: U of Minnesota P, 1995.

Pile, Steve, and Nigel Thrift, eds. *Mapping the Subject: Geographics of Cultural Transformation.* New York and London: Routledge, 1995.

Pinkus, Karen. *Bodily Regimes: Italian Advertising under Fascism.* Minneapolis: U of Minnesota P, 1995.

– '"Black" and "Jew": Race and the Resistance to Psychoanalysis in Italy.' *Annali d'Italianistica* 16 (1998), 145–67.

Piovène, Guido. *Lettere di una novizia.* Milan: Bompiani, 1941.

– *Confessions of a Novice.* Tr. Eithne Wilkins. London: Kimber, 1950.

Piscitelli, Enzo, ed. *Le origini della Repubblica.* Turin: Giappichelli, 1974.

Pitch, Tamar. 'La sessualità, le norme, lo Stato: Il dibattito sulla Legge Merlin.' *Memoria* 17:2 (1986), 24–41.

– ed. *Diritto e rovescio: Studi sulle donne e il controllo sociale.* Naples: Edizioni scientifiche italiane, 1987.

Pompei, Manlio. 'Demografia: Punto e daccapo.' *Critica fascista* 15:9 (1 March 1937), 135–6.

Ponce de Léon, Maria. 'Meccanismi di sopravvivenza: Letteratura carceraria contemporanea in Italia: Poesia, narrativa, teatro 1970–97.' Ph.D. diss., Northwestern University, 1998.

Potter, Joy. *Elio Vittorini.* New York: Twayne Publishers, 1979.

Pratolini, Vasco. 'Testimonianza su "Cronache di poveri amanti."' in *Vasco Pratolini e il cinema.* Ed. Andrea Vannini. Florence: Edizioni La Bottega del Cinema, 1987.

– *A Chronicle of Poor Lovers.* Translator not noted. Foreword John Hersey. Afterword Victoria de Grazia. New York: Monthly Review P, 1988.

– *Cronache di poveri amanti.* Milan: Mondadori, 1993.

Pullini, Giorgio. '*Il deserto dei Tartari* e *Un amore*: Due romanzi in rapporto speculare tra metafora e realtà.' In *Dino Buzzati.* Ed. Renato Bertacchino.

Quazza, Guido. *Resistenza e storia d'Italia: Problemi e ipotesi di ricerca.* Milan: Feltrinelli, 1976.

Rambelli, Loris. *Storia del 'giallo' italiano.* Milan: Grazanti, 1979.

– 'Il presunto giallo: Dalla preistoria alla storia.' *Problemi* 86 (Sept.–Dec. 1989), 233–56.

Re, Lucia. *Calvino and the Age of Neorealism: Fables of Estrangement.* Stanford: Stanford UP, 1992.

Rebay, Luciano. *Alberto Moravia.* New York: Columbia UP, 1970.

Reich, Jacqueline. 'Reading, Writing, and Rebellion: Collectivity, Specularity, and Sexuality in the Italian Schoolgirl Comedy, 1934–43.' In *Mothers of Invention: Woman, Italian Fascism, and Culture.* Ed. Robin Pickering-Iazzi. Minneapolis: U of Minnesota P, 1995. 220–51.

– 'Fear of Filming: Alba de Céspedes and the 1943 Film Adaptation of *Nessuno torna indietro.*' In *Writing beyond Fascism: Cultural Resistance in the Life and Works of Alba de Céspedes.* Ed. Carole C. Gallucci and Ellen Nerenberg. Cranbury, NJ: Fairleigh-Dickinson UP, 2000. 132–54.

Reinert, Claus. 'Beschreibung des Unheimlichen.' In *Das Unheimliche und*

die Detektivliteratur. Bonn: Bouvier Verlag Herbert Grundmann, 1973.
16–26.

Rich, B. Ruby. 'From Repressive Tolerance to Erotic Liberation: Maedchen in Uniform.' In *Re-vision: Essays in Film Criticism* (AFI) 3 (1984), 100–30.

Riegel, Léon. 'Waiting for the War to Break Out: Jünger, Buzzati, and Gracq.' In *Literature and War.* Ed. David Bevan. Amsterdam: Rodopi Press, 1989. 97–108.

Rocca, Giancarlo. *Donne religiose: Contributo a una storia della condizione femminile in Italia nei secoli XIX–XX.* (*Claretianum* 32 [1992], on behalf of *Dizionario degli Istituti di Perfezione.*)

Rochat, Giorgio. *L'esercito italiano da Vittorio Veneto a Mussolini 1919–25.* Bari: Laterza, 1967.

– 'L'esercito e il fascismo.' In *Fascismo e società italiana.* Ed. Guido Quazza. Tuin: Einaudi, 1973. 89–123.

– 'La politica militare dell'Italia fascista.' *Storia d'Italia* 5:2 (1973), 1883–91.

Romano, Luca, and Paolo Sabello, eds. *C'era una volta la DC: Breve storia del periodo degasperiano attraverso i manifesti elettorali della Democrazia Cristiana.* Rome: Savelli, 1975.

Roscioni, Gian Carlo. *La disarmonia prestablita: Studio su Gadda.* Turin: Einaudi, 1969.

Rose, Gillian. *Feminism and Geography: The Limits of Geographical Knowledge.* Minneapolis: U of Minnesota P, 1993.

Rosengarten, Frank. *Vasco Pratolini: The Development of a Social Novelist.* Carbondale: Southern Illinois UP, 1965.

Ross, Andrew. 'Cowboys, Cadillacs, and Cosmonauts: Families, Film Genres, and Technocultures.' In *Engendering Men: The Question of Male Feminist Criticism.* Ed., Joseph Boone and Michael Cadden. New York: Routledge, 1990. 87–101.

Rosso-Mazzinghi, Stefano, ed. *Guido Piovène.* Vicenza: Neri Pozza, 1980.

Rothberg, Michael. 'The Prostitution of Paris: Late Capital of the Twentieth Century.' *Found Object* 1:1 (1992), 2–22

Rowe, Peter. *Modernity and Housing.* Cambridge: MIT P. 1993.

Rubin, Gayle. 'The Traffic in Women: Notes on the "Political Economy" of Sex.' In *Toward an Anthropology of Women.* Ed. Rayna Reiter. New York: Monthly Press, 1975. 157–210.

Ruffolo, Giorgio. *Riforme e controriforme.* Bari-Rome: Laterza, 1975.

Rushing, Robert. 'Il cristallo e il mare: L'enumeracion caotica e l'epistemologia in Calvino e Gadda.' *Forum italicum* 31:2 (Fall 1997), 407–22.

Rybczynski, Witold. *Home: A Short History of an Idea.* New York: Penguin, 1986.

Sala, Alberico. 'Introduzione.' *Il deserto dei Tartari.* By Dino Buzzati. Milan: Mondadori, 1983.

Saraceno, Chiara. 'La struttura di genere della cittadinanza.' *Democrazia e diritto* 28:1 (Jan.–Feb. 1988), 273–95.

– 'Redefining Maternity and Paternity: Gender, Pronatalism and Social Policies in Fascist Italy.' In *Maternity and Gender Policies: Women and the Rise of the European Welfare States, 1880s-1950s.* Ed. Gisela Bock and Pat Thane. New York: Routledge, 1991. 196–212.

Sargisson, Lucy. *Contemporary Feminist Utopianism.* London and New York: Routledge, 1996.

Sbacchi, Alberto. *Ethiopia under Mussolini: Fascism and the Colonial Experience.* London: Zed Books, 1985.

Sbragia, Albert. *Carlo Emilio Gadda and the Modern Maccaronic.* Gainesville: UP of Florida. 1996.

Scaraffia, Lucetta, and Gabriella Zarri. 'Introduzione.' In *Donna e fede: Santità e vita religiosa in Italia.* Ed. Lucetta Scaraffia and Gabriella Zarri. Rome-Bari: Laterza, 1994. v-xvi.

– 'Il cristianesimo l'ha fatta libera, collocandola nella famiglia accanto all'uomo' (dal 1850 alla *Mulieris dignitatem*).' *Donna e fede: Santità e vita religiosa in Italia.* Ed. Lucetta Scaraffia and Gabriella Zarri. Rome-Bari: Laterza, 1994. 441–93.

Scarry, Elaine. *The Body in Pain: The Making and Unmaking of the World.* New York: Oxford UP, 1985.

Schnapp, Jeffrey. 'Epic Demonstrations: Fascist Modernity and the 1932 Exhibition of Fascist Culture.' In *Fascism, Aesthetics, and Culture.* Ed. Richard Golsan. Hanover, NH: University P of New England, 1992. 1–37.

– *Staging Fascism: 18BL and the Theater of the Masses for the Masses.* Stanford: Stanford UP, 1996.

Schor, Naomi. 'Dreaming Dissymmetry: Barthes, Foucault, and Sexual Difference.' In *Men in Feminism.* Ed. Alice Jardine and Stephen Heath. New York: Methuen, 1987. 98–110.

Schumacher, Thomas. *Surface and Symbol: Giuseppe Terragni and the Architecture of Italian Rationalism.* Princeton: Princeton UP, 1991.

Sciama, Lidia. 'The Problem of Privacy in Mediterranean Anthropology.' In *Women and Space.* Ed. Shirley Ardener. New York: St Martin's, 1981. 89–111.

Sciascia, Leonardo. *Il teatro della memoria.* Turin: Einaudi, 1981.

Sclavi, Marianella Pirzio Biroli. 'L'inchiesta sulla miseria in Italia.' *Memoria* 6 (1982), 96–100.

Sebeok, Thomas, and Jean Umiker-Seboek. '"You Know My Method": A Juxtaposition of Charles S. Peirce and Sherlock Holmes.' In *The Sign of Three: Dupin, Holmes, Peirce.* Ed. Umberto Eco and Thomas Sebeok. Bloomington: Indiana UP, 1983. 11–54.

Sedgwick, Eve Kosofsky. 'Nationalisms and Sexualities in the Age of Wilde.' In *Nationalisms and Sexualities*. Ed. Andrew Parker, Mary Russo, Doris Sommers, and Patricia Yeager. New York: Routledge, 1992. 235–45;

Seltzer, Mark. *Serial Killers: Death and Life in American Wound Culture*. New York and London: Routledge, 1998.

Sema, Antonio. 'La cultura dell'esercito.' In *Cultura e società negli anni del fascismo*. Ed. Luigi Dadda and Mario Invernicci. Milan: Cordani, 1987.

Seton-Watson, Christopher. *Italy from Liberalism to Fascism, 1870–1925*. London: Methuen, 1967.

Sheffler, Judith, ed. *Wall Tappings: An Anthology of Writings by Women Prisoners*. Boston: Northeastern UP, 1986.

Shields, R. *Places on the Margin*. London: Routledge, 1991.

Silverman, Kaja. *Male Subjectivity at the Margins*. New York: Routledge, 1992.

Singer, Linda. 'True Confessions: Cixous and Foucault on Sexuality and Power.' In *The Thinking Muse: Feminism and Modern French Philosophy*. Ed. Jeffner Allen and Iris Marion Young. Bloomington: Indiana UP, 1979. 136–55.

Sinopoli, Nicola, ed. *La situazione della casa in Italia*. Milan: Franco Angeli, 1976.

Smart, Carol. *Women, Crime, and Criminality: A Feminist Critique*. London and Boston: Routledge and Kegan Paul, 1977.

Smith, Paul. *Clint Eastwood: A Cultural Production*. Minneapolis: U of Minnesota P, 1995.

Smith, Roger. *Trial by Medicine*. Edinburgh: U of Edinburgh, 1981.

Smitten, Jeffrey, and Ann Daghistany, eds. *Spatial Form in Narrative*. Ithaca, NY: Cornell UP, 1981.

Sodi, Risa. 'An Interview with Primo Levi.' *Partisan Review* 54:3 (Summer 1987), 355–66.

Soja, Edward. *Postmodern Geographies: The Reassertion of Space in Critical Social Theory*. London and New York: Verso, 1989.

Sommavilla, Guido. 'Ierologia di Guido Piovène.' *Letture* 31 (1976), 3–24.

– 'Ierologia di Guido Piovene, II.' *Letture* 31 (1976), 87–110. 147–56.

Spackman, Barbara. *Decadent Genealogies: The Rhetoric of Sickness from Baudelaire to D'Annunzio*. Ithaca: Cornell UP, 1989.

– *Fascist Virilities: Rhetoric, Ideology, and Social Fantasy in Italy*. Minneapolis: U of Minnesota P, 1996.

Spanos, William. 'The Detective and the Boundary: Some Notes on the Postmodern Literary Imagination.' *Boundary 2* 1 (Fall 1972), 147–68.

Starobinski, Jean. 'Il sogno architetto, gli interni di Kafka.' *Domus* 218 (1947).

Sternhell, Zeev. *Neither Right nor Left: Fascist Ideology in France*. Tr., David Maisel. Berkeley: U of California P, 1986.

Sternhell, Zeev, Mario Sznajder, and Maia Asheri. *The Birth of Fascist Ideology.* Tr. David Maisel. Princeton: Princeton UP, 1994.

Still, Judith. '"What Foucault Fails to Acknowledge ...": Feminists and the History of Sexuality.' *History of the Human Sciences* 7:2 (1994), 150–7.

Stille, Alexander. *Benevolence and Betrayal: Five Italian Jewish Families under Fascism.* New York: Pengiun, 1993.

Stone, Marla. 'Staging Fascism: The Exhibition of the Fascist Revolution.' *Journal of Contemporary History* 28:2 (1993), 215–43.

– *The Patron State: Culture and Politics in Fascist Italy.* Princeton: Princeton UP, 1998.

Strazzabosco, Stefano, ed. *Guido Piovène tra idoli e ragione: Atti del convegno di studi Vicenza, 24–26 novembre 1994.* Venice: Marsilio, 1996.

Strelka, Joseph. 'Kafkaesque Elements in Kafka's Novels and in Contemporary Narrative Prose.' *Comparative Literature Studies* 21 (1984), 434–44.

Sweet, J.T.T. *Iron Arm: The Mechanization of Mussolini's Army, 1920–40.* Westport, CT: Greenwood Press, 1980.

Tabet, Paola. 'Imposed Reproduction: Maimed Sexuality.' *Feminist Issues* 7:2 (Fall 1987), 3–31.

Tafuri, Manfredo. *Ludovico Quaroni e lo sviluppo dell'architettura moderna in Italia.* Milan: Garzanti, 1964.

– *The Sphere and the Labyrinth: Avant-Gardes and Architecture from Piranesi to the 1970s.* Tr. Pellegrino d'Acierno and Robert Connolly. Cambridge: MIT P, 1987.

– *History of Italian Architecture, 1944–85.* Tr. Jessica Levine. Cambridge: MIT P, 1989.

Tani, Stefano. *The Doomed Detective: The Contribution of the Detective Novel to Postmodern Italian and American Fiction.* Carbondale: Southern Illinois UP, 1984.

Tannenbaum, Edward. *The Fascist Experience: Italian Society and Culture, 1922–45.* New York: Basic Books, 1975.

Tatafiore, Roberta. 'Le prostitute e le altre.' *Memoria* 17:2 (1986), 101–14.

Teal, Laurie. 'The Hollow Women: Modernism, the Prostitute, and Commodity Aesthetics.' *differences: A Journal of Feminist Cultural Studies* 7:3 (1995), 80–108.

Tench, Darby. 'Quel nome storia: Naming and History in Gadda's *Pasticciaccio*.' *Stanford Italian Review* 5 (1985), 205–17.

Terranova, Antonino, ed. Ludovico Quaroni: *La Città fisica.* Bari-Rome: Laterza, 1981.

Theweleit, Klaus. *Male Fantasies, Volume I: Women, Floods, Bodies, History.* Tr. Steven Conway. Minneapolis: U of Minnesota P, 1987.

– *Male Fantasies, Volume II: Psychoanalyzing the White Terror.* Tr. Erica Carter and Chris Turner. Minneapolis: U of Minnesota P, 1989.

Thomas, Brook. 'Reflections on the Law and Literature Revival.' *Critical Inquiry* 17 (Spring 1991), 510–39.

Thorwald, Jürgen. *Crime and Science.* Tr. Richard and Clara Winston. New York: Harcourt, Brace & World, 1967.

Tölölyan, Kachig. 'The Nation-State and Its Others.' *Diaspora* 1.1 (Spring 1991), 2–20.

Torchiana, Luigi, and Bruno Guaraldi. 'Gravidanza extra-uterina e procurato aborto.' *Archivio di Antropologia Criminale* 51 (1931), 626–34.

Toscani, Claudio. *Guida alla lettura di Buzzati.* Milan: Mondadori, 1987.

Tuan, Yi-Fu. *Space and Place: The Perspective of Experience.* Minneapolis: U of Minnesota P, 1977.

Tucker, Robert, ed. *The Marx-Engels Reader.* New York: W.W. Norton, 1978.

Turner, Victor. *Forest of Symbols: Aspects of Ndembu Ritual.* Ithaca and London: Cornell UP, 1967.

Valentini, Daria. 'Anna and Her Sisters: The Idyll of the Convent in Anna Banti.' *Forum Italicum* 30:2 (Fall 1996), 332–50.

Valone, Carolyn. 'Roman Matrons as Patrons: Various Views of the Cloister Wall.' In *The Crannied Wall: Women, Religion, and the Arts in Early Modern Europe.* Ed. Craig Monson. Ann Arbor: U of Michigan P, 1992, 73–86.

Van der Linde, Gerhard. 'The Body in the Labyrinth: Detection, Rationality, and the Feminine in Gadda's *Pasticciaccio.*' *American Journal of Italian Studies* 21:57 (1998), 26–40.

Vattimo, Gianni. *Transparent Society.* Tr. David Webb. Baltimore: Johns Hopkins UP, 1992.

Villa, Renzo. *Il deviante e i suoi segni: Lombroso e la nascita dell'antropologia criminale.* Milan: Franco Angeli, 1985.

Viotti, Andrea. *Uniformi e distintivi dell'esercito italiano nella seconda guerra mondiale 1940–45.* Rome: USSME, 1988.

Virgilio, Maria. 'La donna nel Codice Rocco.' In *Diritto e rovescio: Studi sulle donne e il controllo sociale.* Ed. Tamar Pitch. Naples: Edizioni scientifiche italiane, 1987. 39–75.

Vittorini, Elio. *The Red Carnation.* Tr. Anthony Bower. New York: New Directions, 1952.

– *Erica e i suoi fratelli.* Milan: Bompiani, 1956.

– *Il garofano rosso.* Milan: Mondadori, 1958.

von Ankum, Katharina, ed. *Women in the Metropolis: Gender and Modernity in Weimar Culture.* Berkeley: U of California P, 1997.

Voza, Pasquale. 'Il problema del neorealismo negli anni Trenta: *Il Saggiatore, Il Cantiere.*' *Lavoro critico* 21/2 (1981), 65–105.

Waller, Marguerite. 'Whose Dolce Vita Is It, Anyway?' *Quaderni d'Italianistica* 11:1 (1990), 127–35.
– 'Back to the Future: Dante and the Languages of Post-War Italian Film.' In *Dante in the Movies and on Television.* Ed. Amilcare Iannucci. Toronto: U of Toronto P, forthcoming.
Wanrooij, Bruno. '"Il Bo" 1935–1944: Italian Students between Fascism and Anti-Fascism.' *Risorgimento* 1–2 (1982), 79–96.
– 'The Rise and Fall of Italian Fascism as Generational Revolt.' *Journal of Contemporary History* 22 (1987), 401–18.
– *La Storia del pudore: La question sessuale in Italia.* Venice: Marsilio, 1990.
– 'Youth, Generation Conflict, and Political Struggle in Twentieth-century Italy.' *The European Legacy* 4:1 (1999), 72–88.
Ward, David. *Antifascisms: Cultural Politics in Italy 1943–46: Benedetto Croce and the Liberals, Carlo Levi and the 'Actionists.'* Madison, NJ: Fairleigh-Dickinson UP, 1996.
Weaver, Elissa B. 'The Convent Wall in Tuscan Covent Drama.' In *The Crannied Wall: Women, Religion, and the Arts in Early Modern Europe.* Ed. Craig Monson. Ann Arbor: U of Michigan P, 1992.
Weil, Simone. *Cahiers I.* Paris: Plon, 1951.
Weininger, Otto. *Sex and Character.* London and New York: AMS, 1975.
Wells, Paul. 'The Invisible Man: Shrinking Masculinity in the 1950s Science Fiction B-Movie.' In *You Tarzan: Masculinity, Movies, and Men.* Ed. Pat Kirkham and Janet Thurmin. New York: St Martin's P, 1993. 181–99.
Whiteman, John, Jeffrey Kipnis, and Richard Burdett, eds. *Strategies in Architecture.* Cambridge: MIT P, 1992.
Wigley, Mark. 'Untitled: The Housing of Gender.' In *Sexuality and Space.* Ed. Beatriz Colamina. Princeton: Princeton Architectural Papers, 1992. 327–90.
Williams, Raymond. *Keywords: A Vocabulary of Culture and Society.* New York: Oxford UP, 1983.
Wilson, Elizabeth. *The Sphinx in the City: Urban Life, the Control of Disorder, and Women.* Berkeley: U of California P, 1991.
Witt, Mary Ann. *Existential Prisons: Captivity in Mid-Twentieth Century French Literature.* Durham: Duke UP, 1985.
Wohl, Robert. 'French Fascism: Both Right and Left: Reflections on the Sternhell Controversy.' *Journal of Modern History* 63:1 (1991), 91–8.
Wolff, Janet. 'The Invisible *Flâneuse*: Women and the Literature of Modernity.' *Feminine Sentences: Essays on Women and Culture.* Berkeley: U of California P, 1990.

Woller, Hans. *I conti con il fascismo: L'epurazione in Italia 1943–48*. Bologna: Il Mulino, 1997.

Young, Iris Marion. 'Throwing like a Girl: A Phenomenology of Feminine Body Comportment, Motility, and Spatiality.' In *The Thinking Muse: Feminism and Modern French Philosophy*. Ed. Jeffner Allen and Iris Marion Young. Bloomington: Indiana UP, 1979. 51–70.

Zaczek, Barbara. 'Guido Piovène's *Lettere di una novizia*: Misreading a Nun.' In *The Flight of Ulysses: Studies in Memory of Emmanuel Hatzantonis*. Chapel Hill, NC: Annali d'Italianistica, 1997. 286–98.

– *Censored Sentiments: Letters and Censorship in Epistolary Novels and Conduct Material*. Newark: U of Delaware P, 1997.

Zanuso, M. 'Adalberto Libera: Unità d'abitazione orrizontale nel quartiere Tuscolano a Roma.' *Domus* 207, 30–7.

Zarri, Gabriella. 'Monasteri femminili e città.' In *Storia d'Italia, vol. 9: La chiesa e il potere politico dal medioevo all'età contemporanea*. Ed. G. Chittolini and G. Miccoli. Turin: Einaudi, 1986.

– '*De monialibus* (secoli XVI-XVII-XVIII).' *Rivista di storia e letteratura religiosa* 33:3 (1997), 643–69.

Zevi, Bruno. *Architettura e storiografia*. Milan: Libreria Editrice Politecnica Tamburini. nd.

– *Giuseppe Terragni*. Bologna: Zanichelli Editore, 1980.

Zincone, Vittorio. 'Politica demografica.' *Critica fascista* 18:8 (15 Feb. 1940), 136.

Zuccotti, Susan. *The Italians and the Holocaust: Persecution, Rescue, and Survival*. New York: Basic Books, 1987.

– *Under His Very Windows*. New Haven: Yale UP, 2000.

Index